Atom Egoyan: Interviews

Conversations with Filmmakers Series
Peter Brunette, General Editor

Atom Egoyan
INTERVIEWS

Edited by T. J. Morris

In appreciation for your help & friendship —

T. J. Morris

University Press of Mississippi / Jackson

www.upress.state.ms.us

The University Press of Mississippi is a member
of the Association of American University Presses.

Copyright © 2010 by University Press of Mississippi
All rights reserved
Manufactured in the United States of America

First printing 2010
Library of Congress Cataloging-in-Publication Data

Egoyan, Atom, 1960–

    Atom Egoyan : interviews / edited by T. J. Morris.

    p. cm. — (Conversations with filmmakers series)

    Includes filmography and index.

    ISBN 978-1-60473-486-7 (cloth: alk. paper)—ISBN 978-1-60473-487-4 (pbk.: alk. paper)
1. Egoyan, Atom, 1960—Interviews. 2. Motion picture producers and directors—Canada—
Interviews. I. Morris, T. J., 1949– II. Title.

    PN1998.3.E334A5 2010

    791.4302'33092—dc22   2009037528

British Library Cataloging-in-Publication Data available

Contents

Introduction

The twelve interviews included in this volume represent the career of an independent filmmaker not yet fifty years of age. Atom Egoyan has played out his artistic vision in twelve feature films and numerous short films. Though his films may not fit the designations "avant garde" or "experimental," he certainly can be described as independent and unique both in his choice of subjects and his approach to filmmaking.

Perhaps his most distinguishing feature is his independence. As the filmography indicates, he often serves as a producer of his films either in his own right or through his company, Ego Film Arts. Moreover, he often writes the screenplays for his films and deserves the name *auteur*. He has, however, written screenplays for three adaptations from novels, giving each his individual stamp. Recently he has directed the screenplays of others; a film entitled *Chloe*, based on the French original *Nathalie* and in post-production at this writing, was written by Erin Cressida Wilson. His experiences with mainstream Hollywood filmmaking have not always been rewarding and he has fiercely maintained his independence. Support from various groups, most notably the Canadian government's support for the arts, and German and British public television, have enabled him to secure funding for the projects he wants to pursue.

Critics often admire Egoyan's novel approaches, although they remark on his dark subjects. Some complain that his movies are opaque, hard to understand. To be sure the viewer has to pay attention and put the pieces of the puzzle together. Non-chronological presentation is a frequent technique. He knows that his films are demanding in this way, but trusts the audience to stay with him and make the effort to receive the reward that psychologically complex films offer. He likes the idea that something hidden or missing will be discovered by the end of the film. It may be a character, as with *Family Viewing*, or a motivation, as with *Exotica*.

Other themes frequently found in Egoyan films are the driving search for identity, the place of the past in the present, difficult families, and unusual expressions of sexuality. Another feature that runs through Egoyan's films is the use of modern technology, specifically electronic media through which characters preserve or destroy their past, find an erotic connection, or present themselves to the world. He has said that at one time he thought of media as separating people, but he can now see it as connecting people. Voyeurism is an essential feature of cinema, which depends on the scopophilia of the audience. What is real, what is remembered, what is recorded—sometimes it takes the audience a moment to discern this in an Egoyan film. Characters are often engaged in the act of making images of each other.

Several of the interviews take place at film festivals where Egoyan premiers most of his films. He's a regular exhibitor at Cannes, the Toronto Film Festival, and New York Film Festival, winning four major festival awards at Cannes, in addition to serving in 1996 as a member of the international jury. Other interviews take place at the Ego Film Arts Studio in Toronto.

From these conversations it emerges that Egoyan had a safe and happy early life with artist/merchant parents, a grandmother, and one younger sibling, a sister named Eve who is now a concert pianist. He grew up in Vancouver and Victoria, British Columbia. The Egoyans (anglicized from Yeghoyan) were the only Armenian family in the area and thus Atom did not grow up in an Armenian community as did his wife Arsinée Khanjian. It was not until he attended college at the University of Toronto that he became actively engaged with the Armenian student organization there. The theme of ethnic identification and history that he discovered in his student days will find its way into his films.

In choosing the interviews I have tried to give a balanced overview of Egoyan's career. He is clearly accustomed to giving many interviews and is generally open, thoughtful, and forthright with his interviewers. He is happy to explain the genesis of films and exactly what he had in mind to convey, always giving generous credit to actors and collaborators. He works regularly with a collection of actors (for example, David Hemblen, Bruce Greenwood, Gabrielle Rose, and Maury Chaykin) and in addition works with Mychael Danna for music, Paul Sarossy as cinematographer, and Susan Shipton as film editor.

The first interview included in this volume is "Emotional Logic," conducted in 1993 by Marc Glassman, an experienced writer, editor, and book store proprietor. Originally appearing in the front of the published script of *Speaking Parts* (Egoyan's third feature film), it discusses most of his film and television work to that time. Egoyan reveals that writing and rejecting scripts is an important part of his process. If the script is not interesting, not worth his passion, it gets rejected. Ideas tease him. "I know that the act of filming people playing these parts is going to bring to the thematic a dimension that exceeds my imagination, and that's an important thing."

Egoyan's interview with Hamid Naficy from December 1993 is a lengthy, in-depth conversation interspersed with Naficy's reflections. His thesis is that the style of independent transnational filmmakers possesses an accent reflective of their ethnic background. He says, "[A]s a cultural hypothesis about exilic cinema, accented style involves the affective dimensions of consciousness such as sensibilities, impulses, restraints, and tones that are not fixed but that are in a continual process of latency and emergence and are evidenced by and expressed in certain forms, conventions, or styles." The interview examines how exile and ethnic identity affect the style of Egoyan's filmmaking.

Two interviews with Cynthia Fuchs are shorter pieces and serve partly as reviews for the recently released films *Exotica* (1994) and *Felicia's Journey* (1999). Fuchs, an associate professor of English and director of film and media studies at George Mason University, writes regularly for the *Popmatters* website. She notes that in *Exotica* the viewer is presented with a puzzle; there's something missing and the last piece is not presented until the end of the film and the triple storyline weaves together. "*[E]xotica* subtly, intelligently, coaxes us to question our own investments in what we're watching and, importantly, how we're reading these complicated, perpetually recontextualized images." In her second interview included here, she and Egoyan discuss some of the interesting points of *Felicia's Journey*, for example, the cliché of the serial killer story and the changes that Egoyan made concerning the mother (played by Arsinée Khanjian) in the film that distinguish it from William Trevor's novel.

Peter Harcourt's interview with Egoyan from *Post Script* investigates a number of interesting filmmaking choices and the motivations behind some artistic choices. Susan Bullington Katz's interview from the 2000 collection *Conversations with Screenwriters* concentrates on Egoyan's seventh film, *The Sweet Hereafter*, based on the novel by Russell Banks. Khanjian had given the book to Egoyan for his birthday and then he, luckily, met the author and obtained the option to film the book. In the interview Egoyan explains what adaptations he made in braiding the four strands of the book together and the difficult task of handling the subject of incest. He also discusses his work as an opera director in this interview.

The interview with Jason Wood ranges widely over Egoyan's work, revealing further cinema influences on Egoyan's film creations, for example filmmakers John Cassavetes, Jim Jarmusch, and Hal Hartley. Wood also explores the notion of what expectations Egoyan has of his audience.

Donato Totaro's interview explores Egoyan's second novel adaptation, *Felicia's Journey*, at Montreal's 1999 International Festival of New Cinema and New Medias. According to Totaro, "*Felicia's Journey* is a serial killer film unlike any other. Rather than the traditional serial killer pile of corpses and bloody mayhem, Egoyan, in his inimitable style, takes us into the nostalgic and romanticized private world of middle-aged catering supervisor Ambrose Hilditch." The interview examines the references to other thrillers by British directors in the film and also discusses Bob Hoskins's preparation for the role of Hilditch. Moreover, Egoyan discusses the adaptations and changes he had to make from the novel, for example giving the mother embodiment in the form of a 1950s television cooking show host.

A lengthy discussion with scholar Rebecca Comay concentrates on *Krapp's Last Tape*, the one-act play by Samuel Beckett that Egoyan was invited to direct for Irish television as part of the *Beckett on Film* archive. The director was especially pleased because his first ambition was to be a playwright (he wrote a number of plays as a high school student) and Beckett and Harold Pinter were his models. In the interview Egoyan recounts his drama influences and the use of tape and film in his works generally. *Krapp's Last Tape* was a labor of love and homage.

Monique Tschofen's "Ripple Effects" is an interview which concludes *Image and Territory: Essays on Atom Egoyan*, a selection of scholarly essays that Tschofen edited with Jennifer Burwell, published by Wilfred Laurier Press. Egoyan explains how he became interested in making films while he was a student at the University of Toronto. This essay covers Egoyan's career, bringing in his television work as well as his work as a director of operas and creator of museum installations. The interview also touches on the film *Ararat*.

The final two essays, both conducted in 2009, appeared first on radio, one on Resonance 104.4 (a British FM radio station devoted to the arts) and the other on the Canadian Broadcasting Corporation's series *Ideas*. Tania Ketenjian, like Egoyan of Armenian descent, concentrates her questions on *Adoration* (his most recent release at the time). They discuss the perspective of immigrants and also the effects of the Internet on the themes of identity and storytelling. The interview that completes the volume is by famed interviewer Eleanor Wachtel of the CBC. Wachtel covers Egoyan's entire career and elicits from him some interesting observations about how he came to be a filmmaker and how he arrived at some of his familiar themes. This interview has substantial excerpts from *Calendar, Ararat,* and *Adoration*.

As with all books in the Conversations with Filmmakers series, the interviews have not been substantially edited from the form of their initial publication. Consequently the reader will at times encounter repetitions of both questions and answers. However, the significance of the same questions being asked and the consistency (or inconsistency) of responses will prove of value to readers in their unexpurgated form.

I would like to thank Mrs. Debby McGary, administrative assistant for the Department of English Language and Literature at the University of Indianapolis for assistance with securing permissions for this book. I also thank my student assistants Nicole Rehman and Shan Hu for research assistance on this volume as well as librarian Lucy Fields.

TM

Chronology

1960   Born July 19 in Cairo, Egypt, the first of two children to Joseph and Shushan Yeghoyan.

1963   The Egoyan family moves to Victoria, British Columbia, Canada.

1978   Leaves British Columbia to attend college at the University of Toronto, Trinity College.

1979   Directs three short, experimental films as an undergraduate; active in Armenian student community.

1982   Graduates from the University of Toronto with a degree in International Relations; also studied classical guitar. Short film, *Open House*, sold to Canadian Broadcasting Company.

1984   First feature film, *Next of Kin*. Receives Golden Ducat at Mannheim Film Festival, and Genie nomination for Best Director.

1985   Directs *Twilight Zone*, TV series episode, "The Wall." *In This Corner*, sixty-minute TV show.

1987   Directs *Alfred Hitchcock Presents*, TV series episode, "The Final Twist." Writes and directs *Family Viewing*, presented at twelve festivals, winning prizes in Switzerland and Sweden.

1988   *Looking for Nothing*, TV.

1989   Writes and directs *Speaking Parts*, six Genie nominations.

1991   Writes and directs *The Adjuster*, fourth feature film. Best Canadian feature film at Toronto Festival of Festivals.

1993   *Calendar* filmed in association with German TV channel ZDF and Armenian National Television. Son Arshile born.

1994   Writes and directs *Exotica*, a "break-through" film, more widely viewed than any previous of his films. *Exotica* wins the International Critic's Prize at the Cannes Film Festival. Marriage to Arsinée Khanjian.

1995   Short film, "A Portrait of Arshile."

1997   Directs and writes the screenplay for *The Sweet Hereafter*, adapted from the novel by Russell Banks. Wins the Grand Jury Prize at Cannes and receives nominations for best director and best non-original screenplay at the 1998 Academy Awards. *Saraband; Yo-Yo Ma Inspired by Bach*, TV (Gemini Award for Best Short Dramatic Program). Knighted by the French government as *Chevalier des arts et letters*. Outstanding Canadian Award (Armenian Community Centre).

1999   Adapts and directs *Felicia's Journey*, based on the William Trevor novel of the same name. Awarded the Order of Canada.

2000   Edits and directs *Krapp's Last Tape*, from the play by Samuel Beckett, for Channel 4, RTE and the Irish Film Board.

2002   Writes and directs *Ararat*. The film garners many awards including five Genie Awards and Best Film on Human Rights from the Political Film Society of Hollywood.

2003   *Citadel*, with Egoyan as director, editor, and cinematographer. Movses Khorenatsi, Presidential Medal from the Republic of Armenia. Elected member of the Royal Canadian Academy of Arts.

2004   Opened Camera Bar, a fifty-seat cinema/lounge on Queen Street West in Toronto.

2005   *Where the Truth Lies*, director and screenplay, based on Rupert Holmes's novel of the same name.

2006   Begins in September to teach at the University of Toronto for a period of three years, joining the faculty of arts and science as the dean's distinguished visitor in theatre, film, music, and visual studies.

2008   Release of *Adoration*, director and screenplay. Receives the Dan David Prize for "Creative Rendering of the Past" from Tel-Aviv University.

2009   *Chloe*, a remake of the French film *Nathalie*, script by Erin Cressida Wilson, funded by Studiocanal, in post-production in June.

Filmography

Feature Films

1984
NEXT OF KIN
Producers: Ego Film Arts, Ontario Arts Council, Canada Council
Director/Screenplay/Editor: **ATOM EGOYAN**
Cinematographer: Peter Mettler
Music: **ATOM EGOYAN**, the Song and Dance Ensemble of Armenia
Costume Designer: Delaine Prasek
Cast: Patrick Tierney (Peter Foster), Berge Fazlian (George Deryan), Sirvat Fazlian (Sonya Deryan), Arsinée Khanjian (Azah Deryan), Phil Rash (Foster counselor), Paul Babiak (Deryan counselor), Margaret Loveys (Mrs. Foster), Thomas Tierney (Mr. Foster)
72 minutes

1987
FAMILY VIEWING
Producers: **ATOM EGOYAN**, Camelia Frieberg
Director and Screenplay: **ATOM EGOYAN**
Cinematographers: Robert MacDonald, Peter Mettler
Editors: Bruce McDonald, **ATOM EGOYAN**
Music: Mychael Danna
Costume Designer: Nancy Duggan
Art Director: Linda Del Rosario
Cast: David Hemblen (Stan), Aiden Tierney (Van), Gabrielle Rose (Sandra), Arsinée Khanjian (Aline), Selma Keklikian (Armen), Jeanne Sabourin (Aline's Mother), Rose Sarkisyan (Van's mother), Vasag Baghbourdarian (Young Van), Hrant Alianak (administrator), John Shafer (private detective), Garfield Andres (hotel bellboy), Edwin Stephenson (video salesman), Aino Pirskanen (mistaken woman), Souren Chekijian (priest

at funeral), Johnnie Eisen (Aline's client), John Pellatt (television voice-overs)
86 minutes

1989
SPEAKING PARTS
Producers: Camelia Frieberg, **ATOM EGOYAN**
Associate Producer: Donald Ranvaud
Director and Screenplay: **ATOM EGOYAN**
Cinematographer: Paul Sarossy
Editor: Bruce McDonald
Original Music: Mychael Danna
Art Director: Linda Del Rosario
Costume Designer: Maureen Del Degan
Cast: Gabrielle Rose (Clara), Michael McManus (Lance), Arsinée Khanjian (Lisa), David Hemblen (producer), Patricia Collins (housekeeper), Tony Nardi (Eddy), Gerard Parkes (father), Robert Dodds (doctor), Jacqueline Samuda (bride), Peter Krantz (groom), Frank Tata (Clara's brother), Patrick Tierney (clerk), Leszek Lis (housekeeper's friend), Sharon Corder (voice), David MacKay (man)
92 minutes

1991
THE ADJUSTER
Producers: Camelia Freiberg, **ATOM EGOYAN**, David Webb
Director and Screenplay: **ATOM EGOYAN**
Cinematographer: Paul Sarossy
Editor: Susan Shipton
Original Music: Mychael Danna
Costume Designer: Maya Mani
Art director: Linda Del Rosario
Cast: Elias Koteas (Noah Render), Arsinée Khanjian (Hera), Maury Chaykin (Bubba), Gabrielle Rose (Mimi), Jennifer Dale (Arianne), David Hemblen (Bert), Rose Sarkisyan (Seta), Armen Kokorian (Simon), Jacqueline Samuda (Louise), Gerard Parkes (Tim), Patricia Collins (Lorraine), Don McKellar (Tyler), John Gilbert (doctor), Stephen Ouimette (Larry), Raoul Trujillo (Matthew), Toni Nardi (motel manager), Paul Betis (man), Frank Jefferson (Simon as a baby)
102 minutes

1993
CALENDAR
Producers: Arsinée Khanjian, Simone Urdl
Director, Screenplay, and Editor: **ATOM EGOYAN**
Cinematographer: Norayr Kaspar
Music: Djivan Gasparian, Eve Egoyan, Garo Tchaliguian, Hovhanness Tarpinian
Cast: Arsinée Khanjian (translator), **ATOM EGOYAN** (photographer), Ashot Adamian (driver), Michelle Bellerose, Natalia Jasen, Susan Hamann, Sveta Kohli, Vica Tsvetnova, Roula Said, Annie Szamois, Anna Pappas, Amanda Martinez , Diane Kofri (guests)
75 minutes

1994
EXOTICA
Producers: **ATOM EGOYAN**, Camelia Frieberg
Associate Producer: David Webb
Director and Screenplay: **ATOM EGOYAN**
Cinematographer: Paul Sarossy
Editor: Susan Shipton
Original Music: Mychael Danna and Leonard Cohen
Costume Designer: Linda Muir
Art Directors: Linda Del Rosario and Richard Paris
Cast: Bruce Greenwood (Francis), Mia Kirshner (Christina), Don McKellar (Thomas), Arsinée Khanjian (Zoe), Elias Koteas (Eric), Sarah Polley (Tracey), Victor Garber (Harold), Calvin Green (customs officer), David Hemblen (customs inspector), Ken McDougall (doorman)
104 minutes

1997
THE SWEET HEREAFTER
Producers: Camelia Frieberg, **ATOM EGOYAN**, Robert Lantos, Andrås Håmori, David Webb, Sandra Cunningham
Director and Screenplay: **ATOM EGOYAN** (screenplay based on the novel by Russell Banks
Cinematographer: Paul Sarossy
Editor: Susan Shipton
Original Music: Mychael Danna
Costume Designer: Beth Pasternak

Art Director: Kathleen Climie
Cast: Ian Holm (Mitchell Stephens), Maury Chaykin (Wendell Walker), Gabrielle Rose (Delores Driscoll), Peter Donaldson (Schwartz), Bruce Greenwood (Billy Ansell), David Hemblen (Abbott), Brooke Johnson (Mary), Arsinée Khanjian (Wanda Otto), Tom McCamus (Sam Burnell), Stephanie Morgenstern (Allison), Earl Pastko (Hartley), Sarah Polley, (Nicole Burnell), Alberta Watson (Risa Walker), Caerthan Banks (Zoe Stephens), Kirsten Kieferle (stewardess), Simon Baker (Bear), Sarah Rosen Fruitman (Jessica), Marc Donato (Mason), Russell Banks (Dr. Robeson)
110 minutes

1999
FELICIA'S JOURNEY
Producers: Bruce Davey
Executive Producers: Paul Tucker, Ralph Kamp
Director and Screenplay: **ATOM EGOYAN**, based on the novel by William Trevor
Cinematographer: Paul Sarossy
Editor: Susan Shipton
Original Music: Mychael Danna
Costume Designer: Beth Pasternak
Art Director: Kathleen Climie
Cast: Bob Hoskins (Hilditch), Elaine Cassidy (Felicia), Claire Benedict (Miss Calligary), Brid Brennan (Mrs. Lysaght), Peter McDonald (Johnny), Gerard McSorley (Felicia's Father), Arsinée Khanjian (Gala), Sheila Reid (Iris), Nizwar Karanj (Sidney), Maire Stafford (Felicia's great-grandmother), Gavin Kelty (Shay Mulroone), Danny Turner (Young Hilditch), Susan Parry (Salome), Jean Marlowe (Old Woman), Sidney Cole (Ethiopian), Barry McGovern (gatherer), Sandra Voe (Jumble Sale Woman), Bob Mason (Jimmy)
114 minutes

2002
ARARAT
Producers: Robert Lantos, Sandra Cunningham, **ATOM EGOYAN**
Associate Producers: Julia Rosenberg, Simone Urdl
Director and Screenplay: **ATOM EGOYAN**
Cinematographer: Paul Sarossy
Editor: Susan Shipoton

Original Music: Mychael Danna
Costume Designer: Beth Pasternak
Art Director: Kathleen Climie
Cast: Bruce Greenwood (Martin/Clarence Ussher), Christopher Plummer (David), Eric Bogosian (Rouben), Elias Koteas (Ali/Jedvet Bey), Charles Aznavour (Edward), Brent Carver (Philip), David Alpay (Raffi), Arsinée Khanjian (Ani), Raoul Bhaneja (photographer), Marie-Josée Croze (Celia), Simon Abkarian (Arshile Gorky), Lousnak Abdalian (Shushan Gorky)
116 minutes

2004
CITADEL
(Mini DV)
Director, editor, and cinematographer: **ATOM EGOYAN**
Cast: **ATOM EGOYAN**, Arsinée Khanjian, Arshile Egoyan
92 minutes
[This film recounts a family visit to Lebanon, Khanjian's first since her family left to escape the civil war when she was seventeen.]

2005
WHERE THE TRUTH LIES
Producers: Robert Lantos, **ATOM EGOYAN**, Chris Chrisafis, Sandra Cunningham, Colin Leventhal
Director and Screenplay: **ATOM EGOYAN**, based on Rupert Holmes's novel
Cinematography: Paul Sarossy
Editor: Susan Shipton
Costume Designer: Beth Pasternak
Art Director: Craig Lathrop
Cast: Colin Firth (Vince Collins), Kevin Bacon (Lanny Morris), Alison Lohman (Karen O'Connor), David Hayman (Reuben), Maury Chaykin (Sally San Marco), Sonja Bennett (Bonnie Trout), Rachel Blanchard (Maureen), Kristin Adams (Alice), Deborah Grover (Mrs. O'Flaherty), Beau Starr (Jack Scaglia), Arsinée Khanjian (publishing executive), Gabrielle Rose (publishing executive), Don McKellar (publishing executive), David Hamblen (hotel concierge), John Moraitis (Irv Fleischman), Michael Reynolds (John Hillman), Erika Rosenbaum (legal assistant), Rebecca Davis (Denise), Simon Sinn (Stanley), Kathryn Winslow (publicist),

Stuart Hughes (journalist), Shannon Lawson (journalist), Sean Cullen (telethon announcer), Aliska Malish (grotto club woman), Brian Frank (club heckler)
107 minutes

2008
ADORATION
Executive Producers: Robert Lantos, Michele Halberstadt, Laurent Petin
Producers: Jennifer Weiss, Simone Urdl, **ATOM EGOYAN**
Associate Producer: Marcy Gerstein
Screenplay: **ATOM EGOYAN**
Cinematographer: Paul Sarossy
Editor: Susan Shipton
Original Music: Mychael Danna
Costume Designer: Debra Hanson
Art Director: Barry Isenar
Cast: Scott Speedman (Tom), Devon Bostick (Simon), Rachel Blanchard (Rachel), Kenneth Welsh (Morris), Dominic Cuzzocrea (Cab Driver), Katie Boland (Hannah), Noam Jenkins (Sami), Arsinée Khanjian (Sabine), Geraldine O'Rawe (Carole), Duane Murray (parking security), Hailee Sisera (Jennifer), Maury Chaykin (third passenger)
100 minutes

Short Films

LUSTS OF A EUNUCH – 1978
HOWARD IN PARTICULAR – 1979
AFTER GRAD WITH DAD – 1980
PEEP SHOW – 1981
CEREMONY AND ALLEGORY OF THE MEDIEVAL HUNT – 1984
MEN: A PASSION PLAYGROUND – 1985
"En passant," episode 4 of MONTRÉAL VU PAR – 1992
A PORTRAIT OF ARSHILE – 1995
THE LINE – 2000
DIASPORA – 2001
CHACUN SON CINEMA – 2007

Television

OPEN HOUSE – 1982

IN THIS CORNER – 1985

"Cupid's Quiver," FRIDAY THE 13TH: THE SERIES – 1987

"The Final Twist," ALFRED HITCHCOCK PRESENTS – 1987

"There Was a Lonely Girl," ALFRED HITCHCOCK PRESENTS – 1988

LOOKING FOR NOTHING – 1988

"The Wall," THE NEW TWILIGHT ZONE – 1989

GROSS MISCONDUCT – 1993

BACH CELLO SUITE #4: SARABANDE – 1997

KRAPP'S LAST TAPE – 2000

[Egoyan directed and edited a TV version of Samuel Beckett's play for RTE, Channel 4 Intl., and the Irish Film Board as part of the *Beckett on Film* project. John Hurt plays Krapp.]

Atom Egoyan: Interviews

Emotional Logic

Marc Glassman/1993

From *Speaking Parts* by Atom Egoyan, Toronto: Coach House, 1993. Reprinted by permission of the author.

MARC GLASSMAN: We're talking at length about your career to date and reflecting it through the prism of one film, *Speaking Parts.* The script takes up the major portion of this book, so it seems reasonable to start our conversation by asking you how much of the meaning presented in the film was already apparent for you in the script. In the film Lisa (played by Arsinée Khanjian) says, "There's nothing special about words." When you were working on the script, how important were the words? How important were the visuals? Where does the meaningful interplay occur?

ATOM EGOYAN: The whole question of meaning is something that I'm constantly flummoxed by. When one has a vision that requires a very precise framework one is always searching for justifications, for the rationale behind any given decision. Yet one is also aware that that could turn against itself. A very well-developed argument is all it takes to paralyze the whole process. If I'm not careful I can become incapable of writing or directing or conceptualizing. On the one hand my approach has been academic (although I resist that because I don't think of myself as an academic or intellectual filmmaker), but I do realize that in order for me to begin an emotional investigation, I have to create a structure that reflects the thematic of the film within the script itself. There has to be an approach, and it comes down to what the camera represents, what the camera is suggesting by its presence, by its absence or by the nature of its gaze.

For me it's not a simple process of recording dramatic action. There is some interplay with the lens which contributes—not in a purely pictorial sense, but in a more mysterious and elusive way—to what is going on. Those are the moments that really draw me to making images: I feel I can create a texture and a resonance through the act of making the photographic representations iconographic and yet not so iconographic that they're overwhelmed by a formalistic conceit. There is still some life in them. But people are aware of the fact that they are being recorded.

That knowledge that something is being recorded can be very overt, as in *Speaking Parts*. In that film a lot of the behaviour is modulated by the facts that Lance is a performer and that films and home videos are being created throughout the film. In many cases, the people are performing for the camera, which they know is recording them and transmitting their images. I think my characters all possess a degree of self-consciousness, and I find that that is in some way the twentieth-century state of being. We're all self-conscious, we're all aware of the archetypes we draw from in our behavioural patterns. We're all aware of images that we've seen that chronicle or depict behavioural states that we try to replay. The question of whether or not that renders our actions natural or unnatural lies at the core of my desire to make films.

MG: Having looked at *Speaking Parts* a lot recently, it seems to me that the apparent confrontation between video and film is a red herring. I don't see video as the pivotal element. Did you intend the video sequences to mean something significantly different from everything else in the film?

AE: I use video as a launching pad when characters veer off from being wholly rational. It can suggest a dream state, memory, hallucinations. It's really a springboard. There are times when it is used in a purely literal way, and there are times when the camera moves in onto the pixels, and one becomes very aware of the construct of the image. Then one has to see it as a phantasmagoric phenomenon.

Sometimes when one watches these scenes one can think of the video in terms of a surrealistic device, but I hope it goes beyond that. In *Family Viewing*, the very texture at times was suspect. The scenes in the condominium were shot on video, but there was no literal mechanical device that could have created those particular images. So they took on a metaphorical significance, they became a reflection of a state of mind. In *Speaking Parts*, video is treated in a more literal way. I think that the moments where it slips into fantasy are much clearer. There isn't as much ambiguity.

I confess that some of the change in *Speaking Parts* grew out of my dismay at seeing *Family Viewing* on video. I realized that when one tries to work with textures, one has to keep in mind that although these films may work with audiences when they're projected, a large number of people will only see the work on video. The problem with video in *Family Viewing* is that the device is too subtle. The film doesn't work on home video on the terms on which it was designed to work. It's easier to watch on home video because one isn't aware of the tension of watching these degraded images and watching the very monolithic cutting style in the condominium scenes. One's not aware that it's strange. It just seems comfortable. But if one watches it in a film theatre it certainly strikes one as being disturbing. In *Speaking Parts*, I wanted the devices I was using to be able to explain themselves even on the television screen. It's possible to watch *Speaking Parts* on home video and get a full sense of what the film is trying to explore. If that means I have to be a bit less subtle about how I'm working with textures, then that's just one of the disadvantages of video.

I'm pleased that *Speaking Parts* is now on laser disc because it's possible to retrieve some of the detailing. A filmmaker is always at the mercy of bad dubs. I do really like those moments in *Family Viewing* where the boy reaches up to change the dial on his monitor in the nursing home. If you're watching on the TV set then he's reaching up for your dial as well. It's a shocking moment. I used to write films as projected images on a screen, not as home video. I'm more aware of video now. It wasn't a market I had in mind when I was making *Family Viewing*. Both *Family Viewing* and *Speaking Parts* have found a much larger market on video and laser disc than they did in theatres.

There are two copies of *Speaking Parts* in every Blockbuster Video store in the States, which gives it the kind of distribution that didn't occur here or in U.S. cinemas. I was speaking in Montreal and someone from a small town in Nova Scotia said that the copy of *Family Viewing* in his local video store was the subject of a lot of discussion. That anecdote suggests to me that there is a viable way of distributing that type of film. I guess a filmmaker starting a career now would take that as a given, but I have been working during the time when that transition was being made.

MG: *Speaking Parts*' plot involves an affair between a scriptwriter, Clara (played by Gabrielle Rose), and an actor, Lance (played by Michael Mc-Manus). You have Lance audition a bit of the script for Clara, and you even have the Producer (played by David Hemblen) act as a re-write man on the script. Let's talk about that alternative script, and the Producer's "re-write." How far did you carry the notion of that script?

AE: That script is something that I actually wrote for Gabrielle to look at. It's really a banal melodrama. One of the curious aspects of our media-saturated society is that we begin to think that a media image has a currency outside of its fairly practical purposes. We think that when things are elevated to the level of transmitted image they gain in importance and significance in relation to our own experience. I loved the idea of Clara's character: someone who had had this phenomenal event in her life and who was plagued by guilt. What could she do to create a tribute to her brother, this missing person? The fact that she ritualistically goes to watch his image in a "video mausoleum" easily segued into the idea that she could take what that image meant and turn it into a commercially viable image, a film.

MG: The environment that you create in *Speaking Parts* is one in which alienation is highly evident. What sort of society were you trying to delineate, or critique, in the film?

AE: *Speaking Parts* tries to chronicle different stratas of people who are infatuated with each other and whose lives are structured through media. There is Eddy, the king of domestic video: he makes home videos and distributes mainstream ones at a store. Then there's the David Hemblen character, a TV and film producer who is obviously operating at a much wider level of distribution. That creates a class structure: the Producer can use the fact that he's made it and take that as a given. Remember when he tells Lance, and I'll paraphrase: "Images that I've made have become part of your subconscious, therefore you must respect me"? That's a fundamental way of outlining a class superiority. His authority as a Producer goes beyond the level of questioning. "I'm here because of certain things that I've done, and you must submit to my authority because those things have become an inexorable part of your experience." It doesn't matter what shows he produced (and Lance becomes too intimidated to ask what they were). In the film industry, that happens all the time. People want to know what you've done. Very often, I don't have to say what I've done, I just have to say who's distributed it, or where it's been seen. What a show is about or what a filmmaker has actually accomplished artistically are secondary to what sort of airplay or distribution a film has had and how many people have seen it. I love that backdrop to the film: all the people are fighting for their own identities, but the currency with which they're fighting is the projected images they're receiving or trying to make. And make on their own terms, sometimes succeeding and sometimes failing. I still continue to present characters who are engaged in the act of making images of each other. *Calendar* is about that. It's endlessly fascinating for me. In *Calendar*, the images include photographs for a calendar, home video, and film. If I couldn't continue to explore these ideas, I probably wouldn't be making films.

In the society I've depicted in *Speaking Parts*, there are producers and there are watchers. There are many reasons why that society is segregated into those two camps, but there are very particular rules in *Speaking Parts*. Why watchers want to be producers is easy to understand, but why they are prevented from doing so becomes a very interesting political issue. It has to do with the fact that certain types of images are more accessible than others. Why is it that certain people are able to channel their feelings through the media and have those ideas and emotions communicated at a mass level while other people are marginalized? Does it have to do with the psychological fabric of those characters? How much of it has to do with the technology they can get their hands on?

In terms of my own situation, I've seen my work grow from very marginal audiences to more mainstream audiences. What is the rationale for that? Is it because I've been able to afford more expensive cameras, better sound systems? Is it because my vision has matured? These are very interesting questions. *Speaking Parts* was a way of exploring them in a contained drama.

MG: The TV talk show, with the Producer acting as the host, is staged near the end of the film. It's an intricate and resonant scene. How did you devise it?

AE: As I was plotting the film, I realized I loved the idea of the TV show, where I could take an issue that is fictional but create a format that people are used to identifying with. On "real" TV talk shows, there's a level of interaction between the audience and the guests. In *Speaking Parts* I'm preventing the audience from reaching that "normal" level of interaction because I've assigned conflicting roles to all of the characters they are seeing. The resulting confusion on the part of the viewer is something that thrills me. The viewer doesn't quite know what it is he's watching.

The most resonant moments for me as a viewer always come when I don't quite know what it is I'm watching. I'm lost in a wash of emotions and feelings that don't originate from something that I can identify immediately. They're the most exhilarating passages in cinema because they come so close to the dream state. Cinema has the ability to transport us into other worlds, but for a number of reasons I'll never understand, we are taught to regard those moments in a film with a lot of suspicion. If something is to be a dream state, it has to be signalled in a very specific way: most obviously, there's a shot of a character rustling around in his bed at night, cut to an image, then cut to him rustling around a bit more, cut to the image. It's so cliched it's absurd, but it's still used as a device. It's as though we can't allow ourselves to disengage our rational selves and just drift with the film.

MG: Did the script for *Speaking Parts* immediately follow *Family Viewing*?

AE: Scripts are developed and rejected between films. I find that the most informative part of the process is writing an entire script that I reject because I've decided that something's just not interesting enough to pursue. It's not worth my passion, or there aren't enough reasons to make it into a film. It exists too neatly as a script; it doesn't necessarily open up possibilities or avenues for exploration as cinema. I'm at that stage right now. I've written a script that I've decided to reject. It's an important part of the filmmaking process.

MG: When you finally started on the script for *Speaking Parts*, how long did it take for it to cohere into something that you wanted to make into a film?

AE: It developed over about six months. I've always had in mind a film set in a hotel because I worked in a hotel for a long time. The original draft dealt with a relationship between two people who work in the hotel housekeeping department. That was the springboard. It was Lance and Lisa originally. It developed from there. I loved the idea of a person being infatuated with someone who fails to recognize that person's existence. The idea of Lance being an extra was always there as well. In the first drafts I made a lot more of Lisa visiting Lance on shoots and always being pushed away. There were scenes of her trying to coax marginal people on the film crew to give him a speaking part. There were a lot more anonymous casting sessions—where Lance wouldn't know what he was applying for but he would be reading various lines into a camera—auditions that never came to fruition. That was the whole film. It didn't have enough resonance. It didn't have the dramatic drive for a feature film. Clara appeared in the second draft, as did the Producer.

MG: How about Clara? Was she a totally original creation or does she have some basis in people you've encountered in the film industry?

AE: Clara is based on a woman who had a screenplay (I get sent a lot of screenplays). In this woman's case, I had to confront someone who had written material that wasn't good but that was obviously based on something that was very close to her. I really tried to find a way of dealing with this person, to communicate that although I was interested in the material I didn't feel the script was well written.

It's difficult to say how things evolve short of giving actual anecdotes about where they come from. *The Adjuster* is very easy to talk about because it was written in the aftermath of an experience that my family had gone through, and it just came in a very lucid flash. The other films deal with figures that are amalgamations of people I know, or are fantasies on experiences I've had. They're riffs. *The Adjuster* is very concrete because the time between the event and the writing of the script was very condensed, a matter of months.

MG: Still *The Adjuster* has "riffs" too: the Censor Board, the Adjuster's house, the bizarre couple who invade that home. I find the layering of the stories in *Speaking Parts* to be quite complex. How did the final script evolve?

AE: The evolution came about through my interest in developing themes. Here is a question: can people live through imagistic representations of life? If they can, do they then need to gain control of how those representations are made? And if these questions can be answered "yes" and "yes," at what point do people fall in love with the representation of the loved one? Maybe they are really falling in love with their own ability to conjure up that image. Does the love then become narcissistic? I find little satisfaction in having characters proposing these ideas literally, so I try to find a structure that brings up these issues.

MG: *Speaking Parts* is a complicated narrative with a number of intertwining plots. Did you have any organizing principles when it came time to structure the script?

AE: It was a question of seeing material and trying to go back to a notion of counterpoint. I'd develop the theme and certain voices that articulate that theme by playing with it and creating tensions between two disparate tracks, which are ultimately reflecting or mirroring a common concern. That's the notion of counterpoint in musical as well as narrative structures.

A fugual structure is a greater articulation of that: in baroque music there's the ground bass, a repeating bass line, which often becomes the foundation of the piece. That's what distinguishes the music of Purcell from that of Bach. Purcell had a heavy reliance on the ground bass, on the repeating theme at the bottom, while Bach—a composer I adore— was able to create as much surprise and variety in the ground bass as in the other voices. I don't know how far I can extend the analogy, but in *Speaking Parts* the repeating theme is people's relationship to each other in a world obsessed by representation. Each element can be seen to heighten the other strand. I find I'm drawn to the fugual form. It comes very naturally to me because of my musical training.

I don't know how much of the structuring is conscious when I'm writing. I think that I work my way through material, and for me it's just a question of what sustains my interest. At what point do I feel the need to switch channels to something else? In fact, one could see my films as fugual, but one could also see them as being structured around channel-hopping. A scene appears for a while, and then one switches to something else. It's almost as though one's switching between two different programs, and at some point they're married. I've been influenced by counterpoint in music, but I've probably been just as influenced by channel-hopping as a kid. I don't know which has had the greater impact on my work.

MG: It seems to me that each film is a process of exploration for you. Do you find that certain characters and situations on the page almost incite you to start filming?

AE: Yes, they're teasing me, and I know that I cannot be satisfied with what they're proposing on a page. I know that the act of filming people playing these parts is going to bring to the thematic a dimension that exceeds my imagination, and that's an important thing. One can read a script and imagine what it's going to be like, but that isn't enough for me. It isn't enough to imagine how these characters could come alive, as the saying goes. I want to become more alive by watching them being filmed, and I want to experience the tension that is going to be part of what I'm going to say. I'm never drawn to characters who just seem to yell out "represent me." I'm attracted to people who are lost in a world that I can navigate. I have to be able to show the characters' attempts at gaining aspects of personality and engage the viewer in a concomitant process of discovery.

MG: You've got the script. Who do you cast? Do you write for particular people? Are you looking for another adventure by exploring these mysterious characters with new performers?

AE: Choosing actors is an absolutely essential part of the process. Some are new to me and some I return to. Actors are phenomenal, because they are there to defend their characters. In *Speaking Parts* that becomes an interesting conceit in itself. I found that the actors would defend what they saw as the emotional logic behind behaviour patterns or activities. I can write stuff, and I can have people go through weird contortions to get to certain points, but the actor is the person who will actually test the character and make sure that it makes emotional sense and isn't just a dramatic contrivance. That's very important for me: that an actor can see his way through a character who (in my films especially) goes through some very extreme states of behaviour. Take the scene with Gabrielle Rose, the one where she breaks down. The way she does that is thrilling to me. I'm just amazed by it. Arsinée's scene with the bride. The way that came across thrills me.

MG: Did you intend Arsinée to play Lisa?

AE: No, that's the funny thing. Arsinée gets full credit for getting the role because originally I wanted her to play Clara, but she wanted to be Lisa. She was so insistent that we eventually auditioned her for that part, and that's how she got it. It was supposed to be the other way around. Gabrielle was supposed to play Lisa. That seems remarkable now.

MG: I find Lisa to be a real stretch for Arsinée: that character is so unlike her as a person.

AE: That's the surprising thing about all of Arsinée's performances. People are always surprised to meet her because she's so open and so spontaneous with her ideas and feelings. In the films, up to now, she's always been trapped in some character. She's not in my new one, *Calendar.* In that film she plays someone much freer with herself, much more easily identifiable. That sense of freedom permeates the entire film. *Calendar* is probably the most enjoyable film I've made.

MG: Do you have a set manner in which you work with actors?

AE: Not at all. There are some actors who want to have a very meticulous, analytical breakdown of why their character is behaving in a certain way, and then there are others who don't want to talk very much and don't want to rehearse. I have to be receptive to both types of performers. I like to rehearse a lot. When we're dealing with a lot of text and ideas it's often very important to develop a whole interior script to which an actor can refer. But there are some performers who I've worked with who will just intuit their way through and don't have to have anything explained to them. I have to make myself shut up—which is not easy for me to do—but sometimes that's what the actors need. Anyone from a theatrical background is used to discussing things, and most of the actors I've worked with have had that background. Elias Koteas, who played the Adjuster, actually prefers to work on the intuitive level. He doesn't want to rehearse too much. He really wants to feel a scene as it happens at that moment. I have to create a space for that. There are people who find the way I articulate my ideas to be completely bewildering. There is an approach to all my films that is very simple and emotional, and they do follow an emotional logic. It's possible to see the films on those terms and not get caught up in a lot of the other issues that I like to talk about.

It's difficult for me to talk about emotional representations on film because I find them to be so self-evident. *Speaking Parts* is almost operatic, isn't it? The way emotions are conveyed, emotional states of mind, notions of need and desire and longing and rejection: these conceits are the basis for making the film. But I don't want to talk about those things because they're beyond discussion. I take those as givens.

MG: I'm intrigued by the character of the Adjuster. How much of that personality was worked out in advance? How much was a response to the intuitive nature of your actor, Elias Koteas?

AE: That character follows a certain pattern which I seem to have established for male leads. They are always people who drift through space without ever knowing their potential to affect other people. What I found strong about the Adjuster was the way his job could automatically transport him to the level of myth. He could suddenly become an angel of reconstruction, of rematerialization, by descending on people's lives and redirecting their energies while they are absolutely devastated. They could completely lose themselves to him for two weeks or so to get their claim and then either stay his friend or drop him. That character was very clear in my mind. It's a character I could understand. It had nothing to do with an adjuster.

Elias was really important, because if that character were played by someone who seemed completely cognizant of his effect on other people, someone who displays his analytical ability through his eyes—John Malkovich or William Hurt, for example—it would not have had the same effect. It would have seemed as if this character knew what he was doing, was somehow driven by it for very clear and perhaps malicious reasons. What I liked about Elias from the other films he'd done was his very open quality. He's emotional but not fixed in any particular type of mindset that could categorize him as being manipulative. That's what the whole film toys with: is he manipulating these people or are they manipulating him? It was very important to have an actor whose presence could keep that ambiguity open. With a lot of actors it would have fallen on the side of him manipulating these people.

MG: The difference between Elias in *The Adjuster* and your other leads is that he is far more intense. An audience does care for the Adjuster in a more connected way than it does for Michael McManus's Lance in *Speaking Parts.* Was that your intent?

AE: It has a lot to do with my relationship with the actor. Elias is a very emotional person. The kind of direction I gave him had to be rooted in that. There are aspects of Elias's personality that I think endow that character with a level of emotionality that really excited me. That's why I wanted to use him. Michael has a different personality that was perfectly in keeping for what I wanted in *Speaking Parts.*

I think actors are receptive to any project. The question is whether one has access to them, whether one can bypass the various screens that they have set up to protect themselves from the public at large. Actors are always really excited about taking risks. I don't think the financial consideration is as important as others think it is. What's more important is letting the actors know that I'm around and that my interest in their participation is not limited to their marquee value but has something to do with what they possess as personalities.

MG: You came to film out of theatre and music. Why not be a theatre director?

AE: Once I got onto the idea of the camera, and the idea of the camera being a possible participant and character, I felt that in some ways it allowed me to become more private. Film by nature doesn't require the same type of interaction as the theatre. It's a much more solitary experience, watching a film, than going to a theatrical presentation. It suited my vision. I also felt that in a lot of the drama I was writing I was just treading over material that other people had done. I was so influenced by Pinter or Beckett that I never really found my own voice in the drama I was doing. It was easier for me to feel confident about my direction and scripting when I was making films. I was able to absorb influences, let them pass through me and grow outside of them more easily than I could with theatre.

MG: Some critics have referred to your scripts as hermetic. Do you think that a general audience can comprehend the motivation behind some of your narrative strategies?

AE: That's a very big question for me. I have to believe that they can. The films become much richer when one is able to position philosophical arguments into the narrative. I realize that people are not necessarily trained to recognize those questions, so my films can also be appreciated on other terms, simple emotional terms. How many people watching David Cronenberg's work are familiar with Cartesian philosophy? Very few. But if a viewer does know Descartes, that adds another level of appreciation to the work. My lack of familiarity with Cartesian philosophy made it impossible to know how seriously I should take Cronenberg's earlier films. At a certain point I just trust myself to the vision of someone whose work I like and respect.

MG: There's something ineffable about the relationship between an artist and an audience. How do you see it?

AE: It's about taking myself and a group of people on a journey to a place that they have not seen or felt before but which rings with a truth or authenticity for reasons that surprise me. There's an unknown energy that either works or it doesn't. And then, when the doors within these rooms open for people to drift in and lose themselves, there is extraordinary potential for interaction. It's an interactive process because there is so much dreaming and projecting onto my images; people want them to operate in so many different ways. They want things to be better paced, or they want some actor to look better, or they want someone to do something that's going to throw them. They cannot change the course of these images; it's inexorable. They have to commit themselves to the way these things unfold. That tension between what the viewer would like to think is happening and what is actually happening can create convergences that are impossible to consider in other art forms.

I don't think the filmmaker is always in control of that tension or interaction with the audience. The films that really excite me are those in which it is unclear if the filmmaker is really aware of how disturbing or moving the image is. The filmmaker just felt the image at that moment, but its implications are overwhelmingly beautiful or monstrous or hideous. The image provokes these reactions because it is calling on something primal.

MG: In experimental films and videos, questions of texture or sound are often preeminent. In your films, although narrative concerns have precedence, similar questions arise out of your aesthetic interests. In fact, some of these issues of texture occur within the script itself. You're making pictures that carry coded messages that move the notion of the narrative forward. Will audiences appreciate and decode your stories?

AE: Well, I hope so. That's why I'm making films. I approach my own subject matter and the way I direct my own scripts completely differently from the way in which I direct other people's scripts. When I apply my directorial talents to someone else's material, the question becomes: how do I best serve the material? How can I convey the ideas in a cinematic way? When I did *Gross Misconduct* the CBC biography of hockey player Brian Spencer, there were aspects of his life that drew me to the project. For instance, Spencer's father was ritualistically shot to death by the RCMP at a TV studio while he was trying to see his son's first game in a national broadcast. The subject matter appealed to me, but it would have been problematic to take my approach and apply it to the script since that aspect of Spencer's history was just part of its structure, not its preponderant reason for being a script. If I were to write that script it would be completely different. When I've directed for other people I have paid close attention to style; the camera has been an active participant but in a more classical way than it is in my own films. My films are, to a certain extent, a reaction against the type of filmmaking I do in a more mercenary way. I make my images and code languages in a very specific way. When I'm making my own films I have the highest possible expectations of my audience. I have to think they look at films the same way I look at films.

MG: In the case of *Gross Misconduct*, did they allow you a fairly free hand to re-write?

AE: To re-structure. The film as it exists is structured quite differently from the original script. I worked on that with Paul Gross, the writer. I proposed my idea of the structure and he incorporated it into the final scenario.

MG: *Speaking Parts* features one of your favourite character actors in a showy role. David Hemblen is superb as the Producer, a slightly sinister figure who always seems to be in complete control of events. How much of your own experiences as a director were worked into that part?

AE: A lot of the things he says I can't help but hear myself saying in my professional life. He says (paraphrasing my own script), "Clara's script was something that was very important to her, something that she went through, but that wasn't what interested me, it wasn't what I felt other people wanted to hear." He embodies that approach of taking certain elements of people's lives but getting rid of their point of view. I find it very funny when he says, "This script is so important that not only am I going to produce it, I am also going to act in it." He's really going all the way. That scene in the TV studio where he has to communicate to the actors who they are, what they're about, that sort of little dance to get them excited, that's what every director does. It's part of the whole absurdity of filmmaking. I could be in the most rotten mood ever and I still have to get a shooting day made. When I am on the set, I find myself twisting in the most extraordinary contortions to get people excited and revved up. The whole issue of manipulating reality and exaggerating and twisting and bending and making things fit one's notion of dramaturgy at the risk of any real authenticity is part of the process. I'm constantly doing it.

Another factor that influenced the creation of the Producer was a very strange experience I had when I was directing the pilot for *Friday the 13th*. I had a lot of conversations with the producer of that series. He was in L.A., and we would have sessions at the end of the day. He would have the rushes on VHS, and I would phone and listen to him watching the rushes. I'd be on conference call. There would be a number of executives from the studio watching the rushes I'd made, and they'd all be commenting freely, as they were watching, to me at the other end. I'd be giving explanations or I'd be taking notes and after a while I thought, this is very odd. This producer was like the Producer in *Speaking Parts:* he had many projects going at the same time and he was very hands-on. He was intimidating as well. I found that character fascinating.

MG: You've already mentioned the fugue as being an important structural element in the film. I've always found *Speaking Parts* to be more visually elaborate than your previous features. Did you intend the visuals, the sets, the music—the production values—to indicate a progression, economically, from your earlier films?

AE: It's important to realize that as *Speaking Parts* evolved I was dealing with a lot of personal frustration with the people who didn't understand that the devices and textures in *Family Viewing* were the result of a very carefully thought-out plan as opposed to budgetary limitation. That drove me crazy. I'll never forget a journalist who, during the Toronto Festival of Festivals, commented that the acting seemed stilted, the sets looked like sets, and the whole work looked like it was shot on bad film stock. Those were three things I had actually paid a lot of attention to, to create! Months later, when the film was building momentum, the same person was doing a profile piece on my work and he asked me, "How do people usually react to *Family Viewing* when they first see it?" I said, just to test his mettle, "Some people say, 'The acting seemed stilted, the sets looked like sets, and it looked like it was shot on bad film stock.'" Instead of saying that was the way he felt the first time he saw it, he said, "Oh really, how could people think that?"

That sort of confusion began to eat at me. I had to create a look for *Speaking Parts* that made it clear that any deviation from the way films normally appear was intentional, and people could not pass it off as "the budget." If I had had three times as much money to make *Family Viewing* I would have made it exactly the same way. With *Speaking Parts*, since it deals so much with people being seduced by images, seduced into the world of the image, it was very important that the film images themselves be seductive. I was drawn to the colonial-style hotel and its old-world panelling because they suggested the sophistication of an earlier time. By placing the main action there, I created a counter-effect to the video technology so a viewer was not able to apply the usual reaction to seeing high tech in film, which is that it's somehow futuristic. In order to get that dichotomy across it was important that the environments seemed lush. We worked on that a lot with the production designer to create an effect that would make a viewer want to be in that elegant conference room. We didn't want the locations to seem sterile or cold, even though what goes on in them—video-sex, for example—might have those associations.

MG: What were the budgets for *Family Viewing*, *Speaking Parts*, and *The Adjuster*?

AE: My budgets have grown slightly bigger each time. *Family Viewing* was made for $200,000, *Speaking Parts* for $800,000, and *The Adjuster* for $1.5 million. Don't forget I'm fortunate to be working with exceptionally talented people. I rely on the artists I work with to pull off amazing feats for meagre amounts of money.

MG: Some of the people who worked on your earlier films have gone on to direct their own features. Most notably, Peter Mettler directed *The Top of His Head* and *Tectonic Plates*, and Bruce McDonald made *Roadkill* and *Highway 61*. You used Peter Mettler as cinematographer for *Next of Kin* and *Family Viewing* and then worked with Paul Sarossy on *Speaking Parts* and *The Adjuster*. Is it different working with Paul?

AE: I worked with Peter early on in my career. Discussions with him about the camera and its possibilities were crucial to my development. Peter's whole sense of being able to use the camera to record completely intuitive moments is a thrilling concept. It makes cinematography a pure art form.

Every working relationship takes a while to get used to, because you can't help projecting the way you formed a previous relationship on to the new one. Paul is someone who doesn't want to discuss things as much as Peter did. He is definitely in synch with what the material demands, but in a very different way than Peter was. One has to understand that some people don't necessarily find much value in the process of discussing things beforehand, or they find that draining, and that's completely valid. It just takes a greater leap of faith for someone like me who tends to over-articulate things.

Film is weird that way. Before a production starts, there are all these meetings. I meet the key people—the costume designer, the properties designer—and I launch into my harangue about my vision of the film. Then what do I do? Do I wait for them to give me something, or try to check out if I have something in common with them at a personal level? It's a very strange process.

MG: You talked earlier about the operatic quality of *Speaking Parts*. Certainly a major element of that "operatic" quality is Clara's story, the film within the film. You've commented that you find her own script to be quite banal. How do you think Clara relates to her story?

AE: What's interesting is that she herself does very little to defend her material on an emotional level. When she's asking Lance to defend her idea to the Producer, she says, "It happened to me and my brother." That's as close as she gets. She does not talk about what she went through. When the Producer explains to Lance that the script is based on the tragic story of Clara and her brother, Lance realizes for the first time that her brother actually died. Clara doesn't capitalize on this when she's trying to convince Lance. She doesn't try to give him a history or a story that conveys the depths of her emotional despair; she trusts that he will sense it. That is a very curious thing for someone to do with Lance, because he's not entirely capable of feeling someone else's emotions. And it raises a curious issue: to what extent can one trust that someone else will, as Lisa says, "feel someone else feeling you" when those feelings are mediated, when they have filters and screens? That's what truly interests me in the film, not the mixing of video and film technologies. To what extent can one trust one's identity to someone else feeling what that identity is about?

MG: That's at the core of the film. And the answer in *Speaking Parts:* nobody does.

AE: It's very bleak. No one does, no one can. The most piercing moments—those with the husband and the new bride, or the father breaking down and crying—are held under such scrutiny because everyone else is trying to glean some truth from them. It's funny and yet completely vampiristic.

MG: You briefly commented earlier on one of my favourite scenes in the film. It occurs when Lance has to let Clara know that the character of the sister has been written out of the script. Gabrielle Rose seizes that moment to create an emotionally pure—and chilling—hysterical laugh that gives the audience a look into the depths of her despair.

AE: Do you notice what's actually happening there at the level of texture? Throughout the film, in all the scenes you've seen Clara, you've seen her on monitors looking straight at the camera. In that scene, the coverage is almost mathematical. It's shot and cut so that Lance and Clara appear to be across the table from each other, appear to be looking at each other rather than at monitors. That is the moment at which her breakdown occurs. For me that is such a great thing. Up until that moment you've been seeing this coverage in which a monitor has been so intrinsically involved. Clara and Lance seem to be looking right at each other across a table, but they are actually thousands of miles apart and are looking at screens. Then, at that point, one suspends one's disbelief; one is watching them watching each other as if there were no barriers at all. I don't think a viewer thinks about that when he's watching it, but it was necessary for me to have that idea in mind when I was directing it.

I think that's a good example of the difference between my approach as a director and yours as a critic. For you that scene is "emotionally pure"; you might not even be aware of all the textural and formally technical things taking place there which for me are profound and very exciting. Yet it was the technical aspect of that scene that allowed me to arrive at that moment of emotional honesty! I could not have come to that moment if I had just thought of it as a pictorial representation of someone breaking down. I need something more to arrive at that emotional moment, to explore something that simple. I have great suspicions about conveying screen emotion. It's my feeling that it can be too easy to just fix the camera on someone going through emotional turmoil. There's something very disturbing about that for me, about my reasons for doing it. I strive to find a structure that allows me to address my own suspicion and still communicate an emotional story. My hope and my dream is that the viewer is involved in all the levels of contradiction and all the levels of complexity that a moment like that actually sustains.

The Accented Style of the Independent Transnational Cinema
A Conversation with Atom Egoyan

Hamid Naficy/1993

From *In Cultural Producers in Perilous States: Editing Events, Documenting Change*, ed. George E. Marcus. Chicago: University of Chicago Press, 1997. Reprinted by permission of the University of Chicago Press.

Situating Egoyan

The conversation that follows is a result of some six hours of taped interviews I conducted in December 1993 in Toronto, Canada, with filmmaker Atom Egoyan. Next to David Cronenberg, he is considered to be the "most original" Canadian director today (Atamian 1991: 70; Ansen 1992). He has been called "the most accomplished Canadian director of his generation" (Johnson 1991) and labeled "Canada's 1st Multicultural Feature Filmmaker, grant-magnet and prize pony" (Balley 1989: 46), a characterization he derides (see below). His films have occasionally received criticism on grounds of being "dishonest and posturing, more like intellectual masturbation" (Kempley 1990) or for being "pretentious" and "elegantly empty" (Maslin 1989). However, overall his films have been such a favorite of the international film festivals that he is regarded as "a child of the festival circuit" (Handling 1993). It is at these festivals that his films have received high praise and almost universal critical acclaim. Calling him one of the most talented directors at the 1987 Montreal Film Festival, Wim Wenders publicly turned over his $5000 award for *Wings of Desire* (1988) to Egoyan for his film *Family Viewing. The Adjuster* won the special Jury Prize at the 1991 Moscow

Film Festival, and the 1993 Cannes Film Festival gave Egoyan the International Critics Prize for his latest film, *Exotica*.

Atom Egoyan was born in Egypt in 1960 to two artists, descendants of Armenian refugees. His parents ran a successful furniture store until the rising tide of Nasserist nationalism and the parochialism of the local Armenian community encouraged their emigration in 1962 to Victoria, British Columbia. Atom was three years old at the time. The only Armenian family in the area, they set up another furniture store, called Ego Interiors (Atom Egoyan's own film company is called Ego Film Arts). Although Egoyan spoke Armenian as a child, he gave that up when he entered the kindergarten to forestall ethnic embarrassment and harassment. He also refused to speak Armenian at home; whenever his parents spoke Armenian to him, he covered his ears. At eighteen he moved to Toronto and became what he thought was a fully assimilated Canadian, graduating with honors in international relations from the University of Toronto. While there he led a socially active life, writing plays, publishing film criticism in the school paper, and working on student films.

His first short film, *Howard in Particular* (1979), was made there, followed by several more shorts. His contact at the university with the nationalist Armenian students exposed Egoyan's hitherto unassimilated ethnic aspects and placed him on a trajectory of increased and deeper ethnicization that has characterized his work ever since. His output can be divided into three general categories: short films, television films and episodic series, and feature films. Despite the wide reception of some of his feature and television films, Egoyan has remained an independent filmmaker throughout his career, relying on funds from Canadian (CBC), German (ZDF), and British (channel 4) public television, regional and local arts councils, private sources, and his own earnings. The overall high production value of his films belies the ridiculously low budgets within which he operates. *Next of Kin* was made for $37,000; *Family Viewing*, for $160,000; *Calendar*, for $100,000; *Exotica* was budgeted at $2 million, the highest ever for Egoyan.

Like most independent transnational filmmakers, he has had to (and has chosen to) take on multiple functions in his films: he has written and directed all of his features, edited several of them (*Next of Kin, Family Viewing*, and *Calendar*), functioned as executive producer in one (*Speaking Parts*), and acted in one (*Calendar*). His wife, Arsinée Khanjian, has also appeared as the star of several of his films, as have other actors of Armenian descent. As I have discussed elsewhere (Naficy 1994), the adoption of such multiple roles and employment of ethnic talent gives independent transnational and exilic directors such as Egoyan fuller control over the content, style, and cost of their projects. At the same time, however, this opens them up to the tensions and chaos of their marginal location, in both the culture at large and the film industry in particular. As such, their films tend to inscribe more fully their own biographies, personal obsessions, and auteurist visions.

Accented Style

Although ethnicity and exile are not dominant themes in Egoyan's early feature films, they are there in submerged and latent forms. As Ella Shohat (1991: 219) has demonstrated, issues of race, ethnicity, and submerged ethnicity are not limited to the so-called ethnic films made by marginalized ethnic directors. In fact, much of the mainstream Hollywood cinema is "saturated" with ethnic and racial resonances. I want to propose here the "accented style" of filmmaking as a way of speaking about the manner in which independent transnational or exilic films make their meaning. Egoyan's films are exemplars of the accented style. One of the marks of difference is the accent in one's speech or the dialect which one speaks. Discussions of accents and dialects are usually confined to oral literature and to spoken presentations. Little has been written about what Taghi Modarressi has called "writing with an accent":

> The new language of any immigrant writer is obviously accented and, at least initially, inarticulate. I consider this "artifact" language expressive in its own right. Writing with an accented voice is organic to the mind of the immigrant writer. It is not something one can invent. It is frequently buried beneath personal inhibitions and doubts. The accented voice is loaded with hidden messages from our cultural heritage, messages that often reach beyond the capacity of the ordinary words of any language. . . . Perhaps it is their [immigrant and exile writers] personal language that can build a bridge between what is familiar and what is strange. They may then find it possible to generate new and revealing paradoxes. Here we have our juxtapositions and our transformations—the graceful and the awkward, the beautiful and the ugly, sitting side by side in a perpetual metamorphosis of one into the other. It is like the Hunchback of Notre Dame trying to be Prince Charming for strangers. (Modarressi 1992:9)

In adapting this concept to cinema, I do not refer so much to the accented language spoken by the actors within the diegesis—although, as you will see in our conversation, that is a mark of Egoyan's submerged ethnicity. Instead, I mean the accented way in which the film is constructed at the level of style. Accented style does not conform to the classic Hollywood style, the national cinema styles of any particular country, the style of any specific film movement, or the style of any film auteur, although it is influenced by them all. It is, rather, a style that is developed by individual filmmaking authors who inhabit certain culturally transnational and exilic locations. As such, accented style inscribes the specificity of the filmmaker's authorial vision, his ethnic and cultural location and sensibilities, and the generic stylistics of postmodern transnationality.

By that definition, all of Egoyan's features are "accented" films. They are accented not in the sense that they follow a certain Armenian, Egyptian, Canadian, American, ethnic, or national film style, nor are they influenced by certain auteurs (for "influences" on him, see Brady 1993). Rather, his films are accented because of the manner in which they inscribe certain Armenian, Egoyanian, and exilic "sensibilities" or "structures of feeling."

In speaking about television shows (particularly *Frank's Place*) that depict African Americans, Herman Gray defined the term *sensibilities* as the "explicit recognition and presentation of the habits, practices, manners, nuances, outlooks," as well as the subtle use of "language, dress, sense of place, the relationship to time, pace, and body movement" that characterize and express African Americanness (1993: 123). Raymond Williams's elaboration of "structures of feeling" deepens this understanding of the term sensibilities. According to him, a structure of feeling is not a fixed institution, formation, position, or even a formal concept such as worldview or ideology (one definition of ideology). Rather, it is a set of undeniable personal and social experiences—with internal relations and tensions—that is "still in process, often indeed not yet recognized as social but taken to be private, idiosyncratic, and even isolating, but which in analysis (though rarely otherwise) has its emergent, connecting, and dominant characteristics, indeed its specific hierarchies. These are often more recognizable at a later stage, when they have been (as often happens) formalized, classified, and in many cases built into institutions and formations" (Williams 1997: 132).

Accented style is one such emergent category not yet fully recognized or formalized. As a cultural hypothesis about exilic cinema, accented style involves the affective dimensions of consciousness such as sensibilities, impulses, restraints, and tones that are not fixed but that are in a continual process of latency and emergence and are evidenced by and expressed in certain forms, conventions, or styles. Even though Egoyan's films are not explicitly about Armenians, they have inscribed certain ethnocultural, exilic, and authorial sensibilities and structures of feeling that give his films their accented style. While this inscription was latent in his early films, it has evolved and become more manifest, emerging fully in *Calendar*.

Armenian sensibilities in Egoyan's films involve looks, expressions, postures, music, and language, as well as certain thematic concerns with family structures, history, religiosity, ethnicity, and diasporism. Added to these ethnocultural sensibilities are Egoyan's own personal proclivities and his transnational, even exilic, sensibilities as a subject inhabiting the liminal "slip zones" of identity, cultural difference, and film production practice. However, the ethnocultural and exilic sensibilities and feelings do not by themselves constitute the accented style, although they are enabling components of it. A third necessary component is the specific authorial style or "accented voice" of the transnational filmmaker that expresses those sensibilities and feelings in certain juxtapositions, trans- formations, and metamorphoses that are at times so paradoxical as to require a "knowing" audience for full appreciation. Furthermore, like all accented speech, the accented film style produces results that can be fabulous or grotesque, that may prove to be surprisingly charming or intensely offensive to spectators. In the case of Egoyan, his accented style is marked by paradoxical and contradictory themes and structures of absence and presence, loss and longing, abandonment and displace- ment, obsession and seduction, veiling and unveiling, voyeurism and control, surveillance and exhibitionism, descent relations and consent relations, identity and performance of identity, gender and genre, writ- ing and erasure, the dense intertextuality of film and video, and the technological mediation of all of reality. Together, the ethnocultural and exilic sensibilities and feelings as expressed through these themes and structures constitute the accented style of Atom Egoyan's films.

As such, the accented film style is an inalienable element of the social material process of exile and of independent transnational filmmaking. Whether it engenders fabulous or monstrous results, the accented style may also create debates about the status of its practitioners and about whether they are perceived as the fairy-tale character of the frog or of the prince. In the case of Egoyan, he clearly plays both roles.

It is important to emphasize here that the identification of the accented style or accented voice in Egoyan's work in no way diminishes
the heterogeneity of his films and the multiplicity of their meanings.
There are many other ways to read and decode his films. As the conversation itself will bear out, Egoyan's films and his statements are richly
textured and palimpsestic. My intention has not been to reduce Egoyan
to an "essential ethnic subject." There is none. It has been to shed light
on some hitherto more or less latent currents in this artist's public image and in his films.

Situating the Interview

The conversation that follows is concerned with Atom Egoyan's feature
films. I conducted two interviews with him in two days. Both took place
in a small kitchen on the second floor of an old three-story house on
Niagara Street, in Toronto. The first floor contained offices and editing
rooms; the second floor consisted of a kitchen, a bathroom, and a large
editing room; and the third floor was an austere but immaculate loft
bedroom. It was a cold mid-December day outside, the tree branches
bare, the courtyard empty.

The interview took place around a white Formica table that was fixed
to the wall at one end. We sat opposite each other with the tape recorder
and my notes between us. There was freshly brewed coffee at hand. The
second day, his three-month-old boy, Arshile, joined us. Although the
baby was asleep most of the time, he woke up and had to be fed and
changed as the interview progressed. I found Egoyan to be somewhat
detached and guarded, like his films; yet he was also warm and engaging—an enigma, like his films.

I have adopted a style of presentation for our conversation that in its
narrative fragmentation, intertextuality, and multiple voices is in itself
an example of accented writing, resembling Egoyan's film style. In doing this I have tried not only to reproduce the ethnographic feel of the
interview situation, but also to reflect and refract that situation. The
write-up is woven from several strands: an edited and reorganized version of our conversation about Egoyan's films and exile cinema, "out-
takes" of our conversations that provide context to the first set (these
are indented and appear as snippets of a film dialogue), and notes that
reflect my own subjectivity during our discussion and the preparation
of this write-up (these appear as indented italicized texts). Throughout,

however, I have tried to be faithful to the interview situation, to the spirit of the conversations, and to Egoyan's and to my own turns of phrases and meanings. The result is more like what the French call an *entretien*, a heavily edited, rearranged, and narrativized interview than a documentary interview that attempts to retain the original flow and the sequence of the discussion. As a result, this is not a real-time interview; it is, rather, a hybrid intertextual "artifact" that combines features of interview, conversation, film script, and annotation. It not only creates a discourse about the contents of my interview with Egoyan but also a metadiscourse about the interview itself as a mode of ethnographic information gathering and creative writing. It was therefore no surprise that it began with him asking me the first question.

Roots and Routes

EGOYAN: Can you tell me something about yourself? I hope this is not an unfair question.

NAFICY: No, it's a very fair question. Right now I'm teaching media studies at Rice University in Houston, in the Department of Art and Art History, which means I don't have many colleagues in my own specific field. We have people who deal with various aspects of the arts and history of the arts. This is actually an interesting context for media studies, but we don't have more than two and a half people who specialize in teaching that. So I tend to teach a variety of film and television studies courses. In the last few years, I've been working in the cultural studies areas, concentrating on the in-betweens of cultures. Right now I'm preparing a book on independent transnational cinema, or on the cinema of exile. Of course, cinema has been transnational from the beginning, and Hollywood cinema is a paradigm of transnational cinema, but what I'm specifically interested in is the independent transnational cinema, particularly the films of recent filmmakers in Europe and America who live in a state of transnationality and exile that is very different from, say, that of Otto Preminger or Alfred Hitchcock.

EGOYAN: Or Rouben Mamoulian.

NAFICY: Do you like his films?

EGOYAN: Well, yeah, but it's very interesting to try and discern his ethnicity given what his background was, how he came to the country, and how he was able to camouflage himself completely, through necessity, I suppose.

NAFICY: How did he do that?

EGOYAN: Well, he was very involved with the Armenian theater in Tbilisi and was very rooted in that culture and was able to come to Hollywood and somehow parlay that into these incredibly beautiful and cinematically radical films in terms of introducing new color and sound processes and camera movements. His work is really quite extraordinary from all of those points of view, but in terms of his own culture, I mean, it's very difficult to discern anything. It was interesting, this past summer there was this big retrospective of Armenian cinema in Paris, and they tried to contextualize him as an Armenian filmmaker, but this is very difficult to do. I have this Armenian filmmaker friend in Paris, Arby Ovanessian, who reads images in terms of motifs and he believes he is able to discern certain things.

NAFICY: A certain Armenianness?

EGOYAN: I suppose, but I find that that is stretching it a bit.

NAFICY: So was Mamoulian involved in a kind of cultural masquerade?

EGOYAN: Well, I think there is that sense of complete evasion.

NAFICY: *Veiling* might be a better term, since masquerade implies a certain tension in the evasion.

EGOYAN: Right. When you are very confident of your place within one culture, the idea of losing yourself into another, total integration becomes very attractive, and I think that applies to a lot of first-generation immigrants who come to North America at a later age.

I am in a very strange situation in that I'm still considered to be first generation, even though I came here at a very young age, and have a mother tongue (Armenian) without having any conscious cultural reference in that language besides my immediate family, who were the only Armenian-speaking people in Victoria, B.C. It was very difficult to have a sense of my culture having a social framework. I associated with the marginality as opposed to, let's say, my wife, who was raised very much within the Armenian community in Beirut and is able to identify the culture as a social phenomenon. When I came to Toronto at the age of eighteen and became acquainted with the Armenian community here, I discovered that there is something about it that I could never take for granted. I think that has given the work a particular tone that I think most Armenians from Armenia would have difficulty identifying with or embracing. In the same way, I am not really from that generation of diasporan Armenians who came from a community which they knew, felt suffocated by, and wanted to escape from. I was never suffocated by an Armenian community, I never felt it was oppressive to me. It was something that was quite exotic to me even though it was something that I came from. I was not raised knowing about Armenian history, and it came to me as a real surprise as I was boarding the plane, leaving my family to come to Toronto to study, when my mother said to me, "You know, you can do anything you want with your life, but the one thing that you could do that would hurt me is if you marry a Turkish woman." That came out of absolutely nowhere. I have no context for it at all. So that gives you an idea of what my parents were going through, I suppose.

NAFICY: I have taken a different tack from you with the issue of identity, and that is to insert myself in it more directly. You are in your films, whether visually or otherwise, but there is an element of veiling, masquerade, and performance. I am present in my works in a less veiled fashion. For example, the introduction to my book *The Making of Exile Cultures* is very personal and each chapter begins with a framing personal narrative. These help to indicate what my own stake is in this analysis of construction of cultures in exile.

EGOYAN: Last night I was reading the introduction to your chapter 1, where you tell the story of the two daughters, yours and your brother's, not knowing a common language but communicating through Disney's *Little Mermaid*. This is so funny because there is one scene in *Calendar* which didn't make it in. Remember, when Arsinée and translator sing a song together? I asked him if he knew any Beatles songs, ironically. Not only did he know every Beatles song, he sang them with a Liverpool accent. I couldn't use that because I couldn't get the rights to the song. The English he knew he had learned from the Beatles.

NAFICY: So he didn't actually know any English?

EGOYAN: He knows it better than he does in the film. But a lot of his English is just from the Beatles music. Incredible!

Calendar is about a photographer who is assigned to take twelve stills of Armenia for publication in a calendar. He takes his wife and a translator on this "return" trip to the homeland. The return, mediated through media, has complex repercussions in the personal lives and identities of the participants.

NAFICY: They must have been protecting you in some ways from contamination by Armenian history.

EGOYAN: They are very complex people. They moved to Victoria because they didn't want to be part of the ghetto.

NAFICY: The ghetto in Cairo or in Canada?

EGOYAN: The ghetto in Canada, and that's a very pejorative term. But they felt that if they moved to Montreal or Toronto, where there were Armenian communities, they would somehow become part of a ghetto. I think my father particularly felt this way. My father was trained as an artist. He had his first one-man show within the Armenian community in Cairo when he was sixteen. He received a scholarship to study at the Art Institute of Chicago when he was eighteen, so he went to America, studied there, went back to Egypt, and just found that after having all these ideas of who he was, or what he was, he wasn't necessarily able to be welcomed back into that community. He wasn't able to take all those notions of abstract expressionism which he had learned in Chicago, bring them back to that community, and be successful. He was quite crushed by that and that's when he decided to leave Egypt.

NAFICY: Was he alone at the time?

EGOYAN: No, actually he met my mother at the art college in Cairo because she is a painter as well. He decided he wanted nothing to do with the community. He was very hurt by them. I think he saw the parochialism as being something very oppressive to him. So where does he end up going? Victoria, B.C., the most Anglophone city in Canada, as though it is the last bastion of the British empire.

NAFICY: Why would he go there?

EGOYAN: He went to Vancouver because he liked it there, the moderate climate, and an opportunity came up in Victoria: there was someone who was selling a furniture design business and he was able to get into that business.

NAFICY: Had he emigrated from Lebanon to Egypt?

EGOYAN: No, no. His parents were directly from the diaspora. His father was from Turkey, and his mother as well. On my mother's side, there were a number of generations in Egypt.

NAFICY: You were born in Cairo, and, I take it, you were three years old at the time of your family's emigration. Was there a particular moment that you remember being Armenian, having the consciousness of being an ethnic?

EGOYAN: Oh, God, it was all through my upbringing, but it wasn't positive. I mean, I went to a very English school where my teachers were quite graphic in what they called me. I was called "little Arab" all the time and I was always aware of the fact that I was quite different.

NAFICY: How did that make you feel being called the little Arab?

EGOYAN: Oh, it made me feel excluded, it made me feel that I wasn't part of something that I wanted to be a part of. I mean, I think as a young child your desire is to be like everybody else, and I think that you only acquire a sense of your cultural identity as being something unique when you are much older. Unless you come from a family where that is taught and they instill in you to be very proud of what you are. I think my parents were probably going through such a reevaluation themselves, and also I think it takes a tremendous amount of effort to force a child to continue to speak a language that he cannot use socially. Armenian was my mother tongue but at a certain point it seemed absurd to me to continue speaking it. I didn't even want to speak it. I remember distinctly my parents speaking it to me, my grandmother in particular, and closing my ears and not wanting to speak it because for me it was part of being called an Arab boy, it was part of what excluded me.

NAFICY: Was the thing that hurt you the most the fact that you were called an Arab as opposed to Armenian? Was there an interethnic distinction in your mind?

EGOYAN: No, no. There was none. My parents were not like some Armenians who did not associate with Arabs. Their closest friend in Victoria was an Egyptian doctor, and I had spent a lot of time at their place. There wasn't that sort of superiority or delineation between Armenians and Arabs. I think my parents, my father especially, have always been quite close to the Arab cultures. No, it was the fact that I was excluded.

NAFICY: Going back to that image of boarding the plane, why is that image particularly memorable for you?

EGOYAN: I had no context upon which to weigh her statement. I knew about the genocide (of Armenians by the Turks in the early decades of this century). I didn't necessarily know in detail what it was caused by or who the perpetrators were. It really made me very curious about that. So when I came to the University of Toronto I became involved with Armenian student association there. I also set about trying to relearn what I had lost in terms of language, trying to read Armenian. Strangely enough, the chaplain there was Armenian. He was quite an important figure to me in those days because he took it upon himself to teach me the alphabet. That was a really important time. It was also around that time, late 1970s and early 1980s, that the seeds of Armenian political extremism were being sown. It was a very, very turbulent time for me. By the time I was eighteen I had really become what I had dreamed of being at a certain point, a completely assimilated young man. I had won the English language prizes at school, which to me was the actual stamp of approval. At the time I was very confident about myself, I was involved in theater, had written a number of plays in school, and was feeling very, very centered.

NAFICY: What you just described occurred in Victoria?

EGOYAN: Yes, Victoria, which is a small city. When I came to Toronto, all of a sudden I realized that I was a small fish in a very big pond. I was overwhelmed and felt very insecure. This is where it becomes very complex for me. I was reintroducing myself into my background; I also came to a point where I maybe began to comfort myself that the reasons for my insecurity were not the result of my not being as talented, as bright, or as curious as I thought I was, but rather the result of this baggage, cultural baggage, that would somehow define me and separate me from the dominant community.

Ethnicity and Assimilation

NAFICY: Why was that baggage so troubling to you if you had assimilated fully?

EGOYAN: That's where it becomes complex. Perhaps because of my own feelings of insecurity and my having to reassess who I was, it became a very opportune time for me to reexplore my assimilation. I think it became quite convenient for me to somehow believe that the reason I was feeling that was because I had lost something which I had to retrieve. It also became a question of performing my nationality. I remember coming here and adopting the persona of the Armenian rug merchant. Looking back on it now it is almost embarrassing that I would assume this persona and play up to it. I would sort of make part of myself be that personality. This is quite humorous!

NAFICY: It seems that by doing so you were engaged in mimicry, not imitation, of an Armenian rug merchant.

Self-consciousness is an aesthetic principle in his films and in his writings about his films, a self-consciousness derived from the idea that one is always being watched and must therefore put on a public face, even in moments of privacy, because of the possibility of being subjected to voyeurism or eavesdropping.

EGOYAN: This interview is almost like therapy! Right. I was hypersensitive to what I thought might be their projections onto me and then playing that back to them, as much in their face as possible. And I was enjoying that and hoping that somehow I would bond with them as a result, and would be able to dispel the pretense. Now, of course, that's always a one-way street. I mean, they would not sort of give me back that image. And I had very strange sort of things happen to me. There were a lot of things going on in my personal life at that time. Oh, God. It's getting very complex!

NAFICY: I think that these things are very important to your films.

EGOYAN: Oh yes, definitely. I would imagine.

NAFICY: And so. I would like you to speak about them.

EGOYAN: There was this woman I was in love with from a very young age, and I sort of idealized her, and she was very inaccessible to me. Her father was very protective. By the time I was eighteen and I came here, I received this letter from her father, written in beautiful English, saying that he was going to come to Toronto to kill me and that he should have known he could never trust me with my "merchant Armenian background." When people ask me what piece of writing had the most profound influence on me, it was this letter. Because the thing that I had thought I had so carefully camouflaged during my time in Victoria was thrown back into my face by the father of this woman I'd loved. I am saying that during this whole time that I was trying to integrate myself into that family, he had in the back of his mind the idea of an Armenian merchant family. This was never brought into the open, but there it was.

NAFICY: He was on to you.

EGOYAN: He was on to me somehow, yeah.

NAFICY: And did that crush you? I mean, did that help you peel off the veneer, and then say, okay, now that I've been found out, so to speak—

EGOYAN: Yes. I guess in my mind, anyhow, it opened the door. Well, I have to say, first of all, that I really did feel at the time that my days were over [*laughter*]. And I also went on this delirious process of just expelling all those things that I loathed most about myself, and one of them had to be this brand, this mark of Armenian rug merchant. What was he deriving that image from? My name? My looks? My behavior, or my mannerisms? What was it about those mannerisms that would have defined Armenian rug merchantness? I didn't know. So I think I went into this whole mode where I tried, on the one hand, to play that out and make fun of it, but on the other hand I was getting quite involved in more political, almost militant Armenian nationalist activities through the student association. So it was a crucial time for me, obviously.

NAFICY: Did that involve a certain element of loathing? Somehow, all minorities seem to go through a stage of loathing.

EGOYAN: Well, definitely. There was this self-loathing, the idea of dirtiness. And it was very obvious in the way it was expressed. It went back to what I experienced as a child in school, having my teachers call me a little Arab. All of that came back. I think I've always had this thing about powerful men with authority. Those are the type of figureheads I am most intimidated by and, I think, it is very much a result of that Victoria stretch.

Victoria is a strange place. They have a hotel there called the Empress, where I worked for a number of years, which has a room called the Bengal Room. They had set it up to look like a colonial outpost, and they hired East Indian young men, dressed up in colonial garb, to serve the predominantly white clientele. I mean, it didn't seem strange to anyone. So this whole notion of Englishness became part of the currency there. And it became part of my way of defining myself.

> *In two of his films,* Speaking Parts *and* The Adjuster *motels and hotels figure prominently. I wonder about the relevance of this experience to that figuration. Later, I find in an interview the following statement from him: "I worked in a hotel for five years and had Lisa's job [in* Family Viewing]. *All my previous films have hotels figuring quite prominently. I was always fascinated by the process of preparing a room for someone to come into, so that the guest would believe it was virgin territory. When I began to make films, I became aware of parallels: both professions have systems to support illusion" (Insdorf 1990).*

NAFICY: If you were to chart a trajectory of your increasing self-awareness, increasing ethnicization—if that's an accurate term to use—how is that reflected in your films?

EGOYAN: See, I would caution against your expectation that I can answer that question. I can't. I am constantly surprised by it. As I articulate my own history I see motifs and parallels that figure in my work. But I'm not aware of them as I'm writing or making a film. I think if I became too aware of them I would paralyze myself, to an extent. I mean, in making my films I don't sift through my own personal history as carefully or as rigorously as I am right now. I think it might serve me well to tap into these things, but I'm not conscious of it. I do find it curious that very few people actually know how complex my particular childhood was. I'm not defined by the most obvious immigrant pattern.

NAFICY: In your feature films, especially in the earlier ones, there seems to be a sort of denial of ethnicity, or better yet, a lack of a strong presence of ethnicity—even though the constructed family in *Next of Kin* is heavily ethnic.

EGOYAN: It's hard to identify. I have always felt very, very uncertain about ever identifying my early films as being Armenian. I think *Calendar* has been a bit of a breakthrough for me. There's no way to camouflage it [*laughter*]. I mean, we were there in Armenia and there was just no way to camouflage that.

NAFICY: That's what I was driving at. In your later films, such as *The Adjustor*, there's a kind of submerged ethnicity. The music in the opening sequence is Armenian, the sister is Armenian, the photographs from Lebanon are Armenian, and the various icons of ethnicity are all Armenian. And in *Calendar*, of course, ethnicity is in your face. So this trajectory of an increasing presence of ethnicity is there.

Performance of Identity

NAFICY: Do you have a sense that you have come around full circle in terms of camouflaging your ethnicity, of not being afraid of being an outsider any more, a sense of being centered again, not as a completely assimilated person, but as a person of your own who has this baggage but is comfortable with it?

EGOYAN: Yeah, except that it seems that at the same time that I might be more comfortable with that side of myself, there's a whole other new baggage that's been acquired, which is the discrepancy I now feel between the image people have of me and the person that I am—and this is ironic given the subjects I tend to deal with.

NAFICY: This brings up a key issue in your films, that of performance of identity—of the self, ethnicity, nationality, and gender. In many of your films, you are problematizing the essentialism of individual and family identity based on descent and blood. You seem to be exploring, not necessarily advocating, consensual relationships, those to which one has to agree to not be born into.

EGOYAN: That certainly is the case in *Family Viewing*. I am definitely sensitive to the idea of our identity being a very, very self-conscious construct and to the possibility that our whole notion of personality is the thing that we choose to represent ourselves as opposed to something that is ingrained. And, as you put it so well, I'm not necessarily advocating that. But I can certainly see that that is what we have become at this point in our century. There are certain advantages to that in as much as you try to cope with dysfunctional families or dysfunctional identities, try to reorganize those people closest to you in a structural model, and try not to live with something you are either biologically, genetically, or sexually preordained to. All that implies that there is a possibility for change. And that theme, or that playing field, excites me tremendously. Because it also relates back to what I as a dramatist am attempting to do. As a dramatist you give life, represent, and explore certain characters. And as you've already discerned, those trajectories come from a very private mythology, a very, very private source.

NAFICY: Except that dramatists and actors leave the stage and go home after their performance. They are not the same people as they play on the stage. In your case, since these themes are embedded in your films, it is no wonder that you are facing a kind of dilemma about who your movies project you to be and who you actually are. The price that you are paying for severing of the ties of identity from some sort of essential self is that people see you the way you perform yourself, not the way you actually think you are deep down.

EGOYAN: But this tension between the idea of who you project yourself to be and who you actually are is a fertile territory to explore, and I think that there are people in environments, relationships, situations where the projection becomes paramount. Noah Render's whole identity in *The Adjuster* is based on what other people project onto him, a sense of need. And that's how he feels alive. He can perform sexually because people need him to. There's not even a real barrier to his sexuality in terms of gender identification. It's really a question of who needs him. So that projection becomes his personality. That's who he is.

Remember the part in *Speaking Parts* where Arsinée is interviewing and questioning the bride who says a lot of things about love that are pulled right from Rilke? Clearly, for her own sense of self-dignity, the bride has taken a relationship that doesn't exist and made it into one that exists in her mind based on a whole set of premises which from the outside seem absurd but which for her become a very particular reality. Also, what happens during the talk show sequence of the film is just projection of fantasy, cross-circuited. You don't know who is projecting what onto whom. In other sequences, the scriptwriter Clara makes a construct of her experience with her brother and through that projected reality she is somehow able to assuage her feelings of guilt for his death. Our society almost rewards our attempts to ritualize emotions through media, some sort of emotional construct which in any other times might have seemed completely psychotic. But, at this point in our civilization, it's quite accepted—and applauded. And I'm very much implicated in that criticism as a filmmaker, as someone who makes images, and I can't deny that.

NAFICY: Do you think that the conditions of postmodernity and exile necessitate this kind of disjunction and discrepancy between the self and its projections?

EGOYAN: I think when you maneuver your way, or when you find yourself in the middle of a culture in which you do not feel at home, you have to reconstruct your personality to some extent. And that process can be either subliminal or very self-conscious. Or, in this culture in Canada, it could be completely subliminal as you can find yourself ensconced within a subculture, or a community, that exists entirely within and of itself. From that position your contact with the dominant society can be very, very fleeting. I know there are people who do not think about these things, who are first-generation immigrants whose sense of what it is there to do is very black and white, very clear. That sense of performance, of persons creating themselves, is really defined by what they have to do professionally from nine to five. When they go home, they're back within the community. There's nothing complex about it for them. It's something that is dealt with with a grudging sense of necessity, but it is not a turbulent factor in their lives. These people have a tremendous sense of nostalgia for that time or period in their lives or in their fantasies when they don't have to put on that cap or that disguise when they go to work to the outside of that culture.

For me, it has never been that simple. I mean, I feel as much tension when I'm in an Armenian community as I feel when I'm in a completely WASP community. I'm really somewhere between those two. As I've said to Armenians, I'm as far away as you can get while still being part of it. I'm at the very periphery. I look at my sister, who was born in Canada, never learned Armenian, and she doesn't have this identification that I do. And that's just a separation of four years. So I really do feel that I'm at the very edge of it all. It's very ironic in some ways that I ended up being with an Armenian woman because that was never, ever in the cards, and I never had any sense that it was something that I had to do or fulfill. Now we have a child three months old. What does that mean? How are we going to raise this boy? There are so many issues. And I can't say that in my heart of hearts I feel that we owe him more exposure to his language. At one point Armenians really felt that if they didn't teach their children the Armenian language, it would die. But that idea has changed radically due to formation of an independent Armenia. The diaspora community right now is in a very exciting phase of reassessing and redefining itself.

NAFICY: The arrival of a child in your life must also have raised questions about the politics of identity and of performance, because children are supposed to be innocent and in need of education and information. Does this not leave some questions about the efficacy, the ethics, of performance of identity?

EGOYAN: Yeah, this is right. I can't afford to be as indulgent as I have been in my way of thinking. I guess I am in the process of having to re-appraise all of that. But that goes to more fundamental questions of: at what point in one's life do you say, Okay, I know these are the issues, I know this is what I've done, I can continue to do that, I can continue to think about these things. Or, I can just sort of put a lid on the issue and say, Well, this is how it is. I don't know how convenient a possibility it is to do that. What has your experience been with these questions? What *is* your experience with these questions? Obviously, they are still very much a part of your life.

NAFICY: I grapple with these issues all the time. I have two children. I was born in Iran, but have been in the U.S. for about thirty years. And since the Iranian revolution of 1979 I have become a lot more concerned not only by my own individual location in culture but also the whole problematic of the locations of cultures, and by what it means to be marginal, hated, and put on the defensive. I am also interested in what it means to have the freedom of the margins to play who you are or what you want to be. It was in the process of writing my book on exile that I became very aware of the cost of this freedom. I became very aware of the distinction that I think has to be maintained between the doubling that we are talking about—that is involved in role playing and performance—and duplicity. I think there is a fine line there. Every performance involves doubling but also a certain amount of duplicity. There's a hair's breadth between the two. And we can go over. What I'm troubled by is the celebration, almost unrestrained, of loosening of identity from all roots in the interest of promoting the free play of signs and signifiers. I am not talking about ethnic roots alone, here. I'm talking about various roots and structures of belonging that may become the basis of one's identity. But I'm very uncomfortable about what that would lead to, because it can lead to very reactionary politics. It can result in alienation and loneliness. While you're in and you're hot, everyone accepts you. But the moment you're not, then what? In some ways, the film *Paris Is Burning* (1991) is a very good example of the vitality of and the empowerment that performance of identity brings, particularly to the marginalia of our society. But you say to yourself, What happens five years from now? What happens when that poseur has a child?

EGOYAN: Well, I don't know. I find it strange that these things which have to an extent tormented or plagued me are now the object of a certain degree of celebration. I ask myself to what extent have I been rewarded for my indulgence in these issues. To what extent have I made a profession out of them? These are very big issues for me.

NAFICY: And to what extent you will be pushed in this direction, into continuing to fulfill the already established expectation?

EGOYAN: Yeah. And then you look back at someone like Mamoulian and you think maybe he really did it the right way, that is, he kept his ethnicity basically at home. But it's just much more complicated for me. I don't know if that's because I've indulged myself and allowed it to become complicated. Well, my life has become an observation, a delineation, and a sifting through of this material. So, you can by no means refer to me as being a model. Did you read that article by Cameron Bailey in *CineAction* on *Family Viewing*? There's a wonderful part where he talks about me as being the prize pony of Canadian multiculturalism. You know, the example of the multicultural boy made good. It's so simplified. That's not who I am. In the films where I haven't even addressed ethnicity, let's say, in *Speaking Parts*, those issues are still there. They form the background for the dramatic action.

NAFICY: How so in that film?

EGOYAN: It's the notion of construction. Just by casting Arsinée, you are obviously casting someone who speaks with an accent. I don't hear her accent anymore because I've become immune to it, but I'm sure certain viewers would see her marginalization as being somehow connected to her accent and her baggage.

NAFICY: Is this a diasporic view? In diaspora one is more aware of the idea that one's identity and one's vision of the world are constructed.

EGOYAN: No. You're aware of it more than I am, perhaps. But you can't generalize about diaspora. Diaspora is such a particular phenomenon, and everyone's experience of it is so different. There are predominant trends or aspects of the diaspora experience, but if you look at my experience, it's very particular.

I think that there are aspects of it that are clear in the work. And I think that the reaction in Armenia to a film like *Calendar* is a reaction like to any film in Armenia: very different from the reaction of the Armenian diasporan community here. What is interesting, and a bit of a revelation, is that these characteristics that we associate with diasporan experience are also experiences that people who have no diasporan history are able to identify with because of their own alienation within society. And, in a sense, we are all members of a much more prevalent diasporan community. I think what identifies them more is alienation, this sense of cultural removal from society. In a weird way, I think a reason that the films have been able to cross over somewhat (such as *The Adjuster*) is that segments of the mainstream audience are able to translate what you and I know as being a source of the film into something else, which is that these people on the screen are just very screwed up. They are screwed up because of other external situations, because of some confusion over their class or place in society. Something other than what we've been talking about. Don't you think?

NAFICY: I think so. Although, I think talking about your films as films of alienation in general is only thinking about them at one level, and that there are other diasporic and exilic levels, which I agree are not necessarily generalizable to all Armenians or to all diasporan peoples.

The discourse of your films somehow seems to be influenced by therapy. Are your films therapeutic?

EGOYAN: I've been reading a lot this past week. One of the things that inspired me in the early eighties and sort of found a manifestation in *Next of Kin* is the whole notion of family therapy in terms of what the therapist does in reconstructing families, reopening channels, and being able to take these archetypes and redefine them. That professional process fascinates me. I think in a lot of the films we see these characters who see themselves as being therapists, or see themselves as being able, as Peter says in *Next of Kin* to have an impact on sorting out other peoples' problems.

In Next of Kin, *dissatisfied with his biological family, Peter adopts another family with a missing boy as his surrogate family. He first "meets" the latter family when he clandestinely views a videotape of their therapy session with his psychiatrist. While his biological family appears to be a typical WASP family, his adopted family is purely Armenian, whose members truly believe that Peter is their long lost son.*

There are always characters in the films that feel their involvement in other people's lives will somehow answer questions which they themselves have. Noah Render in *The Adjuster* seems to have found a job which has certain preordained limits. He is involved in these people's lives until he is able to give them back what they've lost—give them a check or some access to their previous lives. After that, he's gone.

> *Noah Render is an insurance adjuster who appears at fires that destroy people's homes, processes their insurance claims, and places them in a motel until they find permanent lodging. It is in the motel that his sexual involvements with his clients occur. In the last enigmatic scene of* The Adjuster *we learn that Noah himself once lost his own house to a fire and the family he is now living with is an adopted one. He lives with them in the middle of an unfinished housing development in a model show house, with phony books on the shelves.*

NAFICY: There is a certain insincerity in Noah's relations with the homeless people and in Peter's involvement with his surrogate Armenian family. Even though Noah spouts to his clients lines such as "I can help you, this is what I am here for," you sense these are formula phrases he gives to everyone. And when Peter lies down on top of the kitchen table for his surrogate mother to hug and comfort him, this is a very uncomfortable moment because the audience knows that the mother is genuinely feeling that Peter is her son and she truly wants to comfort him. But you know that Peter is not her son and you're unsure whether he is pretending and only playing the part of someone who is feeling close to his mother.

EGOYAN: And that is a moment in the film that is lifted from the type of therapy that I was reading about. It's quite funny, I said to myself, Oh, God, I've actually lifted bits of transcripts from various cases. What really excited me about this therapist is that he actually uses very dramatic concepts, like he asks the father to take off his shoes, and asks the boy to take off his shoes, and then he asks the boy to put on his father's shoes. And asks him, "Do they feel comfortable to you?" It's what a therapist would do to break a situation that interests me.

NAFICY: I guess if you had not become a filmmaker you would have become a therapist.

EGOYAN: I have thought about that a lot, actually. There is something really exciting about the process.

NAFICY: Yes, I also have thought that I could be a good therapist.

EGOYAN: I think you could become an excellent therapist. You pulled a lot out of me in a relatively short amount of time. My God!

Spatial Configuration

NAFICY: There are certain common aesthetic features of diasporic films which I want to explore with you. My contention is that people from various nationalities and ethnicities who live a liminal, in-between life outside of their homelands and make personal independent films of the type you are making are creating a genre of cinema that has its own concerns in terms of themes and topics, as well as its own aesthetics and formal conventions. One of these is the configuration of space.

It seems to me there are a variety of spaces in your films. On the one hand, there's a pervasive claustrophobia, partly because of the closed urban environments and the enclosed spaces of the mise-en-scène. This is a prominent spatial characteristic of your films until we get to your latest work, *Calendar.*

Calendar *charts a trip made by a photographer to Armenia (played by Egoyan himself) whose assignment is to produce twelve stills for a calendar. During the trip, his wife (played by Egoyan's wife, Arsinée Khanjian) develops an intense relationship with the homeland and with their translator. The photographer returns to his base (Canada) alone, where he must deal with videos of the trip, memories of it, and the many phone calls from his estranged wife to him and from his own female "escorts" to others.*

In this film, claustrophobia gives way to a space of immensity. This space, it seems to me, is identified and coded as Armenian space: the long shots of the beautiful landscape, long takes of the flock of sheep that turns into a blurry river of whiteness as the camera placed in a car passes them by. That space of immensity is coded as ethnic Armenian but the claustrophobic spaces are no places. They are the interiors of an urban setting, they are not identified as Armenia, Canada, the U.S., or anywhere else.

The first time I saw Calendar, *particularly these shots of the landscape with*

sheep—that encode Armenia as immensity itself—I was struck by their similar-
ity with another great film Seasons *(1972), made by Armenian director Artavazd*
Pelechian.

EGOYAN: At a visceral level, the notion of space or environment is not
something that I take for granted. For me the idea of people's right to
inhabit space, people's ability to feel comfortable in space, are all part
of the dramatic background of the films. So location becomes very significant. It's not something that is just taken as a given. To me, the
most obvious example of that is in *The Adjuster* which is the first time
I actually used exteriors. In this film the spaces that people inhabit are
either destroyed or rendered absurd because they become metaphors for
something else. You used the word *signifier*; well, what happens when
a house, a place of domestic residence, is all of a sudden decontextual-
ized? There is no neighborhood. The house is just suddenly placed in
the middle of a field. Well, what does it then become? It becomes the
idea of a house. But it's not really a house. And what of the interior, like
the bookcase, which turns out to be just a maquette, a prop. What does
that mean? It becomes the idea of a collection of books. Space is always
transformed into figurative concepts. And this is again a territory that
I find very, very exciting, where things that we think we have a handle
on, things that we think we have identified, are constantly shifting and
are not what they seem. That is really exciting for me.

NAFICY: Thinking about the house in *The Adjuster*, one can think about
a number of words: house, home, homeland. It seems that you are dealing with all of these concepts, not necessarily in a single film, but col-
lectively in all your films. The meaning of home is one of your main
concerns.

EGOYAN: Yes. And what does it take for something to become a home?
Well, it takes a collective projection. It takes a number of people all
believing the same thing at a certain time. Also, there is a certain set of
premises which are somehow able to find root in an environment. But
when they don't come together, what are you left with? Well, for one
thing, a house in the middle of nowhere as in *The Adjuster*. You are left
with a character who feels more at home moving from place to place,
or when he is in a motel, where he places people. I think what it comes
down to is that none of these spaces are ever taken for granted. That
is to say, the characters in the films are always aware of the fact that
the spaces they inhabit are constructs, either because they are physical

constructs—a bookcase, a house in the middle of the field—or because they are constructed very self-consciously as a video or as an image in a photographer's viewfinder, such as in *Calendar*.

So, what other films are you looking at? For instance, I just saw the film *The Suitors*, by Ghasem Ebrahimian. Do you think there's a formal similarity between that film and mine?

Made by an Iranian-American filmmaker, The Suitors *(1989) is about a young veiled woman from Iran who upon arrival in New York City loses her husband to a SWAT team bullet. The film depicts her dealing with persistent suitors and with coming to terms with her new identity in a new cultural milieu.*

NAFICY: In certain respects, yes. For example, the space in that film is also very claustrophobic. The relationships are claustrophobic in that the suitors go after this woman with incredible vengeance, a kind of claustrophobic obsessiveness that one also sees in your films. And if the Iranian director were perhaps truer to himself, he would have included a lot of the issues that you, I think, so boldly put in your films, that structure your films. I don't want to go any further into the specificity of the Iranian diasporic aesthetics. But I've looked at quite a number of exilic transnational films in order to discover their commonality. If you look at the Turkish films made in Germany, for example, *Passages* (Gang Land 1992), by Yilmaz Arslan, who is himself a person with polio, you'll see in it the claustrophobic spaces that I am talking about. The entire film takes place in a rehabilitation center for physically and mentally disabled people that looks like a prison, and the relationships there are also very claustrophobic. Fernando Solanas's film, *Tangos: Exile of Gardel* (1985), is also somewhat claustrophobic.

This film focuses on the lives of a troupe of theater performers—all Argentinean exiles in Paris—who attempt to produce for stage a tragicomic tango (which they humorously call tangedy*). Much of the film takes place in the dark interiors of rehearsal halls and in the exiles' apartments.*

Another spatial feature I've found in transnational films such as yours is an emphasis on transitional spaces, spaces through which people pass on their way to other destinations. We've talked about how in your films home is either not there or is burning or is in the middle of empti- ness, which sort of points to its symbolic aspect more than to its actual presence. In the Armenia you've depicted in *Calendar* there is literally a homeland but there is no home in sight. All we see are ancient ruins without inhabitants. Other transnational films (such as *The Suitors* and *Tangos*) contain scenes of airports, train stations, and other places where people are in transit from one place to another. These are also very emotional places because in them occur the tearful dramas of arrivals, departures, separations, and reunions. Although in *Next of Kin* you have sequences shot in an airport, your chief transitional spaces are hotels and motels (in *Speaking Parts* and *The Adjuster*, respectively), which is very interesting from a different point of view. These are are not usually as transitional or dramatic places as airports and train stations. Could you elaborate about your selection of such places?

EGOYAN: These are places where for a period of time, for an amount of money, you are provided with a place that is sanctuary. Home or sanctuary are things people should be able to take for granted, but they have become market driven, something which you pay for. Of course, there is the notion of prostitution in this idea. Prostitution is also something that figures in the films, the idea that for a certain amount of time, for a certain price, you can have access to another body, and you can lose yourself in the fantasy of what that body may or may not be. Same thing with a room. You can lose yourself to this notion of comfort, only as long as you are able to pay for it. So it's just a construct, one in which we are able to suspend our disbelief. People are suspending disbelief all the time in the films. Ridiculous and artificial rituals from the outside, from the viewers' perspective, seem to be very second-nature to the people inhabiting the films because they have suspended disbelief. When Noah and Hera are showing Bubba around their home, for them it is very normal that the prop books fall out of the shelf.

NAFICY: The use of symbolic space in your films is interesting. The fact that in *The Adjuster* the protagonist is named Noah and he rescues these homeless people and places them in a motel where all four sides look into a central yard reminds one of the prophet Noah and of his ark. In other words, there is another symbolic level from which these places can be looked at. In *Speaking Parts* you never show the outside of the hotel; we see it only from the inside. So we have to have an imaginary relationship to what these spaces are like.

EGOYAN: Because of the fact that the moving image becomes a reality only in people's minds, what you deny them in the experience of viewing becomes as important as what you show. So the fact that there are missing pieces in all the films, and they're very obviously missing, creates a whole other schematic in the subconscious of my viewers, which becomes very important to the films' energy and collective strength.

NAFICY: One way that many transnationals break out of the claustrophobia of their lives is through access to the telephone, which figures large in transnational cinema.

EGOYAN: It's funny. The most memorable moment in Solanas's *Tangos* is that mysterious and almost oraclelike presence of the telephone which gives the exiles access and allows them to make free calls. I love that notion. Telephone is sort of like a gateway.

> *During our two-day conversation, Egoyan kept referring to Arsinée's imminent phone calls, which would supposedly end our session. On both occasions she was late calling, causing him to mutter something about having to meet her somewhere, or to pick her up. A kind of mystery surrounded the phone calls. Waiting for the phone calls, like my photography and audiotaping, mediated our conversation. Waiting for calls is the obverse of the repeated use of the phone in* Calendar. *The telephone plays a crucial role in that film and in* Family Viewing. *It is a means of communication and of emotional exchange, as well as an icon of displacement.*
>
> *Egoyan answered all phone calls in his office upon first ring. When I called him at his home, he answered after the first ring as well, as though he had been pacing and waiting. There was a certain anxiety in the air about the phone.*

NAFICY: The means of communication become important narrative agents in transnational films. For exiles the telephone is not just an instrument used to reach friends and family. It is imbued with magical or very intense emotions.

EGOYAN: Well, that notion of the gateway to another world, that magic door, is something very resonant to me. The idea that access to another kingdom is provided through a television screen or through media gives an almost mythological presence to the media. And that kingdom can be nostalgic or it can be, in the case of a land that doesn't even exist, of course, it can acquire a heightened presence which is fascinating to explore dramatically.

> *In* Tangos *the duress of living and working creatively in exile produces for the performers many tensions and fragmentations, as well as imaginary linkages and connections.*

NAFICY: The other aspect of Solanas's and your works that interests me has to do with characters used in your films. In *Tangos* Juan Uno and Juan Dos are essentially the same person, one is in the homeland (Uno), the other is in exile (Dos); one is imaginary, the other is real. And yet the imagined one affects the one living in exile. So there's the relationship of the real with the imaginary. And there are also the three directors of the *tangedy*, who deflate and split apart in response to the failure of their performance. You, too, have that kind of split or double characters in your films, but they are not as literal. But like Juan Dos and Juan Uno, the relationships between your doubles seem to be based on some process of projection, one projecting the other, with all the tensions attendant to that process.

Another feature that structures diaspora aesthetics and connects your films to Solanas's is the incredible sensuality in both of your films.

EGOYAN: Let's say that like Solanas's film there is romanticism, in my films a definite nostalgia is indulged.

NAFICY: In your earlier films there's nostalgia, but it is nostalgia for images. However, in *Calendar* there's nostalgia for the place itself, for Armenia, even though you undermine it via videotaping, video playback, interaction between cameraman and Arsinée, and all those phone calls. But the nostalgia for the place, for a homeland, comes through, especially in early scenes of the sheep and the later scenes where Arsinée is running in a carefree way through the hills. In fact, if I remember correctly, I think this last scene is the only scene in all your features where there is a sense of spontaneity.

EGOYAN: Definitely. In *Family Viewing* there are moments of spontaneity in the scenes in which the boy is looking at his old videotapes.

NAFICY: This issue of lack of spontaneity takes us back to the claustrophobia again in that there is a sense—even in the acting style in your film—of calculatedness, of previous preparation.

EGOYAN: Yes, yes. I think that it comes out of discomfort, of people not feeling comfortable with being themselves. It comes from being very, very aware and guarded about what they're saying because they're not sure if they should allow themselves to be who they really are. They want to be able to maneuver themselves through situations. That's present in the extreme in *Family Viewing*. I mean, these family scenes in the father's condominium are quite funny and ironic because the acting is so studied and people forget their lines. In the case of *Speaking*

Parts, people are basically lying to each other all of the time, setting up stratagems all based on deceit. When people are being deceitful, I think, they're a lot more guarded. There's not a lot of room for spontaneity. They're very aware of what comes out of their mouths and how it's interpreted or distorted in some way in order to fulfill someone else's motivations. Everyone has a very clear idea of what they need to do to preserve something, and they are very frightened by that.

NAFICY: What is it that is being preserved?

EGOYAN: Their sense of relative comfort. Their sense of what they need to do or be in order to maintain a status quo or to obtain an illusion of sanity. Even though we might be able to observe their behavior as being neurotically inspired, they see themselves as having found a place of refuge, either within claustrophobic environments or claustrophobic relationships. There is a sense of them having found a ritual that answers to certain needs. And usually the dramatic thrust of these films is in dismantling these rituals because of some person's growth. Something displaces those rituals, either someone else's power or a feeling that there's a better world somewhere outside.

Texture and Structure

NAFICY: Besides the spaces of claustrophobia and immensity, there is yet a third space in your films. This is the space of intertextuality, where you enter the video or inhabit the intersection of video and film texts and the tensions that are attendant to traveling across texts. That space is very much like a hall of mirrors, where one surface reflects or refracts another, where one text reflects or refracts another. Because the films' narratives are not as obvious as in the classical Hollywood cinema style, the feeling is very strong that the viewer is caught in a maze of surfaces. In *Speaking Parts* I have a sense that my experience as a viewer is an experience of immersion, not viewing. Because the hotel is not shown from the outside, I don't have a kind of topographical idea of what it's like. Instead I have a subterranean experience of it. I think the idea that viewing your films involves immersion is related to the intertextuality of the imagery of your films. Does it make sense to you? In writing about *Speaking Parts* you have also talked about surfaces and surface tensions (Egoyan 1993: 25–40). Tell me a little bit about the texture of your films. Watching them, one gets the impression that one is dealing with some physical material other than film.

The film/video intertextuality in his films is so strong that I was surprised when I first entered his office and saw only a moviola for editing films but no videotape editing equipment. However, no film editing was going on at the time, either, and the editing room was disquietingly quiet and clean.

EGOYAN: When designing a film I am aware of the tension that exists between a viewer's expectation and what I've the power of subverting, in a number of ways, the most visceral of them being structure. I think it's easy to look at the films and see how the image is being treated, and to look at texture. But what's more exciting to me is structure and how you tell a story.

I take a picture with my disposable camera but the flash does not go on and Egoyan loses his spontaneous pose. Joking goes on between him and me about the "disposable camera."

I love that idea of randomness of film. I like the idea of stating at the outset of a film that what you see are just scenes that are placed together and that the actual glue that holds them together is your own subconscious rather than a narrative action in the classical way. The viewers have to somehow create their own hook, and that's something about my films that I think annoys a lot of people who like to have some sort of narrative. They want to get on with it and have me tell them what the story is. In the previous films it is at this point that I felt it was time for me to introduce viewers into the level of discourse I'm trying to use and raise questions such as, Why do we need to watch images? What is it that you're expecting to see? Why are you expecting to see that? And to question that whole process of watching.

NAFICY: So do you imagine in each film what the audience will be expecting?

EGOYAN: I feel that, I say that. I mean, it comes out of my mouth that that's how I feel structure. The films are not an attempt to play or toy with an audience, but these films are told the way I think. In the films I've found a way of finding a structure that conforms to my own way of seeing things through. You might think I have a linear mind, but somehow I don't think I do, and the structure of the films reflect that.

This confirms the importance of reading the films of independent transnational filmmakers autobiographically. Exilic transnational cinema is both a cinema of authorship and a genre of cinema.

NAFICY: Your films have those kinds of moments, when there's a cut to something, when something replaces another, without an apparent motivation, perhaps driven by a private motivation. Are you trying to reproduce on film the act of perception?

EGOYAN: Yes, but I'm also trying to suggest that there is confusion between moments that are remembered. The differentiation between the process of memory as an organic or a mechanical process has become a bit blurry in our time. *Calendar* brings up interesting questions. There's this photographer who is supposed to be making a calendar. What is this calendar used for? It's used by a community to somehow relate it to notions of national identity. Why do Armenians put calendars with church images on their walls? Because it makes them feel that that aspect of Armenia is there. They're being reminded of that every time they look at a date on the wall. They have a window to the homeland. So this photographer is in a way the originator of these images. Yet how ironic that while making these beautiful images and compositions in Armenia, which will be transmitted to various Armenian communities throughout the world, the photographer himself is completely alienated, is in fact going through a breakdown, and losing his wife in the process. Given the fact that a part of his efforts is a mechanical window into the very profound process which is national identity, isn't it interesting that his own memories of what happened on that trip are somehow blurred between what he may be remembering and what he may be watching mechanically in his living room? We don't know. We have a clue. We know that he's watching them because we see him in front of his monitor at one point.

So the whole question of time as it works in the film is complex: it includes those two weeks he spends in Armenia taking the images, the year after his return which he spends with women he's hiring to go through this wine and telephone ritual. And then the question is, is there one evening when he sits down and watches all his video information, or is it an ongoing process that he's going through? It's up in the air! So the viewer has to identify the whole organization of time. And that is extremely exciting to me. When I make a film, I'm very aware of the fact that I'm providing material for the viewer's imagination. Not at a literal level, not in the sense of wish fulfillment, that this is a character I would like to be like, but rather in terms of their own organizational ability to see and to feel time.

That is the basis of my films, and it's a formalistic concern, obviously.

What I'm talking about has more to do with questions regarding experimental cinema than mainstream film, but obviously there's that other aspect of the work which is the telling of the narrative. As I am between two cultures, I'm also between two worlds of cinema, mainstream and avant-garde cinemas.

Video, Voyeurism, Pornography

NAFICY: You're also between two media, of film and video. Can we focus a little bit on the intersection of film and video.

EGOYAN: Well, when you film a video image and present it on a screen, the viewer is very aware of the construct of the image. The mere act of showing a piece of film doesn't have that effect because there is a tendency to want to believe it's a reality. But when you show pixels on a film screen you're aware of the fact that the image is a construct.

NAFICY: Just on that point, going back to *Calendar*, it seems to me that video images are relegated to inscribing what the photographer remembers from his trip to Armenia.

EGOYAN: Well, that's what I'm saying. Is he remembering it, or is he seeing it? If he is seeing it, is he seeing it as he was seeing it through the viewfinder as he was filming it? Or is he seeing it as an artifact later on?

NAFICY: Or does it matter?

EGOYAN: And is his cultural alienation reflected through this confusion, or is it a result of this confusion?

NAFICY: The ultimate irony in *Calendar* is that the still images that he has created at such personal cost, and with such perhaps shallow understanding of the places he is imaging, will become images for Armenians the world over.

EGOYAN: Yes. And one of the things I was going to do with the film was to show these calendar images on the wall of another family, attracting someone else.

NAFICY: Video brings out the constructedness of image making. In some of your films it is also associated with the absent one. In *Speaking Parts* the most absent person is the dead brother who is made present through repeated replaying of his video images by his sister.

In our conversations, like in all of his films, a key person was missing: his wife, Arsinée. But she was not represented or replaced by a video as is the case in the films. She was present through the many references made to her and her imminent phone calls.

EGOYAN: In all the films, there's an absent figure. In *Next of Kin* it's the missing son. In *Family Viewing* it's the missing mother and brother. In *The Adjuster* ultimately it has to be the missing father. Did you know that the family that Noah has inherited is not his own but a constructed family he has met at a fire? This is shown in the last scene.

NAFICY: It wasn't clear to me the first time I watched it.

EGOYAN: And I regret that it wasn't clear because for me it was quite a powerful revelation that this isn't even his real family. The only way to have made it more clear would have been to put a title saying Two Years Before, or something like that.

NAFICY: Yes. As is, it doesn't really come across. So what is the relation between video and absence?

EGOYAN: In the presence of absence [*laughter*] you have to make up something, you have to fill it with something. In the presence of an image of someone, you reconstruct another image.

NAFICY: So doesn't that give video a sort of magical power?

EGOYAN: Sure, and it also gives it the ability to transform. In *Family Viewing* the video is a means by which the boy sees his history and also a means by which he can activate his sense of history. The role of video in the film is insidious because it seems to be destructive, yet it's the source of transformation as well.

NAFICY: If you look at the obverse of transformation, video becomes a system for controlling others, preventing their transformation. The scenes of the film censors at work in *The Adjuster* are reminiscent of a *1984*-type vision of control. In general, the spectatorship of your films seems to be very different from other films in the sense that if identification is considered to be a main drive in film spectatorship, your films position the spectator as being complicit with the film in an activity that can be characterized by a series of very charged terms: illicit, secret, private, fetishistic, obsessive, voyeuristic. All the terms that come to mind that involve viewing your films are very charged. Do you buy that? Do you attribute that kind of complicit viewership to the use of video?

EGOYAN: There is something very powerful in watching something you feel you shouldn't be watching. That notion of transgression is really compelling. At a very visceral level I can't explain it. There are a number of rationalizations, but I can't come up with a single compelling one. Well, the fascination with pornography, I suppose, is because I'm from a generation in which our first sexual contact was through pornography. This is very intense and intricate; my mind is fried, and I lack sleep. Why don't we take a break and continue it later on. In the meantime you can watch *Family Viewing*.

> *I went to the loft, a neat, clean, austerely decorated bedroom: a double bed and a TV set and a VCR were the only furniture. I watched the film comfortably ensconced on the bed while Egoyan attended to some business downstairs.*
>
> Family Viewing *focuses on the highly mediated life of Van, a boy who blames his pornographer father for placing his maternal grandmother in a nursing home. The boy tries via video to reconstitute the family—by imagining his rescuing his grandmother—while his father is involved in erasing the documentary footage of the family: he records his sexual liaisons not on blank videotapes but on images of Van's childhood.*

NAFICY: Let me pursue the relation between video and pornography. You have said that what interested you about video for pornographic purposes is that the viewer is aware of as much of that which is being taped as the person who is taping it. It is this voyeuristic viewing position that has created so much interest in the U.S. and Canada in amateur pornographic tapes, because while watching them one constantly wonders, Well, who has taped this? Who has allowed himself or herself to be taped in such situations?

> *At this point, I write the word* voyeurism *in Persian in my notebook and the following exchange takes place:*

> **EGOYAN:** That's what I said right there [*pointing to the Persian;* much laughter].
> **NAFICY:** Sometimes it's faster to write it that way. Do you write Armenian?
> **EGOYAN:** No.
> **NAFICY:** Do you speak it well?
> **EGOYAN:** I speak it like a child. That's because I was five years old when I stopped speaking it. I think it will become very curious when Arshile's Armenian becomes better than mine.

NAFICY: Now, you say that you appropriate this vision by figuring its voyeuristic trajectory into your films and by discovering it first for the audience. This, you say, tends to destabilize the pornographic intent. But doesn't it have the opposite effect? You have just added another layer to the pornography in the sense that we must become aware of you also, who's showing us this pornography. You become inscribed in it in a way that you probably don't want to, as a second-layer pornographer, one removed from the first.

EGOYAN: Yes, I can see that, though it will surprise me if that can preserve any eroticism at all.

NAFICY: No, it doesn't have eroticism. It has—

EGOYAN: Prurience?

NAFICY: Perhaps, some sort of illicitness.

EGOYAN: An example of this is that moment when in *The Adjuster* Bubba is explaining to the children, whom he is about to film, how to act naturally. He says, "When the camera is moving, just don't look into it." What's really interesting is, what camera is he referring to? And as he's saying that, we see mikes coming into the frame and a camera is moving behind him. And who is that crew? Has he hired a crew to be there? Who are these people? We see tracks which he begins to describe to the children.

NAFICY: I think it's only there that you realize that he is actually going to shoot a porno film.

EGOYAN: Yeah. It brings to mind this question, When does life become pornographic? I think that *The Adjuster* is very much about pornographic lives, if we see pornography as being the excitement through simulation due to the absence of the real object—a simulation so real that it is able to ignite our imagination, forcing us to become participants. So much of the lifestyles represented in *The Adjuster* are by that definition pornographic in the sense that people have created simulacra of a lifestyle which they don't really have.

NAFICY: But for it to become pornographic it has to not only be simulated but also have a sexually illicit content.

EGOYAN: But look at the whole house. Why is that strange man, who lives just around the billboards, masturbating as he is looking from outside the window into the house where the sister is watching a porno video? The U.S. version which you've seen doesn't show this scene as graphically as the Canadian version, where you see the man's erect phallus and his masturbation very graphically. This scene is absurd, really.

He is almost like a moth being attracted to a light. There's something about that house that has this incredible, illicit sexual energy. What is it based on? To me, anything that's unreal, that's heightened, that's figurative has a sexual power because it means that we have to relate to it through our imagination. And once you relate to something through imagination it heightens the sexuality of that moment. You were talking before about sensuality, and I think the most tangible way of exploring that is sexual release. There have been civilizations and times when sensuality was able to be expressed in other ways, most noticeably, let's say, through food.

> **NAFICY:** In your films, nobody eats.
> **EGOYAN:** It's true. I haven't really explored that, except with *Next of Kin*, where there's an obvious moment when the Armenian family has this incredible feast laid out. Again, filming food and eating scenes is very awkward for me and I don't know why. I find that it's too conventional in a strict sort of way.
> **NAFICY:** Going back to the sexually energized house in *The Adjuster*, it is ironic that there is no licit, unmediated sex going on in there. The only evidence of sexuality are the sounds of the porno videos that the sister is watching or the image of the masturbating man.
>
> *It seems that for Egoyan, unself-conscious, nonironical, unmediated passion for food, sex, or emotionality in general are suspect. The few spots in his films where unmediated expression of passion is allowed to clearly surface are in the scenes involving the Armenian family in* Next of Kin *and the mutual, video-mediated masturbation in* Speaking Parts.

NAFICY: It's interesting that you say that any work of the imagination is necessarily sensual.
EGOYAN: Well, I believe that it requires us to extend ourselves.
NAFICY: Why not intellectual? Why not some other characteristic?
EGOYAN: I don't think that the sensual response denies the intellectual necessarily. There is something extremely sensual about intellectual effort. The two are inseparable. And the thing that has always surprised me is this response to the films that finds them very cold and very detached. A lot of people find the films to be extremely remote. And then there are other people at the other extreme who find them to be almost operatic in their emotionality. I think that the people who find them

cold and remote are generally the people who tend to make a distinction between an intellectual and a sensual response. The people who understand the films are able to perhaps marry the two and not create this kind of Cartesian division.

NAFICY: What elements create the emotionality in your films?

EGOYAN: For me, denial. Quite simply, denial and access! [*laughter*] The more you deny, the moments of access become richer for both spectators and participants.

NAFICY: The use of video within the diegesis, the self-reflexive style of filming, and the fractured structure of your films all tend to create a kind of narrative that constantly blocks the fulfillment of narrative desire, which might intensify that desire. The regime of control embedded in your films may account for your film's high emotionality.

EGOYAN: Yes, but by the same token, people who are satisfied by conventional narrative discourse forget those moments of blockage after the film ends. They don't retain only the glimpses that are not blocked.

NAFICY: That, I think, is part of the pornographic structure of your films. It is the play between blockage and expression, between veiling and unveiling, that guides the movement of desire in your films.

Let's talk a bit about the impact of video technology on your film style.

EGOYAN: To me video is nowhere near as important or original as some critics have made it out to be. There are so many other films that have used that. Maybe it's an easy thing to hold onto and it is in vogue right now. But for me it is really only one element. The locations or shot compositions are just as important as the use of video. You see, in a sense, I feel very betrayed by video because many of the textures I'm playing with on video are not even really appreciated at a conscious level. Many people have only watched *Family Viewing* on tape. As a result, so much of what the video is doing there is undefinable. It can only really make sense when you watch it on 35 mm and can see the video texture. This is also true of the cutting technique used in the condominium, back and forth, back and forth. That kind of cutting is almost natural on TV, especially with soap operas. So you don't feel tension when you watch those scenes on video. But when you see them projected on a big screen, you really feel there is something very brutal about that cutting because it's not cinematic.

NAFICY: Did you shoot that sequence with multiple cameras and cut between them using a switcher?

EGOYAN: It was like a live studio shoot and it was so exciting to do that, it was so transgressive to shoot a feature film using those techniques. But it only makes sense if it is projected; otherwise it's almost banal. That's why I felt so much more betrayed by seeing *Family Viewing* on video than by *Speaking Parts*, which I knew would have a video outlet because it was partially funded by channel 4 in England. In the case of the latter, I was really careful to insure that the pixels or the texture of the video was very obvious.

> Speaking Parts *involves a series of obsessive affairs between a sister (Clara) and her dead brother (Clarance), a woman (Lisa) and an actor she loves (Lance), both of whom work in a hotel, and Clara and Lance—all mediated by videotape, videoconferencing, and voyeurism.*

NAFICY: That is why you went so close into the video screen to make sure TV viewers could tell the difference between film and video imagery. There is also another way that video seems to inform your shooting, and that is through the choice of camera position. It seems to me that in some situations you have camera positions that seem to emulate the surveillance camera angle, from up high as opposed to from a lower, eye level.

EGOYAN: Oh, sure. In this regard, another emblematic moment for me is in *Family Viewing* where we see Arsinée meeting with a client in Montreal, and we see them walking down a hallway from what is obviously a surveillance camera. But the film suddenly cuts from that shot to a similar shot inside the room, where there wouldn't be a camera. So all of a sudden what was literal becomes metaphoric by the cut.

NAFICY: The interior shot is also from that high-angle position.

EGOYAN: Yes. So we're thinking that that shot must also come from a surveillance camera, because why would there be a camera inside? Those moments excite me when we become very conscious of a lens position and think we understand, but all of a sudden our sense of how we understood something becomes confused by context. In that film I was working a lot with video composition, but not so much in the other films.

NAFICY: *The Adjuster* is interesting because video doesn't seem to affect the film's vision. I hadn't thought about this when I viewed *Next of Kin*, but thinking back on it, I want to ask you this question: Does the therapeutic session affect the way you shoot and position your camera?

EGOYAN: Yeah. This is a good point. *Next of Kin* is interesting for me because it doesn't come across the way I meant it. I have become a bit more generous about it in retrospect because so many of the themes are laid out there, and it's also extremely accessible. It's also one of the few films that has been embraced by the Armenian community because it's tangible and because Peter wants to remain with the Armenian family.

The film had a very complex mise-en-scène which really didn't work. It was based on the notion of using a detached camera, not only in the therapy session but also when you see Peter in his family situation. When you see those glimpses of him with his previous family, it's always from a camera that's up high. It starts off with the camera zoomed in on one feature—the birthday cake, hiding in the swimming pool, him playing with the guitar in the bed—then moving out and creating a tableau. So it's all very fixed. I was exploring what it meant to show the detachment. And when you get to the Armenian family, there is a crucial moment which is completely obscure. But when I explain it, it seems very obvious. He's watching the Armenian family and the camera is in the same sort of position, up high looking down, very mechanically moving back and forth between the therapist and the Armenian family. At one point within that tape the therapist says, "Okay, let's pretend I'm your missing son, Pedros." At that point, as the therapist gets up, the camera becomes detached from the tripod and becomes handheld. At this point, what was very mechanical and fixed becomes very fluid and immediate. What I thought that would do is that the moment Peter finds the Armenian family, the handheld camera would have the same effect of becoming the spirit of the missing son, like someone is actually there and watching. So in the scene when he climbs up on the table—which is shot handheld—and he's looking at the camera, I wanted the effect of him addressing the eyes of the actual son who is missing. Well, it doesn't come off. It merely looks like cinema verité because that's a verité technique. And that destroyed me because it was the opposite of what I wanted, which was for people to become self-conscious and uneasy with the handheld camera. In fact, they identified very much with it because it seemed very naturalistic. That was supposed to be a moment that would change the literal into the metaphoric. I realized after that film that you can really miscalculate these effects.

And you know what's painful about those things? Even after seeing that they don't work, I don't know how I'd do them differently. In the case of *The Adjuster*'s ending you almost have to say Two Years Before.

But after you tell people about the nature of the family and they look at that scene again, the point becomes obvious because in the last sequence of the film we see Hera and her sister watching their building burning. We see it is a different place and Noah looks younger. All of these signifiers are there, but somehow it's almost as though that scene has to go on longer.

I've learned something from *The Adjuster* which is that you can't just expect people to respond to a visual cue. Some things have to be expressed verbally as well. I have a major flashback in the new film, *Exotica*, in which I have used that understanding.

> **EGOYAN:** Are we covering a lot of ground for you?
>
> **NAFICY:** Yes.
>
> **EGOYAN:** There's also a book, that I only have one copy of, which was published in France. It's really great, it's called *Atom Egoyan* and I highly recommend it. It's available in English at Pages Bookstore. I'll show you how to get there. The book does not deal with these cultural issues, it is very formalistic, but it is interesting.

You were talking about *Speaking Parts* and the idea of how an image becomes no longer a signifier for anything outside of itself. I find this idea very fascinating. And I think that in *Family Viewing* the image is used as that kind of signifier. There is almost a nostalgia for a world which exists as image, and which has itself as referent. You can always go back to an image. But you can't just go back to a land. The actual artifact of an image presupposes that you can be back in the frame of mind that you were first in when you were in contact with it. So that the idea of innocence and naiveté of watching cannot be returned. A compelling image I have is of someone who has a private piece of pornography, but has somehow become completely dulled to its effect, and then thinks of a ritual whereby he puts it on a monitor in a room and then goes outside the room to watch it through a peephole [*laughter*].

NAFICY: I suppose in some ways one is always trying to reach an originary moment, a moment of innocence before contamination and corruption. In *Family Viewing* it seems that there is no moment before the imaging moment. There's no history before image. In almost every shot, every sequence, some imaging process beyond the relationship of the people is going on within the diegesis. It's as though you don't know you're alive unless you're imaged.

EGOYAN: When you are being recorded you perform or behave differently. This whole interview, the access you've had into my private life, or I've had glimpses into yours, has certainly been heightened by the fact that the interview is being recorded. We both have the sense that there is something here that is artificially heightening this discourse.

NAFICY: Some people say that recording devices have the opposite effect, of making people guarded.

EGOYAN: If people are hurt by them, yes. But I haven't done that yet, I guess. I find it much more comfortable that you have a tape recorder. I'm much more guarded when someone is just taking notes than when I am being taped.

During our conversation, I periodically pulled out my disposable Kodak camera and took a picture of him talking. As I looked through the viewfinder he would become self-conscious and distracted and would look away. He would hold that position until I had taken the shot, then he would look back at me and pick up his previous line of thought. His distraction resembled those of his film characters. Somehow the conversation began taking on the quality of his films. To get around his awry looks, I began asking him to pose for my pictures. He suddenly became more relaxed.

NAFICY: Referring to his film *Chronicle of a Summer* (1961), Jean Rouch told me in an interview that the camera and tape recorder acted as provocateurs in stimulating individuals to reveal something personal that they would not have revealed without them (Naficy 1979). That is a minority view. If you look at the whole history of cinema verité, it's marked by the idea that filmmakers must become invisible, likes flies on the wall, so as not to influence their subjects.

EGOYAN: It's really incredible for me to think of how easy it is to use video technology and how cumbersome it is to use film technology as the Maysles brothers used it in *Salesman* (1969) and other films. You say to yourself, My God how did they do it? I know they had a minimal crew, but there was no marriage between the camera and the sound. And yet the moments they were able to achieve were quite fantastic.

NAFICY: Those are moments of filmic innocence recorded. With the pervasiveness of video today, it seems no longer possible to make images without some imaging technology or mediation inscribed in the act of imaging. It seems that it is not possible to live without mediation. The question is, is mediation more important for a person in diaspora or for a filmmaker who lives in between cultures, even if not in diaspora? It seems to me that for such a person mediation is somehow life itself.

EGOYAN: Well, it's an affirmation of one's belonging to a culture to be placed in the context of that culture. I mean, the most basic impulse is to place yourself in front of a monument and have yourself photographed there. You were there! I was here! You can extend that idea, as you did in your study of the Iranian community living in American culture. You see that acquiring some fluency in the images and systems of that culture is a mark of empowerment in that culture. The fact that there are so many Iranian television programs produced in the U.S. is a remarkably empowering situation to be in, I think.

Film as Empowerment

NAFICY: Is film for you that empowering?

EGOYAN: Not so much at a cultural level, not in my own independent films, but in other films I made for others. I made this film called *Gross Misconduct*, which is about the life of a hockey player who is a popular icon here in Canada. I felt at times when filming in the Maple Leaf Garden, which is this Mecca for the hockey world that oozes with history, I really felt a sense of "I am here. I've made it here." And the fact that I'm re-creating these scenes in this person's life who is a popular figure, I suppose, means that I have finally entered that world. Though, when you look at the finished film, it is so anti–pop culture, so radically made that it was quite strange that it actually made it onto national television. The film is quite fractured and uses all these distancing devices. But there is that sense among filmmakers that if they are re-creating something, a sexual moment, a romantic moment, or a moment of power, that they are somehow demonstrating to the world that they are capable of having those feelings themselves. So that, if I can pull off a really exciting athletic moment, that makes me somehow athletic, or if I can convince you in believing a romance, that makes me a more romantic figure. Well, this is faulty. It doesn't work that way. If by the time people watch they are so consumed with their own identification with that image, the last thing they are thinking of is the status of the filmmaker.

NAFICY: For you, making films is not a way of affirming yourself?

EGOYAN: Oh, yes it is. It's a way of affirming my ego, I suppose. But it's not a way of affirming my cultural status for the most part.

NAFICY: And your personal, individual identity?

EGOYAN: The desire to create, show, and manipulate human beings and to put them into a dramatic situation must come out of a sense of wanting to put order into things that you feel lack order in your own life. Maybe I'm being a bit too glib. I think you can take a position that, looking back in my childhood, there is a tremendous sense of disorder and confusion about identity. And so the ability to make images empowers one, and maybe I'm undervaluing that aspect of it.

NAFICY: In *Family Viewing* childhood is clearly being put to use. Childhood is being narrativized as a way of putting it into order.

EGOYAN: There are situations people find themselves in, such as the sister in *The Adjuster*, where images become empowering. When Arsinée brings home pornographic images to her sister from Lebanon, she is comforting this disenfranchised sister whom she feels is alienated from society. As a censor she has been empowered to prevent these images from being seen, but she herself sees them and now she is allowing her sister to see them. Therefore, as disenfranchised as she is from the mainstream culture, she is seeing the belly of the beast.

NAFICY: And that empowers her?

EGOYAN: And that empowers her. But, again, that type of sibling relationship as a sort of paradigm of Armenian families is quite stretched. So that's why I think Armenians watching my films have to suspend their disbelief.

NAFICY: What has been the response of Armenians to your films? Do they feel betrayed somehow?

EGOYAN: No, I don't think so. Even if the films are not understood for the most part, I think that they are valued, especially with *Calendar*. There's a tremendous sense with this film that the homeland is being shown, that in a weird sort of way, a calendar is being presented.

NAFICY: The iconographical use of ruins in *Calendar* tends to fetishize the ruins of the homeland, making them stand for the lost homeland, thus turning them into sacred icons.

EGOYAN: Sure. Remember the scenes in which the Armenian translator is imploring the cameraman to actually touch and feel the ruins? But the cameraman says something like, "What do you want me to do? Caress them?"

NAFICY: And when he touches, he touches the image of the ruins on his viewfinder. For him the image of the ruin is the ruin.

EGOYAN: Have you seen that film by the Iranian Armenian director Arby Ovanessian called *Thaddeus* [1967]?

NAFICY: No.

EGOYAN: It is about this very famous church site in Iran that is quite phenomenal, where Armenians gather for picnic and ritual sacrifice.

NAFICY: There seems to be a propensity among Armenian filmmakers, especially those in internal or external exile (one thinks of Sergei Parajanov, Arby Ovanessian, Don Askarian, Ara Madzounian, Nigol Bezgian, and yourself), for a kind of use of landscape that defines the nation. Of course, each nation defines itself differently through landscape and topography. For example, the landscape of the "west" defines America even though America is not all characterized by that particular landscape. If you were to think of Armenia, what landscape comes to mind?

EGOYAN: Well, the most obvious one, the most fetishized symbol is Mount Ararat. It's incredible because Ararat is not even within the Armenian territory (it is located across the border in Turkey). I think one of the things that makes it so fetishistic is that it is on forbidden land. And yet if you go up to Yerevan, on a clear day, it has an almost surreal presence. It is quite strange. It's as though it's pasted to the city. It's so large. And yet it's in the forbidden territory.

NAFICY: I agree. Part of that incredible fascination with and the power of Ararat as a fetish lies in its status as off-limits. You have a passing shot of it in *Calendar*. In Ara Madzounian's film *The Pink Elephant* [1988], Ararat figures very large. Under the Israeli shelling of Lebanon an Armenian theater troupe is trying to stage a play and a giant painting of Ararat on the wall begins to weep. Very sad, very effective. For those Iranian exiles, too, who are unable to return to their homeland, the landscape of the country has achieved the same fetishistic dimensions.

> **EGOYAN:** Do you know what I am thinking? We should continue this later, I've got to go now and pick up my wife and son and take them home. I am not sure what is going to happen later on. What shall we do?
>
> **NAFICY:** I am here for the purpose of interviewing you. So I am free.
>
> **EGOYAN:** Maybe it would be good to schedule something for tomorrow. But I don't know what my schedule is like tomorrow until later tonight. How about if I give you a call later. This will give you time also to go over what we've done.

Autobiography and Memory

NAFICY: Is Atom Egoyan your real name?

EGOYAN: Yeah. We changed the name in Canada. It is Yeghoyan, the *gh* sounded really difficult, so my father changed it. The Atom part is interesting because the Western Armenian *d* is pronounced *t* in Eastern Armenian. Adom is a common and classical Armenian name. But my parents who were into modernity named me after this nuclear reactor built in Cairo. They thought Atom was a really neat name.
NAFICY: So they named you after the atom, not Adom?
EGOYAN: Yeah.

> *Film reviewers have had a field day with punning with his name. Examples: "Up and Atom" (Taubin 1989) and "Splitting Atom" (Painer 1993).*

NAFICY: Modernity seems to have superseded ethnicity! Egoyan sounds like a made-up name and in an uncanny way it resonates with the problems of the ego, self, and identity which your films deal with a lot.
EGOYAN: And the name of the production company, Ego Film Arts, is a tongue-in-cheek play on this.
NAFICY: To what extent are your films autobiographical? What are the features of autobiography in your films?
EGOYAN: There are certainly elements from my experience reflected in the films in a literal sense. The parts that are most closely autobiographical are the ones that surprise me by how authentic they are. And usually I don't come to that realization until a film is finished, because I think that if I were aware of how autobiographical it was, I would be paralyzed.
NAFICY: Can you cite any examples?
EGOYAN: For instance, I would say that in *Family Viewing* the relationship of the boy to the grandmother and his wish to get the grandmother out of the nursing home are, in retrospect, clearly autobiographical.
NAFICY: In what sense?
EGOYAN: Well, I had a grandmother to whom I was extremely close. She was my only link to my culture because she never learned English and she could only communicate in Armenian. At a certain point in my childhood she was sent to a nursing home, and I think that must have devastated me. This fantasy of having her escape and my being able to organize that must have been a very deep-rooted wish with me. But I realized this only when the film was finished.
NAFICY: If the grandmother in the film represents your grandmother, does the boy, Van, then represent you?

EGOYAN: Not in a literal sense. If we do examine his family situation, there are not a lot of similarities between that situation and my situation. But, again, you can interpret metaphorically certain things that I laid out in the film in terms of my own life. But that's not really where I'm at. *Calendar* was a very interesting situation because a lot of people felt that it was directly autobiographical. Even people who were close to us assumed that Arsinée and I had broken up. This is great that the film is able to translate that feeling, but in fact it wasn't true. And I would even go so far as to say that the characters that we were playing in the film were actually quite different from what we were in as much as Arsinée was very, very nervous about going to Armenia because of her upbringing within an Armenian community where she was always taught that Armenia was some type of paradise. She was very frightened of what she was actually going to encounter there. In some ways she was almost paralyzed. However, because of my upbringing, having had no projections onto the homeland, I was very excited to go. In that sense, we were really playing the opposite of what we were experiencing.

NAFICY: But doesn't the fact that you are physically in the film change things?

EGOYAN: That wasn't planned. I had not intended to be in the film. I thought that one of the advantages of being behind the camera was that when we got back I would find another actor who could dub over all my dialogs. But it became technically impossible because of the overlap in the dialog.

The most autobiographical element in the films for me is the notion of the submerged culture. The notion of a culture that has somehow been hidden, either for political or for personal reasons. And the notion of the dramatic motor of the film being the escaping from or the redefinition of that culture.

NAFICY: Are you referring to the Armenian culture?

EGOYAN: Yes. But also to the notion of culture as something which is a very strong, identifying feature that has somehow been denied to the characters who are most in need of it. How do we define cultures? Noah Render, living in his house, has in some ways defined his own culture. That is the birth of a new culture. A culture is a system of rituals and collective beliefs, but—

NAFICY: Noah's is not a collective. What he has is his individual image of home.

EGOYAN: But at a certain point he sets up a collection of people. He is setting that up for that brief period of time when he and these people are in a similar state of loss. Even though it is very transitory, it does become a collective. The motel becomes a collective culture, a culture that he lives off of and brings back to the house. And I think that creates a tension in the film.

NAFICY: What is the glue that maintains this culture and keeps these people together?

EGOYAN: Well, in that instance it is fear. Fear and loneliness. But let's say in the case of *Speaking Parts* there is a culture that's being defined there as well, the culture of the mediated. The culture of who has access to making images and who doesn't. There are two cultures in that film: the people who make images and the people who watch. And there are the notions of being excluded from a system or culture and having to gain entry or access to it. This is seen in a passage where the house-keeper explains to Lisa that she uses her employees as children and like children some are more lovable than others. These are strong themes in the films and they are very much from an immigrant's perspective, I think. Though I consider myself to be assimilated to an extent, I certainly watched my parents struggle with that notion.

NAFICY: Isn't it interesting that a lot of the persons who in your films represent the Armenian culture are speechless? The grandmother in *Family Viewing*, the sister in *The Adjuster*, Clara's brother in *Next of Kin*. We don't know that he's Armenian, but if we were to follow this structure that all those who are silent are somehow ethnic, then we would conclude that he was Armenian.

EGOYAN: There's the notion of a silent witness, I suppose. That is, someone who has information, a key, that would give the viewers some access to what is going on, into what was the nature of the relationship between the brother and the sister, the grandmother and the mother, and the mother and the father. These are all people who have secrets but cannot actually express them because they've been traumatized into silence. I think that the whole notion of persecution, of speech being a potential weapon, and of being silenced are obviously things that are part of my history. Either a part of my collective history as an Armenian, or personal history. I think, Why did my parents leave Egypt? There was a tremendous amount of antagonism toward the Armenian population at that time. The direct reason why we came out had to do with our visibility, the fact that we stood out somehow.

NAFICY: As successful immigrants?

EGOYAN: Yes, sure.

NAFICY: So the idea of being invisible or voiceless in your films is a defense mechanism of an immigrant?

EGOYAN: I suppose. This is very interesting that we're talking about this because this idea had never occurred to me until our discussion right now. These things are so latent in terms of my motivation, and I think it takes someone in your position to be able to discern that. I think if I were too aware of these things I would stop. This is a very troubling aspect of this point in my career generally because there is a small body of work that has been accumulated and I am suddenly thrust into the position of having to explain a lot of these ideas. And I am finding that as I articulate them, my desire to deal with them creatively becomes confused. So here we have another situation where the act of speech becomes something which can confuse another impulse, which is the desire to find truth by metaphor, which is for me the beauty of creativity.

NAFICY: Let me just go on with this autobiographical line for a bit longer. My question has to do with the role of video as an emblem of autobiography. Is video intrinsically associated for you—or in our postmodern culture—with biography, autobiography?

EGOYAN: What's fascinating to me about video is that we now have the means to create cinematic records of our lives which are not necessarily selective, which are very free in their recording of time. That is to say, when we had home movies, two minutes cost $25, so one had to be very, very careful about what one was shooting. But now it is quite possible to record freely an entire event without any sense of highlighting or selecting what is important in that event, so that the actual transmission of a personal or a private mythology is profoundly altered.

The role of memory has changed because memory has now been surrendered, at least partially, to a mechanical process. And that, I think, has altered the way we view our own personal histories. I mean, certainly with Arshile I'm terrified to videotape and photograph him. I really don't feel any desire to because I have done so much of that in my life. And I've associated that with a professional realm of my existence. It is really a struggle with me, because I know he will expect those documents. By the time he's eighteen, all of his friends will have video documentation of their childhood. So I need to provide that to him. And I think his will be an entirely different generation, one that will rely not so much on their memory of how things were, but rather on the actual records of what they have seen. I've already experienced that a bit when people ask me if I remember Egypt. I don't remember Egypt consciously. I don't think I do. But my father has taken home movies of my time in Egypt, so I experienced from a very young age images of myself in Egypt. And it's very difficult for me now to distinguish between what I actually remember and what I remember watching.

As a dramatist, that gives me the ability to portray characters not only in terms of their day-to-day behavior but also in how they record that behavior, and how they relate to what I'm doing as a filmmaker. That's fascinating to me. When in *Family Viewing* I show what the father is actually videotaping, or how Van deals with images, I see them doing what I am doing, and that gives me a tremendous sense of access into those men. These similarities make these characters very close and immediate to me because they are being defined by their attitude toward a process which is very personal and direct to me.

NAFICY: This is also another aspect of autobiography.

EGOYAN: Of course. It's quite a remarkable thing. Could Ibsen or Chekhov ever have shown characters entirely defined by how they wrote? No, of course not. It would just be so contrived. But you can at this time show characters—and of course it gets tiresome after a certain point, and you have to be careful about it—but you can show characters filming.

NAFICY: Now, there is a difference, isn't there, between the memory that you hold in your head and a memory that is recorded, because a memory you hold in your head remains private, entirely yours. And a memory that is recorded on tape becomes accessible to others, and in some ways, as we see in *Family Viewing*, it becomes susceptible to erasure, addition, or deletion by others. Of course, we always manipulate our own memories, often without realizing it. But this process of recording it on video renders it an object of individual manipulation and political manipulation by outsiders. I can see, for example, how political images of the homeland can become inscribed in a certain way through careful selection, editing, and circulation so that Mount Ararat becomes, or stands for, Armenia. That image of Ararat is imbued with so much power because it is circulated and recirculated. That image also freezes the multiplicity of meanings of what Armenia is. I have seen this process in the exile-produced Iranian and Vietnamese music videos where a monument becomes a synecdoche for a nation.

EGOYAN: The best example of that in *Calendar* is the Temple of Garni.

Now, that is a very interesting situation, because ten years ago the temple was in a state of ruin, and a lot of effort was put into rebuilding it. To me that's a very important scene. It is where the first fracture occurs in the relationship (between the photographer and Arsinée), but that fracture is also very symbolic because that monument is very often used as an icon of Armenian culture. In fact, it isn't. If you look at it historically, it is Persian, actually. But now it's been appropriated and a whole mythology has worked its way around this pagan temple. Fascinating! Its situation and its context has rendered it iconographically something else because enough people believe it is something else. And what is fascinating to me in *Calendar*, say, is the juxtaposition of the ancient with the modern: the notion of these churches—which symbolize timelessness—with the calendar, which is extremely time-based, and disposable, ultimately.

Production and Distribution

NAFICY: You seem to favor repeatedly working with, if not the same people, at least with a small group of technicians and actors. Why is that? How does that work?

EGOYAN: Well, it's a family of people, I suppose.

NAFICY: What brings you together?

EGOYAN: An understanding of work pattern, a sense of tradition. Because the films are made so quickly, there has to be almost a shorthand where we understand what it is we are trying to do. Let's take for instance the role of the camera and what it is trying to do. The idea that the camera is just not for literal showing of something but, rather, an active participant is very important to me. These are things that I'm able to not have to explain again and again to my cameraperson, for example. Or with the art directors who know I'm trying to achieve a heightened reality, without it seeming like it's a parody. And that distinction is very, very tricky. I mean, you don't want the films to look like *Edward Scissorhands* [1990]. It is really a matter of learning to trust each other's taste. I have directed plays since high school with my art director and production designer. So we've known each other for over fifteen years. That's not necessarily a good thing. It also can be very claustrophobic at times.

NAFICY: Have you found that that's happening to you and that you're about ready to break out?

EGOYAN: I think there is that sense for the crew, that is, in order for them to grow they would like to work with higher budgets. And that becomes a challenge. At what point are you making a film to please what your crew needs? And that's why *Calendar* was a really great experience because I was free of that to an extent because I was filming in Armenia. *Exotica* is sort of a threshold for me.

NAFICY: Do you desire to make a big-budget studio film?

EGOYAN: There's a side of me that loves watching films like *The Fugitive* [1993]. I like it for all the visceral, obvious reasons that everyone else does. And if a script comes my way that allows me to indulge that side of my craft, fine.

NAFICY: One successful Hollywood film might release you from having to do TV shows.

EGOYAN: I don't think it works like that. Once you make a successful Hollywood film, there's tremendous pressure on you. Okay, the production value of *The Adjuster* is very high, but I found this pressure even with *Calendar*. Now I have to explain myself, I have to tell people why I went back to a small budget. And, you know, it's being released in the States in March and I'm very nervous about it because I don't want people who have seen *The Adjuster* and have been impressed by the production value to be disappointed in the fact that this is almost a documentary. I don't want any potential audience that I have found through *The Adjuster* to go to *Calendar* and say, Well, this is like a documentary, and then not go to *Exotica* next year. People tell me, "You shouldn't put that pressure on yourself. You should feel free to do whatever you want." But the film industry doesn't work that way necessarily.

NAFICY: What is your position as a Canadian filmmaker vis-à-vis the power of the American film industry?

EGOYAN: There is a sense in Canada that we are up against tremendous odds in this community of filmmakers because we don't have a domestic market for our films. Our own population is so seduced by American images that our films have less than 2 percent of the screen time on our national cinema, maybe even less. However, Canadians are very comfortable with watching Canadian television programs because they are of a very high standard. And the hockey film I made for television was watched on national TV by one million people, which is a figure much larger than the ten thousand people at the most who watched *The Adjuster* in Canada. The fact that people are tuned into Canadian television and that Canadian television is successful is very encouraging. But when it comes to the cinema, people want the big American experience. They're going to pay $8 to see *The Fugitive* and they have to pay $8 to see *Calendar*. Actually, *Calendar* ended up being quite successful commercially because it had very good word of mouth in this city. People who found the other films emotionally removed and didn't understand them really seemed to enjoy it. So that was encouraging.

NAFICY: Is there an Armenian network for filmmakers in North America?

EGOYAN: Yes. I did organize, I think, the first North American Armenian film festival, in 1985. It was a workshop more than a festival. We invited a number of Armenian filmmakers, such as Nigol Bezgian, from Los Angeles, and John Hovanessian, from New York, to come to Toronto. We had a genuine workshop where we discussed what we were doing and we showed the films in the Armenian community center.

If you look at the catalog of the Armenian film exhibition published in Paris this past year, it's really exciting because it shows that there is an Armenian filmmaking tradition (see Passek 1993). I don't think it is nearly as sophisticated as what has happened in the Iranian cinema in the past ten years. That is because we don't have that background, and we don't have that tension that exists in the Iranian cinema. Talking about illicit images, Iranian cinema is based on that, especially the postrevolutionary films, where the question is, What can you show? The fact that you cannot show certain things is fascinating because obviously those things are so thought about and that tension is very, very fascinating. And I think you can make the argument that postrevolutionary Iranian cinema has a strength that is the result of these limitations. And certainly some fascinating contradictions are brought out in the festival circuit. One of the persons who was sent to represent Iranian cinema in international festivals is that consummate sort of Western figure, a very charming man, extremely approachable. He invited us to the International Fajr Film Festival, in Tehran, where they wanted to do a retrospective. However, the only film of ours they could show was *Next of Kin*. He had seen the other films and he was very excited about them. If we had gone to Tehran we would have faced this strange situation where we participate in a retrospective in which they could only show one film!

Have you seen Arby Ovanessian's *The Source* [*Cheshmeh*, 1971], which he made in Iran?

NAFICY: Yes, of course. That is a great film that was liked by intellectuals, but it was not a box office success. You saw him in Paris this year. How is he doing now?

EGOYAN: Well, you know, he's had a strange nomad's life. He's in the typical situation of exile. What is he? He's living in Paris. He's very, very rooted in Armenian culture, but in the Armenian culture from Iran. Iranian Armenians have a very different sensibility than Armenians from elsewhere. There's a language difference, and Iranian Armenians have a higher level of education. I think their relation to the Iranian population is also very different from Armenians, let's say, from Lebanon or Egypt, where there was a real sense that Armenians were somehow better than their host countries. And I think Armenian Iranians were completely integrated into Iranian culture. They didn't feel that sense of separation. So there are completely different attitudes.

NAFICY: They were not as integrated as you are saying. In Ovanessian's film made in exile in France, *How My Mother's Apron Unfolds in My Life* [Le tablier brodé de ma mère s'étate dans ma vie; 1985], there's no reference to Iranian culture at all. That is completely effaced in the interest of Armenian mythology.

EGOYAN: I think that film is quite hermetic for that reason. It's very strange, you were talking about transnational films, and that film is entirely funded by the French Ministry of Culture, one of the few experiments funded by them which was entirely in another language. And I think he felt that after the film was finished, the minister of culture tried to disown the film by doing nothing to promote it internationally. The film was basically buried.

NAFICY: To substantiate what you were saying about Arby's nomadism, I wanted to show *My Mother's Apron* in the 1993 Los Angeles Festival for which I had curated a series of films made in exile, including a number of Armenian films. To get that film we had to first find Ovanessian in Paris, which was very difficult because he had no phone number and no known, fixed address. We did manage to finally contact him, and he graciously supplied the festival with a print. The point is that he leads not only a kind of nomadic life but also one that is mysterious. There exists in Iran a particular tragic view of exile that considers exile as being banishment to a state of near death, or living death. I don't know whether his lifestyle is playing into that discourse or whether there is another Armenian discourse he is mobilizing.

EGOYAN: I think this is a very interesting point. That would probably separate him from most Western Armenians because I don't think that

Armenians who are in exile from Egypt or Lebanon feel that. I think that that is a very particular view. I mean, I'm not aware of that notion. It's not part of my culture.

NAFICY: This morning [a Saturday] I was flipping through the Toronto TV channels in the hotel. I saw three Hindi programs on three different channels, one Iranian, and one Greek program. But I didn't see any Armenian shows.

EGOYAN: For a while there wasn't an Armenian program. There's one now that airs on Sundays at 11:00 A.M. and that's it. It's actually well produced, by a friend of mine. See, TV is just not that much a part of our culture. It really isn't. There is much more respect for theater in the Armenian community than there is toward cinema.

NAFICY: And for music.

EGOYAN: And for music. There's an understanding of music and of theater, but an understanding of cinema is something that is now being developed. In Beirut, Lebanon, there were three semiprofessional Armenian theater companies.

NAFICY: I guess that's what makes Ara's film *The Pink Elephant* culturally rich, because it focuses on the situation where an Armenian theatrical troupe is trying to put on a play while Beirut is being bombed. It clearly shows the importance to Armenians of theater in diaspora.

EGOYAN: Right. I haven't seen the film, but I think that's a very good example. There is a growing appreciation of cinema now. There is the Armenian Film Society in Los Angeles, where an Armenian film festival was organized by the American Film Institute. I know *Calendar* had a very successful screening within the community in Los Angles. I just think cinema hasn't been nurtured in the same way. Let's put it this way: where and how are Armenian-language films made? Films were either made in the Soviet Armenia, where they were influenced by that sort of system, or they were made with the lowest of the low quality, I mean, really bad B films. And when a film like Parajanov's *The Color of Pomegranate* [Sayat Nova, 1969] is released—I remember a screening of it here organized for the community—people were walking out in droves. They didn't understand it. They thought they were going to see a film about their actual poet, a literal film. They couldn't understand the language of the film because they hadn't been introduced to that.

NAFICY: One wonders to what extent Parajanov's unpopularity with Armenians in diaspora has to do with his unliteralness, as it were, or with the kind of spiritual journey he was conducting with that film. It might also have something to do with the "nonmateriality" of the film in the sense that it doesn't have any fast action, special camera movements, surprises, suspenseful situations, or any of the traditional narrative techniques that people have so accepted that they have assumed a kind of materiality.

EGOYAN: Yes. I think it all comes down to a question of reading. You have to learn to read and people are not taught how to read cinema very often. And so, what they are taught is the most obvious level of apprehension. It's something that needs to be developed. I honestly do believe it is changing. If you look at, let's say *AIM* magazine [*Armenian International Magazine*], which is this glossy new publication for the Armenian community, that looks like *Time* magazine and is published in Armenian and English, you'll see some really extraordinary articles and stories on Armenian cinema, very much in depth. The last issue had a very good critique of *Chickpeas* (Nigol Bezgian's feature film) which was really critical, but in a very satirical way. And if you read it, the writing is so sophisticated, it really shows you how much the community has matured.

    EGOYAN: You should get a copy.

    NAFICY: Where might I get one? Maybe you could send me a copy of the review.

    EGOYAN: Oh, listen, I might have one.

    At this point, we move downstairs, into the receptionist's office, taking the baby with us, who is asleep in his portable car seat. Egoyan goes through various file drawers and boxes, each bearing the title of one of his films and containing reviews, interviews, and publicity material about the film. He finds a number of reviews of his films which he gives me.

    At the end he offers some chocolate bits piled up in a plastic bag on the secretary's desk (she is off today, Saturday). He carefully, almost compulsively, packs the baby's milk bottles and paraphernalia in three plastic bags: one bag gets used-up bottles and nipples; one contains clean, unused nipples; and one receives unfinished bottles. Then the two bags containing dirty things are placed inside a larger one like Russian nested dolls. Control. Frames within frames.

    We take the baby to the car, serenely asleep. I stay by the curb, by Egoyan's gray Volvo station wagon, guarding the baby as he goes back into the building to bring one last thing to the car. I pull out my disposable camera and, as he exits the building, I snap a shot of him, the last.

He drives me off to the subway station which will take me, within half an hour, to one of the parts of Toronto that has a lot of ethnic businesses and restaurants. We bid goodbye warmly. Last night I walked through Queen street, the yuppie main drag in Toronto, and I observed the appropriation of the exile discourse: within three blocks I saw stores called: Exile, Nomad, Exotic.

References

Ansen, David. 1992. "A Holiday from Hype." *Newsweek*, 29 June.

Atamian, Christopher. 1991. "Emotion in Fast Forward: For Filmmaker Atom Egoyan, It's Veni, Video, Vici." *AIM* (Aug.–Sept.), p. 70.

Balley, Cameron. 1989. "Scanning Egoyan." *CineAction* (Spring): 45–51.

Brady, Shirley. 1993. "Atom Egoyan Out of the Margins," *Shift* (Summer): 10–13, 37.

Desbarats, Carole, Daniele Riviere, Jacinto Lageria, and Paul Virilio, eds. 1993. *Atom Egoyan*. Paris/Toronto: Editions Dis Voir and Ontario Ministry of Culture, Tourism and Recreation.

Egoyan, Atom, ed. 1993. *Speaking Parts*. Toronto: Coach House Press.

Gray, Herman. 1993. "Recodings: Possibilities and Limitations in Commercial Television Representations of African American Culture." In *Otherness and the Media: The Ethnography of the Imaged and the Imagined*, ed. Hamid Naficy and Teshome Gabriel, 117–30. Switzerland and Philadelphia: Harwood Academic Press.

Handling, Piers. 1993. "Allegories of Alienation: The Films of Atom Egoyan." *Cinematheque Ontario*, 18 Mar.–27 May, 8.

Insdorf, Annette. 1990. "Image Problems: A Director's Specialty." *New York Times*, 11 Feb., 25H.

Johnson, Brian D. 1991. "Bleak Beauty." *Maclean's*, 30 Sept., 68.

Kempley, Rita. 1990. "'Parts,' Video as Big Brother." *Washington Post*, 3 Feb., D3.

Maslin, Janet. 1989. "On Forging Relationships by Electronic Intermediary." *New York Times*, 29 Sept., C16.

Modarressi, Taghi. 1992. "Writing with an Accent." *Chanteh* 1 (Fall): 7–9.

Naficy, Hamid. 1979. "Jean Rouch: A Personal Perspective." *Quarterly Review of Film Studies* 3: 339–62.

———. 1993. *The Making of Exile Cultures: Iranian Television in Los Angeles*. Minneapolis: University of Minnesota Press.

———. 1994. "Phobic Spaces and Liminal Panics: Independent Transnational Film Genre." *East-West Film Journal* 8 (July): 1–30.

Painer, Jamie. 1993. "Splitting Atom." *Film Threat* (Dec.): 20–23.

Passek, Jean-loup, ed. 1993. *Le Cinéma Armenien*. Paris: Centre de Georges Pompidou.

Shohat, Ella. 1991. "Ethnicities-in-Relation: Toward a Multicultural Reading of American Cinema." In *Unspeakable Images: Ethnicity and the American Cinema,* ed. Lester D. Friedman, 215–50. Urbana: University of Illinois Press.

Taubin, Amy. 1989. "Memoirs of Overdevelopment: Up and Atom." *Film Comment* (Nov.–Dec.): 27–29.

Williams, Raymond. 1977. "Structure of Feeling." *Marxism and Literature,* 128–35. London: Oxford University Press.

Exotica

Cynthia Fuchs/1994

From *Maryland Institute for Technology in the Humanities*. http://www.mith2.umd
.edu/WomensStudies/FilmReviews/exotica-fuchs. 1994. Reprinted by permission
of the author.

Exotica is an excursion into the psychic strangeness of everyday life. Physically claustrophobic while it opens out into remarkable emotional and visual vistas, the movie is at once disturbing and lush. Atom Egoyan's previous films, *Next of Kin* (1984), *Family Viewing* (1987), *Speaking Parts* (1989), *The Adjuster* (1991), and *Calendar* (1993), all explored the intricate intersections of individuals, families, and media (usually reconstituted in domestic space, in the form of video). At the heart of any of these meditations is an investigation of the interdependent relationship of deviance and normality (especially within family structures), extraordinary impulses beneath mundane surfaces, and the ways that video packages, subsumes, and also defamiliarizes such tensions.

Egoyan's latest feature, set largely in a sex club called "Exotica," charts the emotional collision course of several characters who share deep secrets in their pasts. That they deny or are unaware of their shared experiences, and remember them quite differently, provides the film with its careful, intricate pattern of detection, as events unfold as if onto knowledge and understanding. The trouble is, none of this knowledge is secure, even once it's articulated. Images of searching and sorrow accumulate—an airline security check, a field traversed by people looking for a body, video footage of a mother and daughter, men watching women at the strip club—but even as they become coherent as a narrative, their emotional impacts remain elusive and immeasurable.

The characters include a tax auditor, Francis (Bruce Greenwood), his niece Tracey (Sarah Polley), a dancer at the club, Christina (Mia Kirshner), the club's owner, Zoe (Arsinée Khanjian), the club's on-floor director, Eric (Elias Koteas), and an exotic pet store owner whose business is being audited by Francis, Thomas (Don McKellar). The "plot" moves back and forth across time, so that links among events and characters surface slowly, with increasing intensity. It's a movie about watching (like Egoyan's other work), anchored in an ugly story of state and social surveillance. It opens with Thomas being searched at the airport: we watch a guard-in-training watching him through a one-way mirror, as the guard is instructed about the wiley ways of smugglers. Thomas, in fact, is smuggling exotic eggs for one of his clients, but he isn't caught, at least not now.

Thomas's connection to the sex-club plot is at first indirect, until he meets Francis, who solicits his help. Acting on their different fantasies, Thomas is picking up beautiful men at the ballet, while Francis is visiting the club several nights a week. He watches Christina's "schoolgirl" performance: her dance, while familiar enough in its sex-club setting, is weirdly grim and spooky (and it's perfectly set to Leonard Cohen's "Everybody Knows"). She's wearing a plaid-skirt uniform, her gestures seem to parody girlish sensuality, but revealing pain and anger at the same time. Francis is plainly mesmerized, as is Eric, who introduces her act: "What is it that gives a schoolgirl her special innocence?" The film suggests that "innocence" is a problem, projected onto Christina, and made an object of desire in itself, by the culture, by the men who watch her, by Zoe (who watches her as well, while wrestling with her own past: it's her dead mother's club), and by the film's audience. *Exotica* subtly, intelligently coaxes us to question our own investments in what we're watching and, importantly, how we're reading these complicated, perpetually recontextualized images.

That is, rather than offering another indictment of the heterosexual porn industry (all male makers and viewers are "bad"), the film critiques a culture which produces and also demonizes such desire. Making its audience part of the process of textual interpretation and emotional negotiation, *Exotica* makes our complicity less a matter of guilt or innocence (labels which are too easily assigned or assumed), than one of self-consciousness and responsibility.

Interview with Atom Egoyan

CF: Do you think there's a line between innocence and guilt?
AE: Well, there's all this sort of fetishization of the idea of innocence,

you know, what contains innocence. . . . In fact, innocence is never where you expect it to be. So many of the things that we least understand and find something that will contain or give articulation to the idea, and yet the moment you fetishize something, it becomes full of other resonances that you then have to deal with at a later point. . . . I think that in that sense the film does suggest that any attempt to understand or give voice to the idea of innocence, is fraught with all sorts of dangers. It's a really loaded question for this film.

CF: Making people feel guilty is what Francis does for a living, as a tax auditor . . .

AE: Yes!

CF: I thought that as soon as someone comes to audit you . . .

AE: Yes. There's something really pedantic about it. No one can think of an audit without some sort of terror, because of what power that they have to reveal and discover things that you might not have even known you'd done wrong. When I was audited [before writing this film], at first I thought, I have nothing to hide, and I made my books open to this person. But the moment that you get that first question about this lunch that you had two years ago, and as you go over the details of this lunch that you've long forgotten, this person looks at you very blankly, and he nods. And you think, is he onto something? Are they onto something that I don't even know about myself? It was really irresistible, to have this man going to the club, so we were auditing him, taking stock of his private life, and of course during the day he's doing that to someone else.

CF: Can you talk about the multiple storylines, how [tax auditee] Thomas's sense of guilt intersects with Francis's?

AE: Well because most of the sexuality in the film was so fraught with layers of guilt, I thought it was important to show somebody engaged in a form of sexual activity that was flirtatious and quite light. Those excursions to the ballet, where he finds a great way to score dates, I wanted that to contrast with what was happening in the club. And yet, I mean, for all of its lightness, the exchange of money is still very important. The fact that he gives back the money [after scalping the ticket to the "date"] suggests that he's in full control. . . . I love the idea that ultimately, he comes to the same kind of questions that the other characters come to. I really enjoy this type of structure, it's very organic to me, to develop several lines at the same time. And sometimes when you're editing, you realize that you have to let go of some, because certain other things are cooking in a particular way, you don't need to resolve everything that you set up.

CF: Is that how you usually work, you have a script and then you let what happens shape the final product?

AE: Well, my films are really designed, with the exception of *Calendar*, which was improvised. *Exotica* was really carefully planned, but there are things that you only really discover as you're editing. But it's good to have that material there, even if you decide not to use it. It's dangerous to be overly cautious before you start shooting.

CF: So what is "exotic"? Thomas chooses long-haired, darker-skinned men, and Christina appears as the everyday "schoolgirl," but that image is exoticized in the context of the club . . .

AE: To me, the obvious definition of the *exotic* is something outside our immediate experience. So there're all these classic elements of the exotic: the exoticism of race, the exoticism of music, the environment, the exoticism of sexual icons. But ultimately the exoticism that really drives the film is the exoticism that we feel towards our own experience, that point at which our own memory and our own relationship to the things that are closest to us become exotic.

CF: Which is evident when Francis's ex-wife and daughter appear in the home video, very domestic footage . . .

AE: Yeah. Even that footage is so interesting, because when we first see it, we think it's a threatening moment, that the mother is protecting the daughter. But in fact, it's this happy, playful moment, but Francis has fetishized it, and taken it out of context, in order to give meaning or explanation to his anguish. I think that's one of the more interesting things that's evolved [with video technology], our new found desire to make archives of our experiences, and to document them. For all of the potentially healing aspects of that, it also poses a danger, because our memories that are able to change organically, to position themselves within who we become, but technology is fixed. So the images have to be reconfigured in more brutal terms. So you have in *Family Viewing*, for instance, this man who wants to forget his entire family, so he literally re-tapes over old home videos with homemade pornography. That makes him believe that he's able to deal with something psychologically, but in fact it's so brutal and so preposterous.

CF: In this film you've set up different kind of screens, not movies as in *Family Viewing* or *The Adjuster*. Here the screen is "Don't touch." How do you think of your audience as you're setting up these kinds of specific positions?

AE: That's a good question because for me, all the films have been inspired by a need to tell an emotional story. But I think that because the filters were so visceral [in the previous films], like seeing a video image, or seeing something within a frame which removed you, that the audience was not even able to attach itself to the emotional issues. That was always really frustrating. One of the really encouraging things about *Exotica* is that it seems able to reach a broader audience. Even though its themes and ideas are parallel to ideas in the other films, that texture is not there. . . . In a way [the new film] is more traditional, but it also allows the people to access the emotional lives of the characters more directly. They're not as threatened. To me seeing a video image on film is a very seductive and compelling texture, but to a lot of people it's really removed. And I think in some ways it's that removal that I found really hallucinatory. But it's not a feeling that a tremendous number of people share. I can't say that I consciously set out to make this film to appeal to a wider audience, but I think in fact it has, because people are most threatened by the metaphor.

CF: In that context, can you talk about how you've used the incest narrative here, because that's a very hot-button, emotional issue.

AE: Yeah, you know I was aware of that, and in the last scene, the delicate thing was to talk about Christina's abuse, and the household she was coming from, which was really damaging to her. But it's so difficult these days to write that scene, because it's become so cliche. So I just wanted to suggest it in a very suppressed way, in Francis's response. . . . I think that when Christina found that body in the field, so much of her anger at her lost youth was projected onto the body that she found, the girl that she used to babysit for. For her to play that schoolgirl dance, is really empowering to her . . . part of what she was working through. And it ends up being explosive, when what she and Francis are working through separately converge. In a way she's an embodiment of the dead daughter, but it's what Francis is projecting onto her, so she's confused. Why has Francis chosen to do this in this club? He's so desperate; it seems the only option available to him.

CF: Porn theaters or clubs like that are pathologized by the so-called "larger culture," like the Pee-wee Herman business in this country. But these sites exist for that purpose.

AE: Isn't that bizarre? I find that, talking to people, they believe that everyone who works in those institutions is pathological or victimized. That is so unfair. One of the things I understood from my research is that while it's absolutely true that many people who are selling sex on the street have been forced into that situation against their will, it's also true that there are people making a living doing something that they are talented at, and they have control of their lives. That whole issue is so loaded for our society, and there's always a rush to judgment and moral condemnation, so they don't really understand that people work at it for lots of different reasons. And people don't have the time or the imagination to understand how important these sites are in our society.

CF: And video has complicated that too, because porn theaters are rare; the public space is even more condemned, most porn goes to video. I think also that Arsinée [Khanjian]'s position in this film complicates that even more, especially with her pregnancy.

AE: I was at a place in San Francisco, a place that sells sex aids, and this woman there, her job was the opposite of what Arsinée's was in *The Adjuster*: Arsinée was a censor, who decided what society can and cannot see, and this other job was to look at hard porn all day and decide what was appropriate for what [porn] establishment. And one of the tapes was this one called *San Francisco Lesbians*, by a lesbian collective, and it had a scene with a pregnant woman. It is explosive, because it seems so transgressive. We just don't want to think of pregnancy and sex. It's so absurd, how do pregnancies come about? But the moment a woman is pregnant, she's disassociated from sex . . .

CF: Unless she's Demi Moore.

AE: Right. I really like the idea that Arsinée is a woman who's trying to deal with the weight of her mother's influence, and her mother's expectation, and part of her way of coping with that is by having a child herself, she'd be able to empower herself. It's ridiculous, but logical too. So, again the contract is important, the contract with Eric to have the child. And there's Thomas too, who's also traumatized by his father's death, and is pregnant in his way, carrying the smuggled eggs strapped to his belly under his shirt.

CF: And also Zoe's relationship with Christina, combining sensuality and an exchange of parent-child positions.

AE: Yeah. I think that she's confused over that. It's really interesting, to portray characters who are confused about their sexual orientation, or the nature of their desire. It seems to be very challenging to certain viewers, because the moment you show certain things, you have to explain them. I like scenes which point to directions but leave an element of it to the viewer's own imagination. So the kiss between Zoe and Christina, people ask, what does it mean? It really means what it says. There's an attraction there, but it is tentative. . . . And a lot of people ask about Thomas. It's like when you have a gay character it has to be somehow explained. Like he should be coming out, or going through some kind of crisis. He can't just be a character who's just that, without it becoming an issue. But I think that's changing. People are getting tired of gay characters who are in extreme crisis all the time. And what seems to be more provocative to American audiences of the film is the interracial marriage, between Francis and his ex wife. Now in Canada it's not an issue at all, but here I'm asked about it.

CF: It seems to be a question of what constitutes "normal" and "deviant" behaviors, within families and as imposed on them.

AE: This whole idea of parents projecting onto their children their own fantasies of what they may become. It's natural, it's part of what parenting is about. But it's also dangerous. . . . This is one of the motifs of the film: what is natural? The aquarium: it's a little container of the natural world but only as long as it's maintained. So god knows what's growing in Thomas's tanks, because he's not looking after them, you know? It's like the club itself. At what point do you allow natural elements to have their own expression, and when do you make them conform to your idea of what's natural?

A Conversation with Atom Egoyan

Peter Harcourt/1994

Post Script: Essays in Film and the Humanities, 15, no. 1, 1995: 68–74. Reprinted by permission of *Post Script: Essays in Film and the Humanities*.

When talking about the differences between the classic English Canadian and Québecois cinemas in the 1960s, I often talk in technical terms. The English Canadian cinema prefers the telephoto lens, isolating individuals from their environments and allowing anglophone filmmakers to keep their distance from their subjects. The Québecois cinema, on the other hand, prefers the wide-angle lens, relating individuals to their environment and implicating as well the francophone filmmakers in the action. The most consistent examples can be found respectively in documentaries like Don Owen's *Runner* (1962) and Michel Brault's and Gilles Groulx's *Les Raquetteurs* (1958), but these technical preferences also inform the two features that so securely announced our cinema in 1964, *Nobody Waved Goodbye* and *Le chat dans le sac*.[1]

What I have always found amazing in *Next of Kin* (1984), Atom Egoyan's first feature, is that when refusing the anglo-celtic values of his posh West Coast suburban home to adopt the values of the Armenian world in downtown Toronto, the protagonist moves from a telephoto world to a wide angle one. Furthermore, like the disgruntled central character in Owen's *Nobody Waved Goodbye*, Egoyan's character is named Peter; and like the equally disgruntled character in Groulx's *Le Chat dans le sac*, he introduces himself to us.

While working on an article on his films for *Film Quarterly*[2] last year, I visited Atom Egoyan in his offices on Niagara Street off Queen Street in downtown Toronto. The visit took place in March 1994, just as *Exotica* was being invited to Cannes. I asked him if he was consciously referring to the technical strategies and situations of these two seminal films from the 1960s.

• • •

AE: *Nobody Waved Goodbye* was one of the first feature films I saw. There was an NFB office in Victoria, B.C.; and I remember when I first got involved in film, I just loved this idea of being able to project films in my own basement. I used to be able to go there and rent a 16mm projector, and most of the films were, like, McLaren shorts or documentaries, but they had one feature film there and that was *Nobody Waved Goodbye*. So I saw that when I was really young.

The reference is subconscious. But it was a very important experience for me, watching that in my basement. It was one of the first feature films I saw which I could imagine how it was made, as opposed to most Hollywood films, which at that point in my life were completely mystifying.

PH: Perhaps to give himself more control, perhaps to mark his own work off from the Canadian documentary tradition, Egoyan has always built most of the sets for his films. In fact, quite comically, he tells the story that at Cannes he got as many inquiries about the actualities of the strip club in *Erotica* as he did inquiries concerning the rights for the film. It was, of course, a set; but even for *Family Viewing* the old people's home was constructed.

AE: That was built, here, in Toronto. We built that at the Factory Theatre Lab,[3] in the back space there. We just took over that space and transformed it into this home. And the women's hostel at the end was the same location. We just, as you have to do, changed the angle.

PH: Are the photographs on the tombstones at the opening of *Speaking Parts* an invention of yours?

AE: Yes. But I had seen that. If you go to any Italian cemetery you will see photographs, and certainly in an Armenian cemetery as well: you do find these photographs in glass. When we were in Armenia, it was quite amazing, the reproductions that were carved—and they became almost photographic—into granite. This notion of having to preserve an image of the dead is something that I heightened in that scene; but you do find them in cemeteries.

In Hong Kong, when I was travelling there, there are special mausoleums constructed entirely out of photographs that are kept quite apart from where the bodies are kept which are meant to be a place of memory and preservation.

PH: I think you said once that you had actually seen something like your film mausoleum.

AE: No. Someone else told me that they were in Japan and that something like that was being developed. That was a few years ago, and I haven't heard about it again since. But to me, it's entirely conceivable.

The thing is that when you're dealing with technology, you have to question whether or not you're using a device which is contrived or a bit stretched; and I never felt that with the mausoleum. I remember that as I was inventing it, it just seemed to me to be emotionally very resonant and true.

PH: While the mausoleum makes use of video technology, there is one moment when the grieving Clara enters the shot with her now dead brother. She is filming him, but with an 8mm camera. Why did Egoyan employ this device?

AE: Well I was thinking about this the other day. I am fascinated obviously about the process of creativity. I think that within the films themselves there are all these people who are finding a creative means of making images or making scenarios which somehow satisfy these neurotic compulsions. So I think I place a lot of perverse faith in the actual process of creativity. But I think it gets skewed very often, where people lose sight of what it is or why it is that they're trying to do what they do.

PH: And they're all little producers.

AE: Exactly. And I think if you look at the film, you can divide the world in the film into people who are active producers or would be producers, who would like to be producers but who are not quite getting it.

PH: While Egoyan constructs his main sets, there is a strange conglomeration of ancient-looking buildings that form the backdrop for the televisual interviews with the producer in *Speaking Parts*. I asked him about those structures.

AE: At that time, I was doing these gigs as a director and I was directing a *Twilight Zone*. We were shooting at the Kleinberg studios;[4] and as we were shooting there in this field, there was this deserted set that was for a feature film called *Burning Love*, meant to be about the Salem witch burning. The film never got out. It was an aborted project, but this medieval village was there and deteriorating. And I thought, what an incredible backdrop. And so we used that, for free, this location.

I just love the idea of you looking at this and having no idea what type of a film this might be. As the producer says, "I'm shooting three of these suckers right now but this one is very special to me." And so it just is one of these projects, with all these people running around.

PH: It's yet another displacement of the real.

AE: Of course. And in this case, it's so surreal, with the interfacing of this modern technology with this very old communal type of environment.

PH: Another bit of luck occurred with the central location in *The Adjuster*. They managed to find an actual model home stuck away in the middle of a field.

AE: That was one of those things. It was in the script and I thought at a certain point we'll never find the place and we don't have the budget to build it and I thought I was going to have to change it. But one day I got this call from the location manager saying, "I've found it!" It was in Woodbridge[5] and that was the story: they'd built this model home and the developer had actually just left it in a state of suspension. It was phenomenal. And we arrived there one morning and we were shooting these scenes with this wonderful light and this light mist. It worked out beautifully.

PH: Knowing how Antonioni loved to paint his natural sets and noticing an intricate colour co-ordination in *The Adjuster* between the motel itself and the cars in the parking lot, I asked him whether that had been planned.

AE: Yes, sure. Actually, it's probably the most carefully colour co-ordinated film I've done. You probably wouldn't see it on the print but there's great work within the motel rooms as well—this flesh colour and the flame sort of feel and had a very heightened sense of colour. And you know, 'scope lenses have a wonderful way of saturating colour.

PH: On the other hand, about the mythological references in *The Adjuster* that the French critics especially take entirely seriously, he is not too sure.

AE: It's funny because, as you can tell with that book,[6] the French take it very seriously. It becomes a bit scary. The notion of things having references beyond the obvious and alluding to other structures or narrative or story-telling is something which I had a lot of fun with. But that's not to say that you can't interpret at a literal level. To me that becomes so heavy-handed. Noah, the ark, the notion of salvation: to me those are things that become quite funny. So I'm not quite sure what the exercise of taking it seriously provides other than rather an intimidating text for me to have to go through. Because, for instance, Hera: it is also an Armenian name. I've always loved that name and it is the wife of Zeus but I thought well isn't that funny. It the wife of someone who is a god, a king, and yet obviously he's someone who is so completely dysfunctional at a certain level. But I never really took it much further than that.

But with the image of the archer: I mean people do construct mythologies around their own lives; and when you're dealing with notions of pornography and this notion of her creating this very private mythology which she brings back to her sister and exchanges stories and how convoluted that becomes in the film: you know, people's processes of exchanging stories, exchanging histories, exchanging mythologies, creating mythologies, deconstructing mythologies. The notion of having references to classical mythology was irresistible. But I think ultimately it's irresistible to me just because it's so ironic. I'm not someone who would have a lot of patience, I think, with my basing the story on a very direct mythological reference. I don't know what the point of that would be.

PH: The film so much has to do with touch and with being out of touch.

AE: Right. One of my favorite moments is when he leaves the room where he's just had the encounter with the gay man and as he's walking towards his own room, he has this fantasy of stroking his son. I find that moment really strong. As he's walking, he starts stroking an unseen figure beside him and he finds great comfort in that.

PH: The closing shot in *Exotica* is disturbing in the extreme. That cut back in time to Chrissy when she was just a young girl and was baby-sitting for Francis's daughter who was still alive seems to give the film a serial dimension where the actions of loss and of grief will repeat themselves over and over again. The ending of *The Adjuster* is somewhat the same, though not many critics picked up on this rhetorical device.

AE: That really dismayed me and I still don't know how I could have made it clearer. I think the people who didn't pick it up tend to be the most analytical viewers, because they're reading too much into that moment. They're seeing it as a projection, or fantasy he's having of saving his own family in front of the fire or something like that. And of course I never use flash-backs and the first one I use misfires somehow. And maybe it's because of my own tentativeness.

But it is a flashback. It's how he met the family. What I've always done before is that the actual mechanism of the flashback becomes part of the narrative. In *Family Viewing*, the reason I got so excited about that film when it came about is that these flashbacks in the script could be a mechanical device that he actually shows us, and of course that works in *Speaking Parts* as well. There was no such way out of that in both *Exotica* and *The Adjuster.*

Of course, in *Calendar*, I go back to that same technique of the mechanical process creating a blurry distinction between what is a flashback and what is being viewed at the moment. And those shifts and movements in time are fascinating in *Calendar* where you have this idea where it takes place over the course of a year and it also takes place over the course of the two weeks that we are in Armenia and it also takes place perhaps over the course of one evening where he's watching these tapes. But it's never really made clear: that whole notion of time being fluid as opposed to the timelessness of these monuments was something that I found very appealing.

And yet, as a writer, there are times when you have to use a flashback. It rears its ugly head and what do you do about it? In *Exotica* I think it's more explicit. However, I have had one informer viewer tell me that he didn't get it: he didn't get that it was the younger Christine that was being driven home. He thought that it was a different actress.

PH: I asked Egoyan about Bubba's mask at the end of *The Adjuster*, about whether it was devised for the film.

AE: It's a Balinese mask. It's the monkey and it has associations of evil in Balinese culture. But it was a found object. Like the talking teddy-bear—speaking Armenian, actually. It's a sort of Armenian nursery rhyme. It's just a children's rhyme. It doesn't mean anything in particular.

But this idea of other objects becoming allusive, of having the weight to signify something else. I mean, if you look at what he's done to that room at the end, Bubba, it's quite phenomenal, the mask being just one thing. All the props that we've seen scattered about the film have been brought to this location. But he knows exactly what is going to happen. He knows from the moment he sees that house, I think, that this will be the sacrificial site of his own demise.

And why? Why is this house the place he chooses? I think because it is emblematic, it's an icon. It's the idea of a house, with no neighbourhood. And somehow he finds it the perfect metaphor for his state of mind—his crazed state of mind. So he decides that this is the place where this will happen, where the one fantasy that got out of hand will take place. We don't know what went on; but what happened with those boys is probably a fantasy that went too far for him.

PH: But is it really a flashback at the end of *The Adjuster*? Is that the right word for these final moments that call into question everything we have seen?

AE: What I find exciting are movements in time which are not signalled by devices that would lead the viewer to believe we are entering into the subconscious or the memory of the character. Like Resnais, who is phenomenal. What he does with movements in time are not signalled by the classical close-up or the classical music cue. So the viewer has to make this conceptual leap. And it's a huge leap. It completely jars your senses.

PH: I then asked Egoyan about the business of sexual intimacy in his films and about the relationship between Van and Sandra in *Family Viewing*.

AE: I think she's very unhappy in that place and I think she's in love with Van. And I think that they have had intimacy. You know, people talk about why can't there just be normal sex in the films and for me it's very clear that the situations are so unusual and people use sexuality to reflect what is going on inside of them. So if they are dysfunctional, I think their sexuality becomes dysfunctional. Someday when I choose to make a film about people who are completely balanced and who do not have any problems, then their sexuality will be different.

PH: You get that in *Calendar* in a way.

AE: Of course, which a lot of people find very erotic. You don't see much, but I think that that is a healthy relationship.

PH: But there's the whole sense of incest in *Exotica*.

AE: I'm going to have a bit of trouble there. I think what has happened is that, I don't think that he had an incestuous relationship with the daughter. I think that the moment that became suggested during the interrogation that in his mind he is wracked with feelings about whether or not that was what he was feeling for his daughter. That's my take on it. I mean, one day Francis walks into this club and he sees Christina wearing this uniform and it starts this grotesque process.

Again, it's very much like the other films. In order to preserve the memory of someone, you go to this very artificial means. In this case it's not a video or a photographic reproduction, it is a theatrical one. In that sense it's a departure but it's as dangerous as the others. If not more so, because it's a live element.

PH: For all of Egoyan's films, Mychael Danna has composed the music. I asked Egoyan how he would describe it.

AE: He describes it best. He calls it "emotional minimalism." *Exotica's* his best score, and it's going to come out as a separate release. There's also a very heavy use of foreign sounds and foreign instrumentations.

PH: Does he do that all the time? Or is that something that he does for you? The Arabic bit at the end of *The Adjuster*?

AE: No, I think those are things that he's developed for these films. The notion of the exotic. And *The Adjuster* is specifically Armenian. That's an Armenian instrument—a duduk. It's like a flute and it has a particular sound. In *Exotica*, he wanted the sound of a specific Indian instrument called the shehnai and he couldn't find it anywhere in North America. So he ended up going to Bombay and recording it, and bringing it back. That's how obsessive he gets.

PH: And the way those octaves work at the end of *Family Viewing*.

AE: That's a breath-taking score. And you know what I find with his music too is that with *Family Viewing*, if you look at that film without music, it's just too distant. His music is very emotional, and it's music that if it was used in other films, it might be over the top; but because of the emotional place of these films, it just sits well.

PH: Finally, I asked Egoyan about the role that the creative imagination plays in his films. To what extent it can be destructive.

AE: I think this goes down to the very roots of why we make art. We make art to provide order and purpose in a world in which we feel deprived of that in some way. Edward Bond, the English playwright, said that the reason he wrote his plays was to address his frustration in not being able to see the world in an ordered way. He can create order through chaos. Even when his plays are about the most destructive elements in the human mind, someone has written it, someone has actually organized these elements—organized and disciplined his time.

I'm very attracted and always have been attracted to the creative effort. As a child—and you think about these things when you have a child[7]—I wasn't told a lot of stories, I wasn't told a lot of fairy-tales by my parents; but both my parents were painters. It's not that they ended up doing much with this but my father has always painted. And even as a very young child I was always very impressed with this notion of the process of doing that.

So, on the one hand, I'm very attracted to the process; and yet, it's an isolating process. It's something that you do by yourself and it only really makes sense if you're able to share it. But so often, the means of distribution, where you are able to share it, are withheld. For any number of reasons.

So what fascinates me are characters who are very creative but don't know who their audiences are or who have become so aware of the isolating qualities of the creative act that they go a bit mad. And yet, the desire to create is completely comprehensible given what their situations are. Given the traumas in their live that they've had to deal with, given the things that are left hanging, it's the only thing they can do.

There are people who make films about criminals and I guess I make films about artists, but none of them are artists professionally or in a socially sanctioned way. The one person who tries to be, Clara, let's say, in *Speaking Parts*, is so marginalized, maybe because of the fact that she can't really write a good script. I think from the small peeps we get into the script she's writing through the auditions with Lance, it's not very good. And then the producer is probably able to realize that, to realize it is a great story she has but she just doesn't have the particular talent it takes to pull it off.

I think there is some sort of strange attraction I feel towards the artist, let us say, towards the creative person who has a tremendous source of inspiration but is not able to articulate it properly. And that could be a metaphor perhaps for the whole immigrant experience as well—for a person who, you know, never finds that language, never finds the complete control of his new environment.

PH: Whatever the distressed state of his characters, Atom Egoyan is someone who step by confident step has seized control of his chosen environment of cinema. With such a distinguished track record behind him at the age of only thirty-five, it will indeed be exciting to watch his progress hopefully for the next thirty-five years.

Notes

1. See Peter Harcourt "1964: The Beginning of a Beginning." *Self-Portrait*, ed. Piers Handling (Ottawa: The Canadian Film Institute, 1980): 64–76.

2. "Imaginary Images: The Films of Atom Egoyan." *Film Quarterly* 48.3 (Spring 1995): 2–14.

3. A well-known theatre site in Toronto.

4. Quite substantial film studios, located a few miles north of Toronto.

5. An area just west of Toronto—a part of what is now called Mississauga.

6. See Carole Desbarats, Danièle Rivière, Jacinto Lageira, and Paul Virilio,

trans. by Brian Holmes. *Atom Egoyan*. (Paris: Éditions Dis Voir, 1993). See the review of this book immediately following.

7. Egoyan's wife, Arsinée Khanjian, had just given birth to their baby son, Arshile.

A Conversation with Atom Egoyan

Susan Bullington Katz/1998

Funny how our writing often reflects our thought process.

Take Atom Egoyan. In person, he does what characters in his movies sometimes do. Big spaces often sit between his thoughts. Spaces in which you have to listen, wanting to figure out just what it is he's going to say next. Wondering what it is that's going on in that space.

And then, when he talks, it's often in a big stream of ideas, multiple ideas per sentence, things it's clear he's been thinking about for a long time. He's also self-assured enough in his thoughts that he's willing to be open about his vulnerabilities and the paths his work has taken and is taking him.

Growing up in Victoria, British Columbia, he really was named Atom by his parents, and was writing and making movies all along, including four short films as an undergrad at the University of Toronto. He even, at one point, was in a plane crash, and filmed the whole thing.

Along the way he's put together a string of movies which are distinct, writing and directing them all. His eighth, *The Sweet Hereafter*, which he adapted from the novel of the same name by Russell Banks, took the grand jury prize at Cannes this past year.

He lives and works in Toronto with his wife, Arsinée Khanjian, a member of the informal company of actors who often populate his movies. From a mixing studio in Toronto, where he'd been mixing *Sarabande*, a project with cellist YoYo Ma based on the Bach cello suites, Atom Egoyan stopped to talk about *The Sweet Hereafter* and how it fits in with his other projects before and after.

SBK: Your wife gave you the book first?

AE: Yes. In some ways, the project begins with two gifts. My wife actually gave me the gift of the book itself for my birthday, I think, about five years ago, and I just was completely bowled over by the scope and the detail of the story—the ability that Russell Banks had to give urgency to the most banal aspects of these people's lives and the way he was able to create this sense of a moral universe within this one community.

And I felt that it was the first time I read material which had similarities in some ways to my own films, but also was a huge leap ahead in terms of the maturity of the piece and the challenges it presented. I was at a point where I really wanted to surprise myself, and I was convinced that it was the thing to do to try and see if I could honor and serve the spirit of the book and also make it personal.

So the second gift was that I got the option. And that gift was the result of meeting Russell and convincing him that I would be the right person to try this adaptation. I also promised him that I'd be able to actually make the film. I think one of the things that was frustrating to Russell was that all of his books had been optioned, and he's a huge film buff, but he'd never been able to see the screen version of any of his work.

Because I work independently, and after *Exotica* I was quite certain that I could raise the money for this, I promised him that I would make the film. And we talked about the fable-like qualities, and how important it was to make sure that the film could operate at that level. So I then began working on the adaptation of the story.

SBK: You said that Russell's book is similar to things you've done, which I agree. It's similar in its perspective about human beings, and the stance of the narrator is similar to some of your work.

AE: And also the level of discourse it provokes with the viewer in terms of having to question their relationship to time, and having access to the experience of how characters apprehend events, as opposed to just looking at these events in a passive way. That, to me, is a really important part of how I construct movies.

I can look at two scenes in *The Sweet Hereafter* which, I suppose, illustrate this. The scene of incest between the father and daughter in the barn, where up until that part in the film, you're not sure what their relationship is; you might think that he's an older boyfriend. And then you see the scene of him in the barn, and the way it's presented is from the perspective of what a young woman who's involved in that sort of relationship would have to imagine in order to somehow preserve her equilibrium, her psychological equilibrium. She'd have to think that this was a romantic gesture. And I think very often when you see an incest scene, it's shot from the point of view, and it's written from the point of view, of that character, as we understand the nature of the abuse and the violence of the abuse reflecting back on it. But the reality is, at that moment, she would have had to believe it was something else.

So it's a very challenging and complex idea, but it was important for me to situate the viewer in the middle of that and to see what she had to see at that moment. The effect that that has is that we almost sublimate that scene, we forget about it until the very end of the film when she confronts her father, and the father denies the relationship and can't even begin to talk about it. And at that moment, as she mentions in the script, "Do you remember, Daddy, you were gonna build me a stage lit with nothing but candles," the viewer then will retrieve that scene in much the same way that the character would have to retrieve her whole experience of the relationship. And that type of moment, and that type of passage, is really crucial for me. It's why I make films.

There are certain properties that are inherent in the presentation of moving pictures. We believe in a reality, we want to believe that what we're seeing is actually happening. And rather than succumb to that, I love the idea of challenging that and playing with that, and by doing so, maybe entering into the subconscious of my characters and having access to that.

The other scene is the scene of the accident itself, where Billy views the bus crash through the ice. Again, that scene would normally be covered from so many different angles. What was important for me, in the way I wrote and executed that scene, was to see it as Billy would have seen it, within that one frame. Maybe I am talking too much about directing than writing, but it's written that way in the script, too. It's very clear that this is from a static frame, and we actually see what Billy sees, so that later on in the film, he talks about "I was behind the bus, I saw it happen," and we can revisit his experience of it, as opposed to just looking at that moment as an event. We understand it as an experience.

And right after that, we go back to the image of the sleeping family, and we begin to hear Mitchell Stevens's story of his own catastrophe with his daughter. To me, the structure of a film is a question of preparing the viewer for what they need to receive and understand in terms of the underlying psychology of what's happening to these people. And that sometimes means making a choice not to follow linear presentation.

This film had a much broader appeal than *Exotica*, because all you need to know if you are ever confused is that it's about a community before and after an accident. That's all you really need to know. I mean, all the other time periods are really irrelevant at some level besides that huge sense of before and after. *Exotica* was much more abstract in the nature of its construction.

SBK: The book is written in four segments, *Rashomon*-like, in a way. When you went to pull it together into a screenplay, what was your starting point?

AE: What I began with was what it means and why we need to tell stories. What you get in the book are four first-person narratives, and they are written almost as depositions. That form has a huge significance in terms of the film, because it's ultimately through a deposition that a character is able to find redemption. In the book, these stories are being told to the reader, and there's something quite plaintive and quite straightforward about who they're addressing. It's a literary device, a first-person device, and an attitude that we expect and understand as a reader.

But in film, it's a tremendously difficult thing to translate, because you either use voice-over, which is not something that I'm accustomed to, or you have to find somebody that they can address their ideas to within that community, and that meant some degree of reconstruction and contrivance.

The most difficult character, or the one I found most interesting at first, was Mitchell. There's nobody in that town that Mitchell could speak to, that Mitchell would make himself that vulnerable to, I felt. So I created the notion of this airplane trip, being on a trip to visit his daughter and sitting next to an old friend.

That was actually, in some ways, one of the first things I did. And that got me really excited, because I thought, well, this is interesting—here is a major part of the film in another public carrier. I mean, the bus is obviously something which transports this community, and the future of this community. I really do believe that children represent the future, and so every morning, the future of this community is transported in this bus, and I felt that it was very interesting to contrast that with this plane, which is another transporter. . . .

SBK: and another closed stage . . .

AE: And another closed stage, so I felt that there was an interesting thing to parallel and to structure the story around in terms of weaving back and forth from the airplane to the community. So you could almost say the first instinct was almost a sculptural one, of finding a way of positioning and telling the story that would allow me to move back and forth in time, much like the poem, which came afterwards, but allowed me to actually comment and to remove myself from the community while enhancing the ideas I was working with in it.

It's all the people that are repositories of somebody else and the responsibility you have when you carry someone else's history. So to have this other character, Alison, who had a memory of what his daughter was like, and confronting Mitchell with that, was to me a very provocative and identifiable circumstance.

I think we've all been in that situation in an airplane, and it's almost a device. It was funny to see *Private Parts*, where that's sort of used as a framing device in that movie, too. [Howard Stern] gets into an airplane and sits beside a woman who hates him, and he basically defends himself by the end of the trip, which is also intercut within the film. It's a place where you are forced to speak, you're forced into a relationship. What I found interesting about that choice was that here's a man who insinuates himself into a town, and forces himself into these people's houses and into their rooms so that he can get them to speak and get them to believe in what he has to present, and suddenly the tables are turned and he's in a situation when he has to speak to this young woman who is confronting him, asking questions about his daughter, asking questions about his past.

And in a way, there is a sense of how we can heal ourselves by talking about our experience and our circumstance. And by revealing the truth, and by sharing a truth, and by delineating what the truth is, we come to some sense of resolution. And that is a very important thread in the film, so anything I can do to enhance and emphasize that was really helpful.

In the case of Billy, because of who Billy Ansell was, there wasn't really anyone he could talk to. He's someone who keeps to himself. So what we're prepared to accept as a literary device had no meaning, really, in film convention. I decided not to have him speak to anyone, but his story would be told in a greatly simplified way.

With Dolores, she tells her story to Mitchell as he comes and conducts the interview, and that was in some ways the most straightforward.

Nicole was a challenge, because I seized on the idea of the Pied Piper and that would serve as her narrative, and yet I felt that I needed more. So I did create a voice-over in an early draft in which she is talking to Mitchell in her imagination. We get a glimpse of that in the end now, when she sums up and she is speaking to Mitchell. But in the first rough cut, we had a voice-over which wasn't working at all. As inventive as I thought it was, it was actually thunderingly banal and reductive. But the advantage was that shot these close-ups of Sarah Polley, anticipating the voice-over, and when I took the voice-over away, I was left with these extraordinary images which I wouldn't have shot otherwise, so I'm very thankful that I wrote the voice-over, because it meant that I had this coverage of her, including these very slow dolleys onto her face, which I probably wouldn't have dreamed of if I hadn't thought there would be voice-over over them.

Ultimately it's a story about people constructing narratives. And that became a very interesting device in the film. Because the most extraordinary gesture Nicole makes, when she's in the middle of this deposition when she's supposed to tell the truth, she suddenly finds a way of controlling her own narrative by lying, and thereby empowering herself.

So even though the seeds for Mitchell's story are laid, she's able to disrupt that and give herself dignity in the process.

SBK: You mentioned earlier about Allen Bell and the Pied Piper. The Pied Piper doesn't appear in the book, but it provides a real interesting visual metaphor for the story. How'd it happen, and who's Allen Bell?

AE: Well, when I first showed my first film, *Next of Kin*, in a small theatre in Victoria, British Columbia, [a man named] Allen Bell came up to me, and the things he said about the film were just so lucid and inspiring that I felt that I would like to work with him. He's a poet, he was a lit professor for many years, and he is now living in semi-retirement. He's just an extraordinary resource. He's somebody that I can trust to be unblinkingly honest about my work and he likes to sculpt my scripts. He likes to take out any extraneous words. He likes to make sure that everything is reduced to what is absolutely essential. I resist that sometimes, because I think in the process you might take away some of the character of the piece, but he's a great person to work with. It's a wonderful relationship that way. And he is absolutely clear what his responsibilities are, and he has a tremendous amount of respect as to what I will do as a director, but he has an unflinching belief that the script is paramount, and he wants it to be in its best shape before it goes before camera.

SBK: And what exactly happened re the Pied Piper?

AE: I went, as I often do, to tell him what I was doing next. And as I told him what the story was about, he said, "I think we're about due for a modern version of the Pied Piper." And I just got goose pimples and rushed out to get my tattered version of Robert Browning's poems, and it was such a gift! It was just so amazing to see how the ideas of that poem—the themes of a village that loses its kids, the idea of a person who comes in promising to solve the problems of the town and not getting a reward, and the themes of annihilation and punishment—all those are woven into the poem and found resonances with Russell's story. So it suddenly gave me, also, a sense of authorship.

I think that was very important to me, having written seven films based on original material. I needed to feel as though this was something which, at a certain point, I could become the author of in spirit, and the poem in some ways gave me that angle and that point of entree.

SBK: And it worked beautifully.

AE: It's uncanny how well it works. The only thing I had to do at the end was . . . I felt that with her lie at the end of the deposition, I wanted to make clear that we all knew she was lying, so I invented some poetic text based on Browning's rhythms at the very end of the poem, which was intimidating, but I think it works.

SBK: Do you remember the lines?

AE: Yes. "And why I lied, he only knew, but from my lie this did come true, those lips from which he drew his tune, were frozen as a winter moon." It's so bizarre because I'm in the lab, mixing another movie, and they are playing the film in the background. The moment I said that, I heard the flute of the Pied Piper coming from the other room.

SBK: One of the things I've noticed about your work, and this is probably more a directorial comment than about writing, but you allow silences between the words.

AE: Yes. I can't tell you how frustrating it is sometimes, and they won't do this with this movie, but with the other films, sometimes the criticism is that it's removed or that it seems I've sucked any emotion from these people. And I've always found that really frustrating because to me there is nothing more emotional than what is unspoken or what is repressed and held back. Very often the journey that my characters find themselves in is getting to that point at which they actually identify their emotions because the circumstance or fate has robbed them of the ability to express and has taught them that they need to hold back. That frustration and that desire to find communion is really what fuels a lot of the drama in my original stories.

I think in my earlier films, especially, I was so intrigued by the emotions that were kept back—the things that people couldn't say. That came from, I suppose, my theatre heroes, like Beckett and Pinter. I've always loved the silence and pause where there would be extended moments where the viewer or the reader would have to imagine what was unsaid. And it made you aware of how frail the process of communication is.

In many films, one of the things we love to amuse ourselves with is how effortlessly people can communicate with one another, and very often, in real life, there are moments of hesitation and uncertainty. Part of our job as screenwriters is to construct dramatic situations which warrant an exchange of words and ideas, but I still think that when we can define those moments where people lose words and don't know what to say, and trust that that will be as dramatically convincing as a barrage of sound being emitted from someone's mouth, that that is a way of accessing people's interior landscape.

So a lot of it has to do with working with actors, because when you choose to work that way, you have to rehearse and make sure the actors know what it is they're suppressing and what it is they're not. But it's also in the script itself. One of the characters in *Speaking Parts*, Lisa, a character who's returning a videotape at one point, is obsessed by this man she works with who's an extra. And when she's admonished by the video store owner [for being] obsessed with someone who's an extra, who doesn't have a speaking part, she retorts by saying, "Well, there's nothing special about words." And maybe there isn't. Maybe ultimately it's how words can sometimes convey a feeling and sometimes they can't. And I'm just as interested in those moments when they can't.

The difference between the characters in *The Sweet Hereafter* and my own [earlier] characters is that all these people in this town know who they are, they have a very clear sense of how they are rooted in this community. That's thrown into question after the accident, but they always are able to refer to what they were. In my other films, I think people's experiences have been so shattered and fractured that they are in the process of trying to understand what constitutes their own identity. The viewers aren't allowed to identify with any of my other characters because [the characters] don't even know who they are, and you are much more aware of what it is they need to do in order to piece themselves together. Those films are about finding that moment, and finding a sense of discovery. In *The Sweet Hereafter* it's very different. The characters are identifiable, they are very vivid, and we see them through their darkest hour, but we understand and are given enough idea of what their routines and their habits and their relationships are that we can invest ourselves in them in a more direct way.

And that was something I needed to do. I really felt like I was getting tired in some ways of my own way of drawing characters. It seemed as though I needed to learn more about what a novelist does, and this was a great, great experience that way. I don't immediately want to go back to one of my own scripts, and my new project is another adaptation.

SBK: *Sarabande*? Or another?

AE: Oh, no. I just signed with Icon to do an adaptation of *Felicia's Journey*, by William Trevor, the Irish writer.

SBK: So you didn't want to go back to one of your own scripts right away?

AE: Not right away. I just think that I'm entering a period in my own development where I am very open to collaboration. So with this experience I had with YoYo Ma where we spent a lot of time talking about what it is he tries to do with his art form and what music means to him, and listening to him, I created this drama, or a comedy, based on a number of circumstances that happened around a performance of the suites. You know, someone in the audience begins a coughing fit, and the tension as to whether or not he should interrupt or keep playing; a master class he gives with a very troubled student who had to give up her cello to become a doctor; and then intersections and parallels in all these different lives—all that was a response to listening to YoYo and hearing what he felt, and trying to interpret that, and collaborating with him on this unique project.

The operas, I had an incredible charge last year when suddenly I had the opportunity to direct *Salome*, which is, I think, a totally forgotten play by Oscar Wilde, and maybe in some ways it makes a better libretto than it does a play, but suddenly to interpret that material and to interpret it in the context of Richard Strauss's music, that was just so thrilling and so educating. I felt that I was apprenticing myself to these other people's visions, and learning from them and applying my own ideas.

I've been involved in a number of art installations which have also had a high degree of collaboration, and my next opera projects are both new operas. One is in London at English National Opera, with the English composer Gavin Bryars and the poet Blake Morrison. It's an adaptation of a Jules Verne short story called "Dr. Ox's Experiment."

The other one is an original libretto that I've written, called *Elsewhereless*, and I'm working with a Canadian composer here for a presentation in 1998. In opera you work very closely with a designer, so I'm working with this extraordinary theatrical designer, Michael Levine, and we're coming up with a concept for "Dr. Ox's Experiment" together.

I think for so long in the early part of my career, up to *Exotica*, I was just really concerned with making sure that people understood what I had to offer, making sure that people understood what my voice was. And with the profile and success of *Exotica*, I felt that I could loosen up on that a little bit, and perhaps develop my own talents by working closely with other people.

Atom Egoyan

Jason Wood/1998

From *Talking Movies: Contemporary World Filmmakers in Interview.* New York: Wall-flower Press, 2006, 54–63. Reprinted by permission of Wallflower Press.

One of contemporary cinema's most distinctive voices, working also in television, opera, and installation pieces, Atom Egoyan's work blends detachment and compassion to explore themes centring around identity and alienation, familial and personal dysfunction and sexuality.

Born in 1960 to Armenian refugees in Cairo, but relocated at an early age to Victoria, British Columbia, Egoyan initially grew up consciously rejecting his own ethnicity in favour of assimilation into his adopted culture. It was this experience that would later come to exert a profound influence over his work and thinking. His work is also marked, both visually and thematically, by a consistent exploration of the manner in which personal experience is mediated and manipulated by digital or video technology. A final key facet to the director's work is the key collaborative relationships he has formed from his first feature, *Next of Kin* (1984) to *Where the Truth Lies* (2005). Key personnel include Egoyan's wife and muse Arsinée Khanjian, producer Camelia Friedberg, editor Susan Shipton, cinematographer Paul Sarossy, and composer Mychael Danna. Egoyan's most recent work is the fascinating *Citadel* (2006), a video-diary exercise in which he charts his wife's emotional return to Lebanon. As one would expect with Egoyan, in the film nothing is what it seems.

He has also ventured into more mainstream territory with the Academy Award–nominated *The Sweet Hereafter* (1997), from Russell Bank's novel, wherein he utilises a fragmented narrative to convey a sensitive and poetic treatment of grief; *Felicia's Journey* (1999), another adaptation (this time from the novel by William Trevor) also effectively exploits the landscapes of the Midlands of the UK as *The Sweet Hereafter* does those of parts of western Canada.

I have had the pleasure of interviewing Egoyan numerous times throughout the years. The following exchange took place in London whilst the director was combining post-production work on *Felicia's Journey* with his directing of an opera, *Doctor Ox's Experiment*. The interview formed the basis for my film, *Formulas for Seduction: The Cinema of Atom Egoyan* (co-directed with Eileen Anipare, 1999).

JASON WOOD: I wondered if we could begin by talking about *Calendar* [1993]. It's a hugely personal work that also seems to encapsulate the search for identity that punctuates your films.

ATOM EGOYAN: It is a really personal work and it is, along with *Family Viewing* [1987], the most autobiographical piece. It was so liberating to go to those church sites and to shoot those scenes and to realise a fantasy. As a young child in the diaspora your only contact with your culture is with those church images that are sent out every year and it was fascinating to actually tell the story behind those images and to situate myself behind some of the things that my character is saying. Specifically, I really thought that I was from here but being here has made me realise that I'm from somewhere else. That's so true.

As an Armenian born in Egypt, so much of what I thought was Armenian was actually Middle Eastern, but that's the culture I was raised in and that my parents were raised in and certainly that my wife has been raised in. Arsinée Khanjian was raised in Lebanon and what we share as what we think are Armenian are actually Middle Eastern traditions and when you go back to Armenia you realise that it's not a Middle Eastern culture at all. It's a Caucasian culture and their habits and their social manners are really different to what constitutes Armenian; and that was a shock.

When we went to shoot that film in Armenia, one of the reasons I designed it so that I was behind the camera the whole time was that we'd be able to come back and find another actor who could then dub over my questions and dialogue and then put those in those other scenes, but for technical reasons it was not possible. There was so much dialogue that was overlapping, and that meant that I had to play the part. It was such a low-budget film that we couldn't think of re-dubbing the whole thing and I was put in the situation where I play a character who I think was involved in my own worst nightmare of who I might be.

JW: And did you find acting that part to be in some way therapeutic?

AE: I don't find acting anywhere near as therapeutic as making a film. It was a character that I could almost see myself falling into should, heaven forbid, something like that ever happen to me.

JW: And what about some of your primary filmmaking influences?

AE: Well, next weekend I'm going to Belgium where they're presenting my imaginary cinematheque. I had to choose a hundred films and they're all over the map. There's certainly the great Italian masters like Antonioni, Pasolini, and Bellocchio, and Fellini, of course. There's also certainly Bergman, Buñuel—a huge influence—and, of course, David Cronenberg. I'd also say a lot of the American cinema of the 1970s.

JW: I know that you're an admirer of Coppola's *The Conversation* [1974].

AE: *The Conversation* to me is a magnificent work and a moment of pure adulation was when I was on the jury in Cannes and Francis Ford Coppola was president of the jury and I actually took him the jacket of my video cassette of *The Conversation* to sign. All you have to do is remember what that work meant to you. I also had a close contact over the last year with Michelangelo Antonioni because I was supposed to be back-up director on his new project. No matter who that person is one can't forget the enduring effect that their work has had on us, and how it inspires us to be who we are. It's important to do things that keep that excitement alive.

JW: An incident that continues to reverberate is Wim Wenders gifting prize money he had won for *Wings of Desire* [1987] to your own *Family Viewing* at the 1987 Montreal Festival of New Cinema and Video.

AE: Truth be told, Wim hadn't seen the film at that point and he liked the idea of giving away his prize money to a film to which the jury had given an honourable mention. The great myth that I was circulating for a long time, and certainly didn't put an end to, was that he had seen the film and was so moved by it that he gave it the money. He did see it subsequently and thank God he liked it. I mean, he didn't ask for the money back, which would have been embarrassing.

That gesture of Wim's in 1987 in Montreal has had enduring ripple effects. For example, we're still talking about it. It was just so unexpected. I really do believe that one of the things that one is indebted to do is to help introduce new talent. If you have some sort of status as a filmmaker and you are able to use that to support projects that you believe in, such as first features, then it is incumbent upon you to do that. I was lucky to start making my first films before *sex, lies and videotape* [1989] came out; that was the film of course that changed everything, the whole independent scene.

To me the incredible heroes of the independent scene are people like Hal Hartley, Jim Jarmusch, and certainly Alan Rudolph and John Cassavetes before them. These people were somehow able to make their films in a system that was hostile to subsidies. There is also someone like Jon Jost who is one of the forgotten heroes of the American independent scene. Jost was a huge inspiration to me, making feature films for under $10,000. I think I'm in a really privileged situation because I'm able to make films that look and sound the way I would want them to be even if they had millions more. I'm working with a really dedicated crew and I'm working in a system that is able to cherish and support the films as a cultural product.

I have to also say that the films that I have loved have come out of similar situations. Bergman was working in a similar situation with the Swedish Film Institute and certainly a lot of the French cinema of the 1970s. There was subsidisation. It's very much like opera; people expect it to be subsidised in Europe. In America they don't and it's very much based on what the public wants, but that can be so inhibiting. One of the reasons that I really love working in Canada is that it's very difficult to be caught up in this momentum that has happened around first features coming out of the States, where there is a whole mythology about what that means and it has become the trademark of capitalism. You make something from your own ideas and you make it cheaply and suddenly it brings back tons of money; well, that's such a terrible pressure to put on someone at the beginning of their career.

JW: Do you try and deal equally throughout your work with issues of a national consciousness? *Gross Misconduct* [1992], which you made for Canadian television, deals very specifically with these issues, no doubt as a consideration for the audience who you were making it for.

AE: I felt that was a great Canadian gothic tale. That's why I was so excited about that project and it's still one of those projects that lingers in my mind. I always think should I remake it as a film. It is a great story and it actually did happen; it really is death by time zone. It is about this father who dreams that one day his little boy would become a hockey star and that he would watch him on television and on the night that all this happens the country decides not to show the game in his part of the country but to play another game, and this father just went crazy.

He walked into his TV station, held it hostage, demanded that they play his son's game and took a pistol to the TV programmer's head and said, "There's something wrong with CBC programming and something's got to change."

JW: And how do you react to a charge frequently levelled at you that your work is purely cerebral, structurally complex and thus somehow lacking in emotion?

AE: My reason for making films has always been emotional and I have never understood the claim that the work is cold, because it's really about people who are holding back emotion, but what they are holding back is torrential in a lot of situations. I look at *Speaking Parts* [1989] or *Family Viewing* and the experiences that these people have endured and are trying to cope with are operatic, but they have arrived at a point where they cannot afford to express those feelings. So I was confused by that accusation because I thought that there was something that wasn't getting across. Also, the films do use humour and there is an irony, which if you don't perceive the films that way then I don't think that you are getting the full experience. I do think that my strength is in setting up formulas for seduction based on structure, more so than on the image itself.

JW: How did you come to Russell Banks's *The Sweet Hereafter*?

AE: From the moment that I read that book I was aware that Banks has the ability to inhabit the voices of people other than himself and to find patterns to their speech and their mannerisms which means surrendering yourself completely to somebody else. I can't do that with my writing. I think I'm very good with strategies and structures and I can represent characters to a certain degree but after that I really want the actor to inhabit them. But here was this great material about a town—which I didn't know as I wasn't raised in a town like that—but Russell made me believe that I could create that town. I saw that novel as a gift.

JW: You've always worked closely with composer Mychael Danna but I think his contribution to *The Sweet Hereafter* is especially impressive.

AE: Mychael's contribution has been huge because in many of the films where you are not quite sure what the emotional life is, Mychael's music always tells you that there are emotions that are beneath the surface and there are times—and I think this is really powerful—where the music gives you more of an emotional feeling than the images do. And the shift and the movement of the film is to reconcile what you feel should be happening, through what the music is telling you, with what the images are saying, as opposed to film music, which just tries to elaborate what you're already seeing. That's something we're both keenly aware of and try to explore with every film.

If you look at *The Sweet Hereafter*, the use of early music is not what you'd expect. It has very specific associations, but to hear those medieval instruments suddenly paints the whole film as a Brothers Grimm fairytale. There are associations of a crusade, but you have a sense of it being of another time which gives it a timelessness when, in fact, it's very, very reality-based.

One of the fears that we had about the film was that it wouldn't be a TV film about an accident, because we can get all that by watching one of those incredible parades of emotion that you see on a Jerry Springer or a Phil Donahue show where people just let emotion out. Here, when you tell people what the story's about, it's as if they can see something that they can see on television but through the music you are able to heighten and give different direction and surprise people and disturb people as well. It's not what you'd expect to hear.

JW: Your work is also marked by your collaborations with cinematographer Paul Sarossy, editor Susan Shipton, and Arsinée Khanjian. Would you be able to comment on the creative import of these relationships?

AE: Paul and Susan are essential to what I do. I trust Paul completely with light, Susan to find the internal rhythm of a scene. Arsinée is the source of so much of my creative energy, and her face is an object of complete fascination.

JW: You have your own repertory cast of actors such as David Hemblen, Gabrielle Rose, Maury Chaykin. How did you come to work with Ian Holm and how did you find the experience of working with a "star"?

AE: Ian is an extraordinary actor and somebody who I think is greatly undervalued. He's also a wonderful person to work with. He's so generous. When I announced the cast, that it was going to be Ian Holm, there was a stunned silence because they are all from theatre and what he means to theatre actors is very similar to what I feel about Pinter or Antonioni.

Ian, from the moment that he came into the unofficial repertory company, was so impressed by the actors and let them know that and felt that he wasn't up to their standards and was quite genuine about that and he just made himself vulnerable. So much about this system, this star system, is about making people as detached and as invulnerable as possible.

I've always done my own casting and it's always been through theatre. I watch a lot of theatre and a lot of them are actors that I've seen in
theatre or I've seen as character parts in other people's films and they are
people that I have a really strong attachment to. When you respect an
actor from what they've done on stage, I think that means something
to them because that's when an actor is most in control, much more
than in a film when it's the director who orchestrates things. On stage,
you really see that is the actor's medium. So when you're taking them
from stage and when you're not even subjecting them to the process of
auditioning, because that can be disastrous when you're asking actors
to audition and come back, because they should feel from the moment
that they read a script and when you offer that role to them that they
are the people who should play those parts. That's the best way to start
off a relationship with an actor, to say, "This role is for you, you don't
have to audition for it, it's yours." I think that allows the actor to feel a
tremendous sense of confidence.

Unfortunately, what happens a lot of the time is that because an actor has to go through so many hoops and so many executives approv-
ing them that there is this lingering sense that maybe they shouldn't
be playing this role. This can find its way into what you see on screen
ultimately.

JW: After *The Sweet Hereafter* and many years of writing your own material you tackled another adaptation, William Trevor's *Felicia's Journey*.

AE: I again fell in love with the book. I think Trevor is a writer that I
can learn a lot from. I've met with him and I think that he is a master
storyteller. Again, he's one of these writers that has this superhuman
gift of being able to inhabit people other than himself. I find this story
so compelling.

The film is about two people who are timeless and yet very much
of this time: one being this monster of a character who is completely
influenced by modern technologies and media and yet doesn't seem
to be, who actually seems to be a relic of a previous time and that is
fascinating; and this young woman who comes to England and is a relic
of a time when people still write letters. It's just about people finding a
consciousness. I've always been attracted to the thriller as a form as well
and this allows me to explore something that I don't think I would have
been able to come up with myself and make it my own.

JW: As you work with bigger budgets and larger production companies
with rafters of executives, do you fear your films having to be subjected

to test screenings and market research? I can imagine there being resistance to your somewhat elliptical narratives.

AE: If you were to show *Exotica* [1994] or *The Sweet Hereafter* to a test audience and ask them what would they change, you would come back with a list too heavy to carry. Everyone would like to see these films follow a cohesive, narrative, linear pattern, but I just can't make them that way and I just don't think that way. The relationship we have to a finished film is very different to something we think we can change, so I'm really frightened of that process and I just don't know how I could cope with it. It's this idea of surprise, of not knowing what the result will be, and of trying to find a way to keep the process alive for yourself.

Sometimes I can read a really linear, well-written script and go yes, this is a movie that I would really love to see but I could not for the life of me spend a year laying out what's already there. There has to be an element of surprise. I have to feel that I don't quite know how pieces are going to fit and manipulating the question of time seems to me to be so seductive—that we can drift and actually address thematic issues through people's relationship to time. Film is a medium that first and foremost records time and gives the illusion that it is projecting time. It's an extraordinary book—Tarkovsky's *Sculpting in Time*—but that is your material and to not question the natural impulse to linear and narrative consequence and sequence is I think really limiting. It's just not the way I think. I like to remain excited by the process and one of those ways of remaining excited is by not knowing, even as I'm writing sometimes, where something will lead. That's why I can't write a treatment.

JW: Very much to the forefront in *Family Viewing* but a recurring motif in your films is the recording and manipulation of memories and experience. This strikes me as quite a sinister concept.

AE: It's sinister and yet it's also so touching. When someone tries to destroy or enhance their experience by a natural manipulation of the recording of it it's such a frail and vulnerable thing to do because it's not dealing with a real issue. It's like a cry of despair or pain, it's like saying this is what I'd like to be able to do; I'd actually like to go back and change the course that events have taken but we can't. But to think that we can somehow deal with that through a secondary source is very much a part of the specific moment in our cultural evolution and it's something that I find fascinating and sad and quite funny sometimes: that we can actually think that we have control over our fate by exercising control over the most obvious representation of our fate.

JW: To quote from *Family Viewing*, the people in your films "love to record" and commit to tape. For many of the characters in your films it offers both a form of frequently sexualised therapy.

AE: I think that this has become so persuasive, we all have systems where feelings and ideas can be transcribed to pieces of tape and through various types of technologies. There's something almost casual about it. The way in which we surrender our process of organic memory and our sense of how we can objectively block out ideas or retain certain images. Now that has become quite suspicious to us because we give everything to an undiscriminating technology which just records and we have to deny those processes because we don't know what we are keeping or throwing away because everything is stored and that has changed the way we behave, I think.

I'm interested in seeing how human beings react under pressure and I'm interested in people who think they have systems that deal with neuroses, and I'm really fascinated by this notion of therapy. I'm attached to this idea of creativity and there are people who can be very creative about things in their own lives and that might include finding a sexual practice that can help them release certain things or it might mean actually finding a pattern which others might see as being diverse or deviant, but it allows them to cope with something. Sometimes that pattern may not be the best thing that person can do, but they are almost aware of that and you want to applaud them for the effort and there's something very human about their desire to come to terms or find a way of dealing with their pain.

JW: Do you have a defined Atom Egoyan audience in mind when conceiving and constructing your films?

AE: No, but I also have the highest expectation of my audience. I have to. For the type of films I make your point of departure is the belief that your audience is infinitely curious, exploratory, and trustful, that they are able to trust what you are doing. For instance, I love films that start off and set a tone of mystery; that start off and say you have to be prepared to go on a journey and you cannot expect that it's going to follow a formula. I'm attracted to that type of film. The criticism I've always received for all the films is that they start off slowly. What people mean is that they don't necessarily tell you who it is that you are supposed to identify with or why.

You have to be able to understand that very often a reviewer or even a jury—having been on a jury myself—what they extend to is the result of an immediate impression and what endures is something that you won't even know until weeks, months, or maybe even years later. I have to believe that people are going to the films prepared to be there for the hour and a half that the experience will take and if they drift at certain moments, that's fine. It's something that I find quite pleasurable. I love to drift. There's no better place for me to just let go than in a dark room that's projecting images at twenty-four frames a second. It's one of the essential powers of cinema: images that suggest that what is happening is real and to not question that seems a great shame.

JW: You like to diversify. You have worked on art installations; written librettos [for a chamber piece called *Elsewhereless*] and have directed operas such as *Doctor Ox's Experiment*.

AE: Directing *Doctor Ox's Experiment* and working with Gavin Bryars's music was a thrill and a huge honour but I can't help but feel that it is a sideline to what is my vocation ultimately. The more I work in other media the more I understand what I'm attracted to in film. With cinema you're given an instrument which can actually reflect a point of view and which can situate the viewer in a really dynamic way which any other medium, including opera, well there's just something antiquated about the theatrical experience. When it works and when you have a genuine sense of transformation and transfiguration it's really spellbinding and yet those moments are really rare. It's something that I'm drawn to because it was my initial passion and love. With the camera, from the moment I started playing with the camera, well you are able to reflect one's way of seeing the world in a really literal manner. The issues it provokes, the issue of why we need to record images, why we need to transmit images, what we expect to get back from those images, those are all so crucial to our society. It's impossible to feel irrelevant when you are working in the film medium while all these other professions somehow risk a sense of being outside what are our most crucial and pressing issues. That is, what do we expect to see or how has technology changed our sense of what experience is and what constitutes experience.

Felicia's Journey
Atom Egoyan Speaks about His Latest Film

Cynthia Fuchs/1999

From *Nitrateonline*. www.nitrateonline.com/1999/ffelicia.html. 19 November 1999. Reprinted by permission of author.

Atom Egoyan speaks softly and carefully, in complex sentences. Unexpectedly, this makes our interview difficult, because we're stuck with a phone line that cuts in and out, so that our voices intersect and overlap. ("Hello?" "Are you still there?")

Egoyan is home in Toronto, looking after his six-year-old son, while his wife, actress Arsinée Khanjian is away working in France. He and I have spoken before, first when *Exotica* was released in 1994, and again on the occasion of *The Sweet Hereafter* in 1997. In the past we've talked about his explorations of voyeurism and exhibitionism, memory and repression, desire and fear. This time, we can't help but note the irony of this crackling, sputtering connection, because we're talking about his new film, *Felicia's Journey*, which is all about gaps in communication and the ways that modern technologies—namely, video and audio recordings—shape recollection, identity, and meaning.

These themes have surely informed Egoyan's previous films—including *Family Viewing* (1987), *Speaking Parts* (1989), *The Adjuster* (1991), and *Calendar* (1993)—but in *Felicia's Journey*, they seem honed down to a skeletal precision. Where the earlier films (save for *Calendar*) involve multiple characters, with intersecting expectations and disappointments, the new movie focuses narrowly on two characters, the middle-aged British serial killer Hilditch (played by Bob Hoskins) and the Irish teenager Felicia (Elaine Cassidy). Their histories and their goals divide them, but chance brings them together in a dance of self-delusion and attempted redemption.

114

While the themes might be Egoyan's own, the basis for this script is a novel by William Trevor. I asked Egoyan why he decided to use another novel—as he had for the first time with Russell Banks's *The Sweet Hereafter*—as the basis for his script.

ATOM EGOYAN: I wanted to focus on a simpler, more classic structure after *The Sweet Hereafter*, and Trevor's book seemed perfect. I was fascinated by the characters, both suspended in a kind of period piece. Felicia [played in the film by Elaine Cassidy] is coming from a sort of nineteenth-century rural culture, and Hilditch is removed from his own time. They shock each other into recognition of who they are and what their current situations are. It has many different levels—cultural, familial, psychosexual—which come together in a compelling story.

CYNTHIA FUCHS: Serial killing is by now almost mundane in popular culture. How did you approach the topic?

AE: That's true. It's almost become a job. The representation of serial killing in contemporary film culture makes it an occupation, like lawyering, which I explored in *The Sweet Hereafter*. That's the only way I can understand the preponderance of this particular abnormality. We're fascinated by it because it represents the most extreme moral transgression, but it's done repeatedly. The seriality of the action becomes interesting to us structurally, because it alludes to fate and inevitability and our ability to stop it. In typical serial-killer movies, you have these acts unfolding and a character trying to stop them. That's the dramatic point of tension. *Felicia's Journey* is different; it's not constructed like a thriller. I consider this more of a drama than a thriller.

CF: It's even more like a melodrama; it's so domestic in location and spirit.

AE: Exactly. I'm really trying to represent his actions the way he perceives himself. I don't think he sees himself as a serial killer. He's convinced himself that he's something other than what we eventually gather he is. That interests me as well, his denial, his ability to live in that state, and its intersecting with Felicia's denial, which is simpler and more identifiable. She's seventeen years old and she believes that this young man loves her, and clearly he doesn't. But she has to believe that and repeat that to herself.

CF: I have to ask you this. One of the cliches in serial killer imagery—from *Psycho* to Ted Bundy—is the bad mother. How were you thinking about Hilditch's mother, Gala [Arsinée Khanjian], in this context?

AE: But, *how* bad a mother is she? I think it's a complex relationship. One of the things that Arsinée and I discussed was the difficulty of her position. Given what she was doing, at that particular time, she had to be so focused and so driven to succeed. She was probably quite preoccupied with her career. One of the main differences between the film and the novel is that the book sexualizes the relationship between mother and son, and that struck me as being reductive. I am of the belief that some of us are genetically encoded or hardwired in a certain way that manifests itself at a young age. What interested me more in blaming the mother, is that now, because of the lack of attention that Hilditch felt, he has a ritual where he can command Gala's full attention. He can play her films and redirect her gaze electronically, to be watching him. He can pretend that this relationship was completely nurturing. And that ritual has perverted him more than anything she ever did or didn't do.

CF: Like using her opera glasses to watch her on TV from the dining room, giving himself control of look?

AE: That's right. I tried to avoid the bad mother cliché, but I think you've really identified the problem, which is that we're so predisposed toward the bad mother, as the site of blame, so that anything that even hints of that is seized on. People talk about her cruelty to him in the garden. But it's not that extreme really: she just asks him to move out of the range of camera. And the moment where he chokes on the liver: my question is, did that actually happen? There's a fuzzy line between the video as a document and his state of mind.

CF: So, we only have access to that relationship through his memories?

AE: Yes. It does fascinate me, as you know, this blurred line between the tape as a way of representing memory or the tape as a way of representing the archiving of reality. The mere act of having that subjective, fetishized moment, leads to its own behavioral pattern. He's a product of technology as a means to memory. He's of the first generation who would have been brought up by and in mass media, so he's chronicling the first gestures that technology was making in recording childhood. And the other thing that makes this character disarming is that normally, when we have these technically oriented characters, they live in sleek, modern looking homes, like the Baldwin character in *Sliver*. But Hilditch doesn't fit that mold, he's not *au current* with the latest technologies, and yet he's a product of technology as a means to memory.

CF: While images of Felicia's past, appearing as flashbacks, seem to be more direct?

AE: That's exactly right, but she comes from culture rich in oral traditions. Her father tells her stories about 1916, and her only maternal link is her grandmother, who speaks this ancient tongue. Felicia's still living in this world where she has to write letters by hand for her boyfriend and have his mother deliver them. It's really a nineteenth-century world; she has a romanticized vision of the world she lives in. It's shot to look pastoral and traditional.

CF: At times Hilditch seems almost to romanticize his relationship with her, as if she's his "daughter," to whom he would give advice.

AE: Yes. And the fathers are awful in the film: the most violent action we see on screen is Felicia's father banishing her. That's unspeakably cruel. The moment that Hilditch realizes that Felicia is carrying a child, I think this forces him to self-consciousness. I don't think he's used to receiving the sort of attention that she gives him. He's become accustomed to not being someone you would look at.

CF: And he's looked at ferociously by the women who come to sermonize him in his own garden, when he's digging a grave for Felicia, whom he plans to kill. The women stand over him and summon the all-knowing, all-punishing Lord Father as a means to get him to repent, even though they have no idea that he's got many bodies buried all around them.

AE: That's right. But any message that those women are purporting to spread is only as strong as they are as messengers. When he finally admits to a theft, which is really the least of his crimes, the women can't even begin to fathom what he's really telling them. I think the garden is important here, as a place offered as a refuge or sanctuary, but it's only as safe as the gatekeepers, who are inept in this case.

CF: Hilditch seems ever-ready to cut deals. But his sense of fairness is so warped, like when Felicia is concerned about the money for the abortion, he says, "It's my treat," which it's obviously not. It's such a dark and funny line.

AE: Yes, that *is* hilarious. *And* he's paid for the abortion with her stolen money. I love that line. But no one is laughing at it. Because of what he does—serial killing—there's this set of genre expectations placed on the film, and that's difficult to navigate. Except for the scenes of Arsinée on the cooking show, which is so clearly signaled, the film seems less forthcoming with giving people permission to laugh, so the humor is elusive.

Egoyan's Journey

An Interview with Atom Egoyan

Donato Totaro and Simon Galiero/1999

From *Offscreen*. 8 February 2000. http://www.horschamp.qc.ca/egoyan.html. Reprinted by permission of the author.

Atom Egoyan's latest film, *Felicia's Journey* (1999), is a serial killer film unlike any other. Rather than the traditional serial killer pile of corpses and bloody mayhem, Egoyan, in his inimitable style, takes us into the nostalgic and romanticized private world of middle-aged catering supervisor Ambrose Hilditch (played by Bob Hoskins). Playing alongside Hilditch is a young Irish woman, Felicia, who has come to Birmingham, England, in quest of her boyfriend and the father of her expected baby, Johnny. Instead of finding Johnny, she finds the timid, fatherly figure of Hilditch, who leads her into quite another type of journey. Egoyan presented *Felicia's Journey* at Montreal's 1999 International Festival of New Cinema and New Medias. Egoyan was nice enough to find time in his busy schedule to indulge us with the following interview, which took place at the festival headquarters, Ex-Centris.

OFFSCREEN: First off, I was struck by Bob Hoskins's performance as Ambrose Hilditch. I was wondering whether he did anything special to prepare for the role?

AE: Well the most important thing was in establishing a system of references and motifs during the rehearsal process that you can then draw on as you're shooting.

OFFSCREEN: So you spent a long time on rehearsals?

AE: We had a lot of discussion. And Bob had to do a lot on getting the accent right, because that particular accent, the Brumie (Birmingham) accent is very unusual. His character is in such a state of denial, that

118

we had to be very specific about what it was that he was holding back. I think it is also a question of organizing the shooting schedule in such a way that allows that process to become organic. Because you can talk about rehearsal a lot, and that is crucial, but I'm finding that for the type of performances that I've been using in my later films, where there is something more immediate and accessible about the emotionality of the characters, that it is what I do on set that is more important. For example, in the earlier films, where I was trying to find a very repressed, held back performance style, they required almost a theatrical type of rehearsal process.

OFFSCREEN: And speech is so important in your films, the timber, inflection, going all the way back to *Family Viewing* (1986).

AE: Yes, that took a lot more rehearsal, because that is a more theatrical presentation. And when you are using dialogue that is so sparse and so reduced, and where everything is being held back, you have to be very specific about how loaded every statement is, and what is being held back.

OFFSCREEN: Do you know whether Hoskins was patterning his voice after any other filmic characters?

AE: No, because I'll tell what is unusual about the Brumie accent, which is never heard in British cinema, even though it is the second largest city in England. Unlike Manchester, Liverpool, or Sheffield, there's no fantasy that exists in London about Birmingham. The reason the accent is so nasal is that for many years, because of the industrial waste in the air, they couldn't breathe through the nose. And because of that, this very particular accent was developed, which grates the English ear like you can't believe. So it was a real journey for Hoskins to immerse himself in that particular voice.

OFFSCREEN: Well I mention it because it reminded me of the real-life character John Christie from the film *10 Rillington Place* (1972), played by Richard Attenborough. In both cases the voice is so unassuming, it is the last person you would consider to be a serial killer. *Felicia's Journey* also seems to me like a collection of some of the most perverse moments in films made by British directors, like Michael Powell and Alfred Hitchcock.

AE: Well certainly Michael Powell, I mean you have to re-watch *Peeping Tom* (1959) if you are making any movie about a child who is traumatized by the profession of a parent! And then who ends up killing people! I mean it is the über-serial killer film to watch. So I was certainly aware of *Peeping Tom*. And then I re-watched a lot of Hitchcock, but Hitchcock to me, where I find that I've been most inspired by Hitchcock is in the way he deals with perversion and obsession. But the actual science of the way he creates suspense is not something that is very compatible with my way of filmmaking, because I'm always trying to find a way of showing how these characters see themselves. Which means that the viewers are not necessarily in a privy position. The viewer does not necessarily know something that the characters don't realize themselves. And Hitchcockian cinema is almost founded on that principle. In some ways it is anti-Hitchcockian in science, but very Hitchcockian in tone.

OFFSCREEN: Well there's of course the moment you reference from *Suspicion* (1941), where he's walking up the stairs with the glass of cocoa (instead of milk).

AE: Well that was a direct nod for a couple of reasons. First of all, I think that at that moment, I love that moment, because we realize that he [the Cary Grant character] is about to murder her [the Joan Fontaine character]. So that whole sequence is suspenseful in a classic way because at that point we know what is in that glass of milk or cocoa, plus with the stuff happening in the garden. So that was a way of acknowledging that we were about to enter into that zone. But also, there's also something Hitchcockian about the way he would look at the camera and implicate the viewer quite directly. But it is troubling because there is nothing pleasurable about that. It is very unsettling because we realize at that point that we have no idea who this person actually is, and he has no idea who he actually is. And also the idea of the regard, the direct camera address, has—hopefully—been subtly worked into the film. He clearly has wanted his mother's regard, which he has never received, and now electronically is able to. Through this ritual of the tapes, she's able to look at him all the time. And it is a very intimate, very adoring relationship that they have, which never existed in his childhood. So he's become very used to this look. I think ultimately the power of the gaze is so unsettling to him. I mean, look what happens to him in the garden with the crazy women. It has nothing to do with what they are saying, but I think it is just because of the fact that they are looking at him that way. He is just not used to receiving the gaze. So that when we then are presented with his gaze, it is very unsettling.

OFFSCREEN: It completely emasculates him, the way he falls to his knees in the garden scene. You actually feel for the character at that point. There's also the paranoia that Hitchcock creates in that scene, I like the way you used that and modified it.

AE: Well the other classic English film, I guess you can call it English, is *The Collector* (1965), the William Wyler film. Which is probably the closest film I can think of to *Felicia's Journey*, more than *Peeping Tom*, with the way it is set in the house. I love all those classic films. Another one is *Séance on a Wet Afternoon* (1964). I just love the mood of those movies.

OFFSCREEN: And *Psycho* (1960) as well in a way, with the mother figure. And I was also struck by a similarity between a line of dialogue, which is probably purely coincidental, but after Hilditch and Felicia have had dinner for the first time, he says something like, "we all do terrible things sometimes." Is that a reference to the line Norman says to Marion after they have lunch, "we all go a little mad sometimes"?

AE: Oh no, that's interesting, though I've never thought about that. I'm really proud of that scene. Everything he is telling her in order to convince her to have the abortion makes so much sense. He's almost like the monster of pro-choice. In fact it is probably the smartest decision she can make in terms of her own life. But of course his reasons for convincing her are so skewed.

OFFSCREEN: Sticking to the serial killer motif. I like the way you take the traditional serial killer text and subvert it by not showing any murders or deaths, except his own.

AE: Well he doesn't see those things. He doesn't see himself as a violent man. The whole question about how much he remembers is up in the air. I think he's beginning to have a connection with his organic memory as he is stealing her money. Because there is something about Felicia as a mother which really jars him. The moment he realizes that she is carrying a child and that she's a mother, that puts him into another state. And those images of him in the garden are probably the first glimmerings of consciousness he is having. So every other image is a mediated one. And they are not images he is remembering, but rather they are archival moments he's actually preserved. It is similar to *Family Viewing*. Have you seen *Family Viewing*?

OFFSCREEN: Yes, I love that film.

AE: Well I'm flattered. It's probably still my favorite film. I really love that film, especially when it is the 35mm blow-up projected. Because we did a blow-up from 16mm to 35mm. And it is texturally so perfect that way. Because all the stuff that takes place in the condominium, which was shot in one-inch Beta with live switching, suddenly you really see the texture of it as video. Which on tape you never quite get. You get it through the cutting style, but you don't really see the texture. And on 35mm, not even 16mm, it is really cool. All those textures work really well. Where the technology serves as both a metaphor for the notion of experience but also as a way of having characters deal with their neurosis. Where the manipulation of recorded experience allows them to rearrange and re-orient themselves to experiences which are unresolved and dysfunctional. I think *Felicia's Journey* can exist very well on a double-bill with *Family Viewing*.

OFFSCREEN: Yes I agree. Just the way *Felicia's Journey* begins with the extremely lush dolly shot, the lighting, the mise-en-scene, it is so warm. And then that is contrasted with all the other video footage.

AE: Yes. Felicia's sense of time and her sense of experience is so much more immediate. She has complete access to her life. And the way those images drift in and out is so much more vivid and lush. Though she's living in a nineteenth-century type of world, in a rural, pastoral village. She is still delivering letters by hand to the mother of her boyfriend. And Hilditch is living in his own period piece.

OFFSCREEN: Yes, well you captured that well. I mean, I couldn't decide what period the film was set in!

AE: Well, I love that. And then you realize that he's very much a monster of our times. And what was really cool about this was that we had a whole sequence where we showed him setting up his little spy camera in his car, and then we realized, we actually don't need it. In fact we are living in a culture where we just consume images. Images are everywhere. And it is a real shock when we see this person who is still putting on LP records! And dealing with old technology. But it makes complete sense. He was raised on mediated imagery. Actually, it is very interesting. When I made *Family Viewing* I had to have the character Van deliver this very awkward line in the film where he has to explain to his stepmother that his dad had all this technology when it first came out. I made that film in 1986, and even that was a bit of a stretch, that a boy who was sixteen at that point would have access to color VHS home movies. But in a way Van is of that first generation of kids who might have had their childhood videotaped. In this same sense, Hilditch is of that first generation of kids who had their childhood mediated, through this very bizarre participation on his mother's cooking show. So Van and Hilditch are cousins.

OFFSCREEN: In terms of the mise-en-scene, was there a lot of that period stuff in the William Trevor novel?

AE: No. The mother did not exist in the book. There's no cooking show, or video in the book. That is completely constructed.

OFFSCREEN: Well you've been to England, and I lived there for a while, and it is amazing the way that cooking shows are so popular there. And they don't cook very well!

AE: Well in the 1950s I think Gala would have been an extraordinary pioneer. You can understand how she would have been a cult figure. And in fact, the biggest shock was in going there and finding out that there was a Gala in the 1950s England, this woman called Fanny Cradock, who was this mythical figure. She wasn't French, but weirdly enough for one of her shows taped at the Royal Albert Hall, she put on this fake French accent.

OFFSCREEN: Why did you give her a French accent?

AE: The whole notion of how culture is represented in the film kind of fascinates me. The way the father gives all this cultural baggage to Felicia, about the Anglo-Irish history, and dwelling on 1916. And the idea that she is somehow the repository for all this history. And I like the idea that in Hilditch's past there was this forgotten culture, or a culture that was perhaps fabricated in the first place. What the mother's cultural orientations were and her legacy that she left to her child is so mysterious. And also I love the aspect that the mother was possibly a construct of what, to the British, a French woman would be like in the 1950s. And that she made a career out of playing a stereotype.

OFFSCREEN: Back to the video imagery. I remember in *Family Viewing*, at first the video image was always put on or started by someone, but by the end it comes on autonomously, by itself. And in this film, which I've only seen once until now, it appears to me that there are moments when the video images come in and you are not quite sure what the point of view is?

AE: Right. Well, in particular, like when he is watching the cooking show, he's watching the show, and suddenly there's an image where the mother is looking at him on the show. There is a confusion as to whether those are really part of the show that he's watching or whether or not the imagery at that point slips into his state of mind. I love those passages.

OFFSCREEN: Did you do any research on serial killers?

AE: Yes. There was quite a bit of research because I wanted to make him unusual. And he is unusual for a number of reasons. First of all, with most serial killers, there is a pattern to the way the victims usually look, and the type of people that they are. And I wanted to show that there wasn't that type of regularity. That there is no similarity in the way these women look. And so he doesn't fit that pattern at all. And research has shown that there is a genetic encoding, like young kids who pull the wings off flies, and burn things with magnifying glasses, there's the beginnings there.

OFFSCREEN: O boy, I think I did that when I was a kid!

AE: Well, the thing is that there are upbringings that can allow one to deal with those issues and then there are other types of upbringings that maybe enhance those characteristics. But I don't think there are any simple reasons or explanations as to why people become serial killers.

OFFSCREEN: Yes. What's also interesting is that a high percentage, like 90 percent or higher, of serial killers are white males, which is a pretty alarming statistic. But there are the stereotypes that are completely anal and ordered, and others that are competely disordered. And that Hilditch would fall under the anal and ordered type.

AE: Yes, but I remember reading about Jeffrey Dahmer, where he kept victim's bones in his house, and one of them escaped, they found him running down the street with like a knife sticking out of his back! He got away. And they asked him later on, well explain what was going on with Dahmer, and what he said was that Dahmer was the nicest man, he was warm and kind, and the moment he turned was when I wanted to leave. So, like with Dahmer, the moment these women want to leave Hilditch turns. He can't stand the fact that they will go away. At that point he needs to keep them. And I think his video archive is as disturbing as Dahmer's bones. And he's been taught to believe that with his skewed relationship with his television mother, that tapes keep his relationships current. With his mother never giving him attention as a kid, and suddenly through this ritual of the tape, he is able to maintain an intimacy in a relationship. He's able to construct an electronic gaze where there wasn't any attention directed to him as a kid. He's able to make that happen. It's similar to the situation in *Family Viewing*, with the father trying to erase over the tapes of the home video. I'm very interested in those points where the technology, as I said, can serve as a metaphor but also as a way of having these characters think they are dealing with issues of experience.

OFFSCREEN: Yes, because Stan the father never watches the tapes he records. The cooking show was set in the 1950s right?

AE: Yes.

OFFSCREEN: Yet it was shot on video?

AE: It was shot live, on kine, which is how those things are preserved, and why there are scratches and stuff [ed. kine being the term for a film recording made from a picture tube].

OFFSCREEN: Well, there's been this huge influx and interest in serial killer films in the past five to ten years.

AE: Well, I think in cinema the serial killer has become a profession, it's like showing a doctor or lawyer character. Serial killers have become another one of the ways in which a character might conduct their lives. It is odd to say that but that's the only way we can deal with our public fascination with them. Just think of all the thrillers that are based on lawyers. And what a lawyer has come to represent in our film culture is someone who is seeking truth. And usually has to deal with notions of personal truth as opposed to objective reality. And it has become a controlling metaphor in many narratives. And the serial killer, in a similar way, has found an occupation, killing people, which serves to represent latent issues in a very convenient way. I think we are all obsessed with the notions of fate, and of course in a conventional serial killer film, there is seriality involved in the actual structure of the film. There's a sense of the inevitable, who will be the next victim? And there is usually an investigation to try to stop what would seem to be the inevitable. It's an interesting occupation to represent. And I think in a weird way, maybe this is one of those films where there is a serial killer, but it is not a serial killer movie. It's actually a drama about a serial killer in the tradition of, maybe, *The Collector.*

OFFSCREEN: In terms of the non-linearity of the narrative, which is something you've always done and more so in your later films, I think the way it works in this film is different. Can you talk about that a little, what you were attempting to do with the non-linearity?

AE: Well, I'm trying to find ways of accessing history. And in her case she's on this particular journey. She's made this momentous decision to leave her home and she's playing back these scenes to reinforce this story she has to believe, which is that Johnny loves her and is waiting for her. But she is also sifting over the information of the father, the obligations and the burdens the father places on her to remember history. So she is trying to sort out what history means, what her history means. So there's that sifting through the evidence, that she's trying to come to terms with. And that is contrasted with Hilditch's story, which is actually told in a very linear fashion. From point A to point B he is not moving backward and forward in time, except when he's actually putting on a tape which gives him access to the past. Otherwise his sense of narrative is quite clear. So there is that play between the two. And because of the interplay you get the sense that the film is less linear than it actually is. It is not as complex, by any means, as *The Sweet Hereafter* (1997) or *Exotica* (1994). I mean, *The Sweet Hereafter* has something like thirty-five different time periods! This is more classical.

OFFSCREEN: A more general question. Do you think filmmakers need to do more work in training or educating the public in how they watch movies?

AE: I think the main work is just to read. That images are to be read and that the greatest way to invite that process is by giving space, and time. I'm really painfully aware of that with my movies, because of their pacing. If you are not reading into the images then the films become almost unbearably slow. But I come from a generation where the models that I have are people like Andrei Tarkovsky. It is all about creating a space where you need to read into the image. If you are not reading, then there is nothing else happening. Anytime you hold a shot and you linger, there is an intention there. And you are saying to the viewers, that it is ok to take time. You don't have to feel that you are caught up in a parade of images that don't invite further investigation.

OFFSCREEN: So do you agree with Herzog when he said that there are no more images?

AE: I don't think it is a question of images, but of creating space.

OFFSCREEN: As a Canadian, do you find any differences between shooting a film in Quebec as opposed to somewhere else in Canada?

AE: Well, filmmakers like Jean-Pierre Lefebvre, the way he made films and makes films, his philosophy and his use of time was really inspiring to me. He was the first Canadian filmmaker that I found an affinity with. Obviously there was a time when making films in this province was viewed as an artisanal activity, and I have a very romantic image of that period. In terms of the status of how films are made here now, I don't see as great a split between English Canada and Quebec. I think there are more similarities, maybe unfortunately, than there was before when there was a huge difference in philosophy.

OFFSCREEN: Do you think Quebec films lack a certain universalism? As opposed to, for example, watching an Egoyan film or a Kiarostami film?

AE: Well, there are great films, but I think it is a question of continuity, of being able to make many films. I'm not sure what happens to those filmmakers who make one good film. I'm not familiar enough with the process here to know why films aren't being made quicker. I remember with Lefebvre in his golden period, he was making so many films. I think maybe there is a pressure here, of course . . . but no, if you think of Léa Pool and her latest film *Emporte-moi* (1999), which I just saw and think is brilliant, she's as universal as anybody and is working under a similar system.

OFFSCREEN: Back to your film. When you talk about space and time, I love the way you coded your opening and closing shots. Both are long takes of roughly the same lengths. The opening shot with Hilditch's character, the last with Felicia's character.

AE: Yes, it is there to read when the camera takes that much time. One is charting an interior space, one an exterior space.

OFFSCREEN: Well I hope you continue shooting in that way, taking that time.

AE: Thank you!

Krapp and Other Matters

A Conversation between Atom Egoyan and Rebecca Comay

Rebecca Comay/2001

From *Lost in the Archives*, ed. Rebecca Comay. Toronto: Alphabet City, 2002. Reprinted by permission of the author.

This discussion was recorded in March, 2001 at Atom Egoyan's studio in Toronto, a few months after the festival release of his recent production of *Krapp's Last Tape* (starring John Hurt)—part of an international film series commissioned by Irish television to film Beckett's entire dramatic corpus.

COMAY: *Krapp's Last Tape* seems to have been made for you. Both in its formal encrypting of one medium within another—a tape recorder placed within theatre like a little play-within-the-play—and in its thematic exploration of the uneasy nexus between technology and memory, Beckett's play seems to anticipate many of the moves you make in your films. Your work obsessively explores the various textures created by the incorporation or layering of mnemotechnic devices—video, television, photography, answering machine, tape recorder, at times even cinema itself—within the frame of cinema. To what extent has this play been an overt inspiration for your other work?

EGOYAN: Totally. When I first encountered the play, I was going through a period in my adolescence when I was overwhelmed with the theatre of the absurd. It matched a certain disenchantment I felt with a lot of things. *Krapp's Last Tape* was the first text I encountered in which a piece of technology could have a dramatic force that was at least as important and profound as the human character on stage. There was also a play by

128

Elmer Rice, *The Adding Machine*, from the 1920s—one of the first plays that dealt with technology: in this case the effect of the adding machine. The play had emerged from a whole movement of American Expressionism, and involved an oversized adding machine on the stage, with a man jumping from one key to another—remember, this was 1920. There was also, of course, Cocteau's play *The Human Voice*, in which we observe a woman having a telephone conversation with various people, all expressing different points of view but which we ourselves never directly hear. And finally, there was that wonderful moment in Arthur Miller's *Death of a Salesman*, where Willy Loman walks into the office of the new manager and is surprised by the presence of a dictaphone—completely overwhelmed by it.

COMAY: I'm reminded here of one of your very early short films, *Howard in Particular* [1979]—a spoof on *Krapp*, bananas and all—in which an entire corporate machinery is set up to theatricalize a mass firing, human labour having been made redundant by technology: each employee has to march into an empty office and listen to a tape-recorder issuing his marching orders (along with ritualized humiliation). Let's talk specifically about *Krapp* and the relationship it dramatizes between technology and memory. The machine gives him access to a past which appears essentially as a storehouse of repressed possibilities and gestures towards a future riddled with loss. I'm wondering how technology, with its own futuristic dreams of progress as well as its inherent tendency to obsolescence, also reflects (or compounds) the experience of the past as a site of lost possibility.

EGOYAN: What *Krapp* does so brilliantly is to anticipate a time when our imagination and memory are entirely dependent on our surrendering to a recording device: there are certain aspects of our experience which we will have organically filtered out or forgotten, and this machine comes back and reminds us in a startling way, not only of the forgotten experience, but of our way of understanding the experience. Krapp at age sixty-nine is reflecting on his past self at the age of thirty-nine, who is in turn reflecting on his past self at the age of twenty-seven, and so on. He once had poetry; he had been able to speak of experience in a language to which he doesn't have access any more—this makes it doubly cruel. He would never have to encounter this particular pain if he didn't ritualistically go through the taping process once a year. On the one hand there is the ability of technology to enhance our experience, but it can also trivialize it. Why do we need to record? I think Krapp believed that he was going to be a writer of some note—this is a powerful fantasy that he has, or that he had had—so he must feel, or have felt, that these tapes would be of some value to someone, sometime. . . .

COMAY: But there's also a real circularity here: the recording feeds on itself in an infinite loop. Krapp is recording not just for the sake of the present, or to take stock of the past, or even for the sake of future listening. He is essentially recording in order to record again, in some unspecified future. The purpose of the birthday ritual of listening to an old tape is as a stimulus to enable him to record another tape: he can only record on the basis of listening to previous recordings. At some basic level, Krapp is taping simply in order to keep on taping. This is also what makes the ambiguity of the "last tape" so palpable. Can there be a final tape, logically speaking? Or is every "last" tape only the "latest" tape, the most recent tape (which thus already puts itself under erasure by anticipating its own obsolescence, its ultimate lack of finality)? All this takes us into familiar Beckett territory—*Endgame*, the impossibility of dying, the failure of a final testament, the *Trilogy*—"You must go on, I can't go on, I'll go on." . . . Strictly speaking, a final tape could not be heard: all hearing is in the context of a further recording. Which raises the very disturbing question as to our position as audience, listening to Krapp's "last tape." Are we in the position of the aging Krapp having to assume the burden of a memory which is not ours to assume?

EGOYAN: That's right. And Krapp's recording is a response not only to what he hears in the previous recording, but must also be a response to the very fact of having his memory ignited—he is forced to deal with the loss of memory, the loss of love, the loss of ambition, the loss of hope . . .

COMAY: . . . the loss of language . . .

EOYAN: . . . the loss of language! All those things. . . . Is he being optimistic by going back through this old material, is he still trying to challenge his present state? Is he hoping to shock himself into some sort of recognition? Or is he torturing himself: is it an act of masochism? Those are interpretive issues for the director. Very often I see productions of the play—and perhaps Beckett himself was also a bit misleading in this, because he talks about the voice that comes out of the machine as being pompous and arrogant, not to be taken entirely seriously—where what's on the tape is glossed over, rushed through and almost dismissed. But I thought it might be interesting to take time with the language and to make it clear that this is someone who actually loved and still loves language, and to make it quite tender: this might impart an entirely different sense of his motives for wanting to hear the tape.

COMAY: We hear and see pathetic remnants of that love of language, in the old Krapp's exaggerated mouthing of the word "spo-o-o-o-o-l." It's a complicated articulation, both infantile and parodic—as if language is showing itself as pure carnal gesture, on the one hand (the brute sensation of a word in the mouth, the jubilation of a baby filling its mouth with sound), and ironic self-awareness, on the other (the sense of an absolute loss of meaning). There is a kind of bitter pleasure there, even at the end—a pleasure both in the sound itself and in the ironic awareness that it is only sound (a pleasure in disillusionment itself?). On the one hand, this infantile enjoyment, and on the other this curiosity, tinged with disdain and a perverse enjoyment of his own lack—is there defence there? Of course that it's the word "spool"—the signifier of the machine—that he lavishes his tongue and lips upon is significant, and this libidinal relationship to the machine has many other manifestations in your film that we might want to come back to. There's also his pedantic obsession with dictionary meanings, which is both infantilizing, schoolboyish, and a mark of his senility.

EGOYAN: Yes. So he still does have a certain curiosity, he still has pleasure, even if it's a bit twisted: are these the last embers of what might have been a really great mind? The issues that this play deals with are so profound at many different levels, and touch on everything I've always been attracted to in literature, film, and installation. It's fascinating that it was written by a man who had no idea how to operate a tape-recorder. He actually had to ask a friend of his in Paris to send a manual so he could understand how the fast-forward and rewind functions worked.

COMAY: Not to mention his own apparent phobia of transcription—refusing to let interviewers, for example, even take notes during the interviews. So now of course there's a whole army of fetishists hoarding these little snippets of his recorded voice culled from their answering machines—the only place he got captured. . . .

EGOYAN: Yes: despite or because of all this ambivalence, it's astonishing that he could anticipate so many of the issues that we're still dealing with today: it is in some crucial ways a work of science-fiction. It was written at a time when it would have been physically impossible for a man in 1958 to have access to tapes recorded some thirty years earlier, and earlier still. . . .

COMAY: Hence the sci-fi setting of the play "in the future," which superficially removes the problem of that anachronism. But that literary conceit can't fail to raise the spectre of another, perhaps even more virulent form of anachronism: it inevitably anticipates the future obsolescence of the recording machine itself, which starts to appear as an antiquated dinosaur, even in its pristine, postwar newness. Obviously this is how it looks to us, now, in the twenty-first century, with our ever-evolving panoply of digital recording devices—and your film accentuates this sense of a clunky monster, the physical heaviness and clumsiness of the machine, its oddity and awkwardness—but there is a sense that Beckett himself has already captured this sense of obsolescence by virtue of the futuristic fantasy embedded in the play's very setting: the machine projects a vantage point from which it will inevitably appear outmoded.

EGOYAN: The anachronism recalls *Family Viewing* which I made in 1986: in that film an eighteen-year-old character plays back home colour videotapes of himself at the age of four—which would have been physically impossible at that time. The way we tried to fudge the issue was by having the boy's father work for the company that manufactured the machines, so that he would have had very good access to all the equipment when it first came out, before it went on the market. But in much the same way in this production of *Krapp's Last Tape*, it somehow makes perfect sense that you have a seventy-year-old man reflecting on the recording he had made thirty years earlier, which in turn reflects on a previous recording, which in turn presumably reflects on an even earlier recording. . . .

COMAY: I wonder if there is any sense of redemption in this movement. Does obsolescence only make itself felt as the rush of newer-and-better? Or is there a non-linear sense of time captured in the experience of the obsolescent that disrupts the idea of progress, even as it evokes it?

EGOYAN: I'm constantly thinking about all this. I'm going to be presenting an installation next summer at the Musée d'art contemporain de Montréal, inspired by this experience of *Krapp*, called *Hors d'Usage* (*Out of Use*) which tries to reflect on this old technology, on what it means for an instrument of this sort to become out-of-date. I had the idea of making an appeal to the community of Montreal asking for individuals to find these old reel-to-reel tape recorders in their family attics and to donate them to the gallery for the period of the show. I plan to have some fifty block pedestals displayed in this huge space, with all the various machines that have been donated set on top of the pedestals, with a small archival plaque indicating the name of the family and the year the machine was last used. Then there will be a recording—a digital recording—of the owner of the machine recalling the last time they remember it being used. So when you walk into the gallery you'll see this huge array of machines, each with a kind of Boltanski-like lightbulb hanging from the ceiling, barely illuminated—you'll be able to press a button on each pedestal, and you'll then hear a digital recording of a voice discussing the last time the particular machine was used.

COMAY: This idea of a specific date is interesting—that you can identify the "last tape" in retrospect—which would make the mortuary associations explicit: a cemetery of tape recorders—and an escalation of Boltanski, in that you turn the spotlight not on the dead or vanished referent but on the very medium of recording itself, its own pastness relative to the digital forms that have superseded it. For Krapp, the lastness of the "last" tape is more ambiguous. . . .

EGOYAN: I love the idea of obsolescence—the idea of a technology which has become unnecessary or unworkable. And I love this idea which we're playing with now of backwards-compatibility: that when you introduce a piece of technology it is able to use the encoding devices of the technology that immediately predated it. For example, we have it now with 8 mm video: now that we've gone over to digital, there's a new camera system that allows you to play back your old tapes. But there are technologies which have completely fallen by the wayside—Beta, for example. It's very difficult now to play a Beta tape; it's very difficult to play a quarter-inch tape. What's shocking about computers is that those old punch cards we all remember from university have become completely illegible: the information encoded on them simply can't be processed anymore. A friend of mine brought in an expert to find out the best way to preserve computer information, and it was hilarious: this expert said that the only way you can be certain that something is going to be interpretable in, say, a century from now is if you actually write it down. I thought that was remarkable—that we are still fundamentally reliant on the notion of the graven image. What fascinates me about the period we're in now is that up until this point, with image-production, we were still in some sense operating with the Biblical notion of the graven, and therefore with all the suspicion that's aroused by the graven image. Until now, all images have required the displacement of properties or materials—whether on silver, on a negative, on magnetic oxide on a tape, and so on—but we are now at a point where these images are not graven anymore: there is no displacement, it's all become numeric—a digital process.

COMAY: This shift from the "graven" or inscribed image—which involves a kind of indexical relationship between what is registered and the actual registration itself—to an information-based image store also seems to signal the end of medium-specificity: the digitalization of storage seems to suggest an immediate interconvertibility of every medium into every other. The sense of interface between mediums would radically change, from being a kind of limiting membrane between radically disparate modes of experience to being a complete porous or transparent switching station between essentially homogeneous or continuous modes, distinguished only at the level of information. Since so much of your own film practice is about the permeability (but also the distinction) between mediums—video-within-film, photography-within-film, and so on—I wonder how, from the perspective of complete digitalization, these textures will mutate and play themselves out. Is your film aesthetic essentially dependent on medium specificity? Does it speak of the (lost?) possibility of inter-medium graftings, transpositions, incorporations—of a world in which the ontological difference between mediums is still thinkable, still operative at the level of experience? I'm also intrigued by your decision to use an old-fashioned analogue editing table—a Steenbeck, the last model of its kind, effectively now out of work—to work on *Krapp*. Rather than editing with a mouse on a computer, it was a question of physically manipulating the tape, running it through the reels, fast forwarding, rewinding, cutting, splicing. . . .

EGOYAN: That was just irresistible. It's a machine I have not cut on since *Exotica* [1994]. I love the machine. I now keep it in my studio as a permanent installation. There is something entirely physical about it. I would say it's more satisfying, and it is in some ways, except I'm also aware, having gone back to it, how completely cumbersome it is. In terms of sound, for instance, you can't begin to compare it to a digital system, where you can do all sorts of sound interpolations and essentially mix it at home. I loved the feeling of threading it, the ritualized aspect of working on this film, and I derived great pleasure from seeing the spools turn on Krapp's machine as the spools were turning on mine, and the fact that if I turned off my machine or slowed it down, that would have a concomitant effect on the image of his machine. I felt incredibly close to what he was doing.

COMAY: I'm intrigued by the logic of cutting, which is so palpable in an editing table of this kind, but which seems to rupture the superficial homology between the film reels and the audiotape reels. The editing process is wildly different in the different filmic mediums. I'm struck by how differently one experiences negation or loss or erasure—deletion— as one moves from celluloid film strip to magnetic audiotape to video- tape to digital disk or card. With the film-strip, in order to delete you have to physically cut into the thing: you literally have to remove the discarded matter, which then poses the problem of disposal—do you store or throw away the excess? Regardless of what you do with it, the waste matter nonetheless persists, as residue and reminder of the pro- cess of deletion itself—a kind of ineffaceable trace of the very act of ef- facement. But with the magnetic audiotape or videotape, as well as with the digital file, the process of erasure is radically different. You can erase with a flick of a button, you can re-record over previous recordings— which amounts to a deletion—or you can delete accidentally. In the case of a digital file,you don't need to delete, strictly speaking—you sim- ply remove the filename, mess up the catalogue, and the text becomes lost in the archive of the computer: lost is as good as deleted here. What is cut, in all these last cases, leaves no necessary or tangible remainder, unlike celluloid, which always produces leftovers. This somehow seems terribly evocative in terms of Krapp's various antics of deletion: his ob- sessive attempt to rid of residue, the constant editing or cutting that is implicit not only in the layers of abbreviation operative in his selective listening activity—the ledger book summarizing the highpoints of each tape, the annual choice of a specific tape to listen to, the choice of spe- cific moments within a given tape, and so on. There's also cutting im- plicit in his stop-and-start method of recording his "last" tape. There's a systematic erasure or blanking out which is necessary for him both to access his own memories and to construct future ones: it's as if every memory is surging up from a sea of oblivion which he himself has to activate, has to actively produce. This is reminiscent of the compulsive deleted bits that are continually tripping Krapp up. Whatever he tries to throw away keeps coming back, like the banana peel he can't quite get rid of like his own excremental name, like the constipation he suffers—a constant return of what is being evacuated. . . .

EGOYAN: This sense of physical cutting is certainly true of the photo- graphic elements within film—not so much with the magnetic audio elements, which you can record over and over again. Again, going back to *Family Viewing*, I'm thinking of that strange character who erases, and who can only get sexually activated by taping home-made porn over the home videos of his family. There are sometimes features of technology which mirror or trigger a psychological process in an intriguing way. There are aspects of our life that we need to ritualize, and technology gives us an opportunity to do that effortlessly, in a way that's socially acceptable. It's not such a big thing to record. . . .

COMAY: So much is at stake in the father's compulsive erasures in *Family Viewing*: the experience of immigration, for example, as if the moment of naturalization—the tabula rasa of a fresh start—gets eroticized in the very act of deleting the past. The revelation of that blackout is what is so traumatic to the son. Then, of course, there's the censor in *The Adjuster* [1991] who smuggles away the censored films—censorship being the prime act of deletion—to show to her sister, again, an immigrant: taking what the dominant culture needs to expel and finding a new kind of experience in this discarded residue. . . .

EGOYAN: I'm still thinking about the notion of deletion. . . . Everything Krapp does is made physical. The material is stored in these boxes, so there's that whole process of bringing the boxes to the table, all so physically rendered. . . .

COMAY: Fumbling, dropping, losing, hurling. . . . There's another striking moment of erasure in the film—actually, it's a fast-forward, but it amounts to the same thing: you're watching Krapp as he suddenly begins to hear his past self waxing on about inspiration, genius, the "memorable equinox," and so on—a shocking eruption of this unbearable reminder of vanished possibilities. Krapp frantically tries to speed over the passage, punches the fast-forward button, his arms are moving in a kind of parody or imitation of the reels, as if he's magically connected, scanning with his whole body. At this point, you become more aware than ever that an entire section is being effaced, and this only accentuates the power of what is being skipped over. This is radically opposed to the experience of a digital random-access scan-point-delete: in this latter case the wipe-out—the fact that you're deleting—is completely effaced, physically speaking. . . .

EGOYAN: There was also a real chemistry with the camera. I'm thinking especially about the very slow track when Krapp is beginning to hear the story of the day in the boat: the camera follows him with a very slow gesture; when he stops the machine, the camera stops; then he rewinds back, and the camera goes back into the starting position. And then the whole movement begins again. That single shot went on for twenty minutes. We were all completely aware of—and how—we were techni-cally encoding this: we wanted to test cinematic notions of endurance. I think a huge part of old reel-to-reel film technology is that there are physical limits to how long you can record. Normally, 35 mm film can shoot a ten-minute stretch—that's the maximum length for a single shot. We had to order a special magazine from Panavision in London—absolutely immense. In the end, the physical bulk of this magazine was so oppressive—one had the sense of a medium that has become so obso-lete. Nowadays, if you want to record something, whether on VHS or on digital video, you can record up to six hours, easily, of continuous time. There's nothing particularly rare, with the new technologies, about be-ing able to record an immense continuum of time.

COMAY: This lengthy shot almost seems to be pushing celluloid film be-yond its limits—making it try to do what video does so effortlessly. On the one hand, this pushes traditional cinema into the future, as if forc-ing it to anticipate possibilities beyond itself—possibilities that would only occur to us in a video age. On the other hand, it only emphasizes the finitude of the medium, its obsolescence: it gestures towards a pos-sibility which will not ultimately be its own to realize.

EGOYAN: Yes, and you know, I love the cumbersomeness of this: I love the fact that as Krapp brings the boxes over, as he's searching for Box 3, Spool 5, everything becomes so physical—there's such a weight to tackle. . . .

COMAY: The burden of a memory which is ultimately not one's own to appropriate—it's always outside. I was also fascinated by Krapp's li-bidinal relationship with the machine, which is so accentuated in your film: the shouting, the staring, the caressing, the gesticulation, the hesi-tations, the assaults. . . . The character's fate is caught between these two spools, and at a certain point his face as well, when he almost lies over the machine. At the very moment when the voice on the tape is remembering lying on top of his lover in the boat, his face between her breasts, the old Krapp is at that moment seen hovering, lying over the machine with his face virtually down between the two spools, which take on an erotic, anthropomorphic aspect, becoming like breasts or eyes. (Of course the erotic connection is implicit in the French render-ing of *La derniere bande*—the last hard-on—something Beckett himself refers to in his production notes, when he describes the taping ritual as masturbatory.) There's also an extraordinary moment at the beginning of the film—I don't know if this was deliberate or not—when Krapp is in effect winding himself up to start listening to the tape. He circles the desk twice, counterclockwise, in the direction that the spools will eventually be playing. It's immediately prior to tripping on the banana. He's signaling this rotary movement with his whole body. As if he himself were setting the machine in motion, becoming the very machine into which he will deposit his life, as if his whole body is anticipating the movement of mechanical memory, as if he is becoming nothing but a conduit for his own memory tracks, a living prosthesis of himself. . . .

EGOYAN: In the stage-directions for the play, the character is supposed to go back and forth on the stage, which somehow just didn't feel right in my frame. I liked the idea of circular movement. I would not have explained it the way you've just done when I set out to shoot the scene, but this notion of intentionality is always vexed. I love the moment when Krapp is circling the desk, and at one point glances at the machine, and taps it almost fondly. There's something that seems organically right about that movement, and now that you put it this way it makes perfect sense, but it wasn't necessarily what I had in mind at the time.

COMAY: There is also a crucial ambiguity as to whether he himself is here assuming the automatism of the machine—turning himself into a mechanical instrument wound up at will—or, conversely, whether he's humanizing the machine by trying to circumscribe and anticipate its motions, translating these into the terms of a sentient, living being, disarming the uncanny threat of the machine by feigning its movements.

EGOYAN: Yes. . . . I can't help but feel that there is a touching personality to this machine . . . the design of the machine, which shows the year it was made, the fact that it is so physical, the gesture of threading, right down to the sound effect we introduced of the whirring pause as the tape is going in. One of the obvious ways to deal with this subject matter is to make the machine sleek and threatening and anonymous, but in fact I don't think that's his experience of the machine at all. And certainly it's not my experience of the machine. My father had a Sony from the early 1960s. This is a man who kept a diary of his life from the age of thirteen; at one point, during my early adolescence, he began to tape all his diary entries. I was very aware of this practice. He would go off to his private space, he wanted to make these recordings alone. Later we had this huge fire, which is documented in *The Adjuster*. My father was in a complete state of shock. I was able to retrieve all of the written material, but it's still a mystery where those tapes went. I think he still somehow feels that I did something with those tapes, which is quite bizarre—I have no idea where they are. But it's interesting that he remembers them, and that he's kept a note of what those recordings are, recordings which I've never heard. But that machine was terribly formative for me in other ways as well. When I was twelve or thirteen I would go to the library in Victoria and take out play performances which had been recorded on vinyl LPs; there were a couple of plays which then I re-recorded with a microphone and my parents' old stereo onto my father's reel-to-reel tape-recorder, so I actually have a magnetic audiotape of Donald Davis doing *Krapp's Last Tape*, as well as *Who's Afraid of Virginia Woolf?* and *Rhinoceros*, and various other plays. It required an enormous effort to keep a record of drama at that time. I remember ordering a copy of Beckett's *Film* from Grove Press in New York—it arrived in Victoria in a 16 mm print form. I loved it, and wanted to keep a copy of it, but there was simply no way to copy at that time. So I borrowed a friend's Super-8 movie camera and projected the film onto a white wall and refilmed it off the wall. So I now have this Super-8 re-recording of it. It was a difficult thing for a kid at that time to record something that they wanted a copy of. Which is so strange today—it's completely effortless to make copies, far easier than to actually watch the thing. I still sometimes wonder how much of my ambition to make images came out of my wanting to have access to something which was distant and hard to possess—essentially inaccessible.

COMAY: The old experience of film was so bound up with the experience of loss: you're sitting in the theatre, the film is relentlessly moving on, you can't stop it, you can't play it back, you'll possibly never see it again—all you'll leave with is the after-image in your memory. Even broadcast television used to be that way, although it seems that film has a different relation to loss than television—the winding of the spools imparts a very different sense of temporality. And that film is a medium of reproduction only compounds this sense of loss: we're doomed to keep on living through the loss, again and again. I wanted to talk about the effect of the film medium on *Krapp*. Clearly you're not producing the documentation of a play or a simple transcription of theatre into cinema. One is constantly aware of the camera in relation to the tape recorder, of the extra layer of memory produced by this second-order recording device. We watch the camera tracking Krapp as he operates his tapes—there's a kind of surplus reflexivity generated. This resonates with your other films, each of which involves the encrypting of some kind of recording technology within film, whether it's video, television, photography, audiotape, or film itself. This kind of layering probably reaches its peak in *Speaking Parts*, in which there's a vertiginous stacking of mediums: a TV talk show which incorporates a video screening of the hospital bed is in turn incorporated into a movie made for TV, for which the auditions have been videotaped, and which involves an extensive panoply of mediated experiences throughout its production—directorial teleconferencing, video-conferenced sexual encounters, endless trips to the video-archive mausoleum, and a frenzy of (unanswered) answering-machine messages. But there seems to be something radically different going on in *Krapp*. In your other films, it is for the most part a question of incorporating some kind of televisual medium within film: there's a basic audiovisual homology between the two mediums, which of course only accentuates the differences and produces specific textures. But the only medium being incorporated in *Krapp* is the tape recorder: here we have an audiovisual medium encrypting a purely auditory one. And the resulting texture is very different.

EGOYAN: But at one level, the tape recorder does function exactly like a video monitor: both contrast very similarly to film. When I think of a video or a tape-recording, I think in both cases of spontaneity, of an unreflected moment being captured—something completely immediate and intuitive. When I think of film, I think of preparation, of the apparatus of production, of the whole machinery gearing up: it's totally unspontaneous—it requires such reflection, such consideration, such elaboration. And the difference arises not only because of the technical exigencies of film production. It also has to do with the resilience of a film image—the ability of the image to last, as opposed to a video image which we think of as being disposable, re-recordable, something that is infinitely malleable and almost evanescent.

COMAY: There's also a private-public distinction. . . .

EGOYAN: Yes. Perhaps the most extreme expression of this contrast is in a film like *Calendar* [1993], where there's this constant tension between the video image and the still photographic image (which may in at least this respect be compared to cinema). The calendar image requires the perfect light—it's a static image, the photographer is obsessively waiting for the light to be absolutely perfect. Behind the camera lens there's a stubborn desire to believe that if you concentrate on something long enough its essence or truth will make itself manifest to you—as opposed to the video image, which is just about letting things go, taking them as they come, haphazardly. And in that film we witness the corrosive effects on the relationship between a personality who needs to wait constantly and consider and reflect—and who perhaps paralyzes himself with these compulsions—and the free spirit who wants to respond to things as they are, immediately, without delay. In *Speaking Parts*, again, there is a medium which suggests the possibility of a spontaneous production of desire—I'm referring to the video-sex teleconferencing. It's interesting to watch the film today—it's possibly even more relevant now in the age of internet sex: all the things you can now spontaneously explore, the fantasies and desires that you have immediate access to, knowing that there's this immediate trading of image technology and information—it's like a transfusion. There's an experience of transfusion in digital and video which you simply don't have in film. Film is not at all about spontaneous transfusion—it's more about a witnessing. . . .

COMAY: But it seems to me that the actual video activities that you've been transcribing within your films are not just on the side of immediacy: they themselves in fact expose a certain tension between spontaneity and calculation—as does the audiotaping activity in *Krapp*, for that matter. I'm thinking, for example, of the videotape of the wedding in *Speaking Parts*, when Lisa seizes the video-camera and aggressively turns it on the bride, trying to extract a confession. What's striking about that scene is the tension between the desire for a constructed image, the desire to lay down memory traces for the future, and the desire (in this case the camera operator's) for an unrehearsed revelation—which would strictly speaking make the wedding event impossible.

EGOYAN: Yes, this is true, but it's the actual filming of the video that introduces or exposes this layer of reflection. It's also important to think of this in terms of space and installation—the physical situation of the machines themselves. I have a great interest in the spaces in which we encounter screens and monitors—what it means to watch an image in a contemplative setting, whether in a gallery or in another kind of room that burdens you with the responsibility of introspection: you can't just be passive. I'm thinking, for example, of the video therapy in *Next of Kin* [1984]: this is in many ways an installation. You have these TV monitors in the therapist's office, and then you have the film camera recording the recording. And within this setting, not only are the participants of the therapy supposed to go back and reflect on those tapes, to look at themselves, but we too, as the audience, are set up to feel self-conscious about the presence of these monitors—the way they record behaviour, the way they reflect our need to identify and classify behaviour, and so on. All this becomes completely self-conscious: this is one of the most crucial effects of putting a frame within a frame—you suddenly become aware that it is a captured image. If you look at a video image on its intended playback system, you tend automatically to believe in its immediate referentiality—you don't think of it as a considered gesture, or that the medium itself is determining what you see. Similarly, even when you watch a film projected, you tend to assume that the image is caught by the truth of the camera—that it is real. But the moment you show a video monitor within a film, you become aware of this being a decision that someone has taken: that both images are constructed. This awareness comes about precisely by becoming conscious of the interface between the two mediums.

COMAY: So let's get back to the tape recorder, which is not a visual medium, and which thus has a different relationship to the film that's filming it than an image of a screen within a screen would have. In his tape-recording activities, Krapp seems to display an intense oscillation between an editing mode, on the one hand—separating the wheat from the chaff, studying his notes, already relating to the tape recorder in some sense like a cameraman, adjusting, assessing, selecting, filtering, deleting, and so on—and, on the other hand, a sort of aleatory, haphazard mode. Thus his indecision, so exquisitely portrayed by Hurt, as his hand hovers over the machine, hesitating whether he's going to turn it on or off, or making the mistake of recording silence, or not recording what he is trying to record. And then of course there's Krapp's ultimate, fateful decision to throw away the envelope on which all his recording notes are written—come what may. . . . How do you think the presence of a tape recorder within a film differs from the presence of a video monitor?

EGOYAN: That was one of the great challenges of the film: to treat the recorded sound in such a way as to make you become fully aware of it as being framed or constructed—to defamiliarize that sound. We had to decide whether we wanted the recorded voice to sound as though it were coming from within that machine—to locate it within that room, within that piece of technology—or whether to make you aware of it as being an artifact of a recorded voice which was separated from that technology, precisely by virtue of that technology. We decided that the recorded voice would be completely clear, and would actually be emanating from the surround speakers rather than from behind the screen.

If you see *Krapp's Last Tape* in the movie theatre—and you can't really get that effect on videotape—there's something completely unworldly about the voice you are supposedly hearing coming from the tape-recorder: it's not coming from that machine at all. It's suddenly coming from all around you, and you're hearing it in its full digital glory: it's very resonant, it's very present, there's nothing at all fragile about the voice. So then you have to reconcile that with the image you're seeing of Krapp listening to that tape. In fact, his voice making the last tape is much more frail than the recorded voice that we're hearing, which is purportedly coming from his machine.

COMAY: The voice is doubly disembodied. As a recording, it's disembodied from its original speaker. And as a projected filmic sound, it's disembodied from the visual image of the recorder itself, which no longer tethers it to any place. Simultaneously everywhere and nowhere, unlocatable: it has a spectral quality, even or especially in its liveliness and veracity, its living authenticity and presence. . . .

EGOYAN: That's a beautiful word—that's the word that I was searching for earlier, disembodied—it's such an interesting notion. At what point does something become disembodied? That is, released from the physical. . . .

COMAY: It's an interesting paradox: the more living the voice becomes (the smaller the acoustic gap between the original and the reproduction), the more damaged or dead that same sound becomes (the more untethered from its source, free-floating in space and time). There's a kind of strange intertwining of life and death here, which takes us back to the very earliest fantasies stimulated by the invention of the tape recorder at the beginning of the century—the fears of the soul being stolen, the fantasies of communicating with the dead, all the spiritualist overlays—similar to early photography and early cinema in this respect. There's also a crucial relationship with language itself, which is becoming mortified for Krapp: he's failing to understand his own mother-tongue—language itself is turning into a dead mother (which nonetheless won't go away: the withdrawal has an obtrusive force). It's telling that the experience of hearing-oneself-speak—which one tends to associate, at least within a certain philosophical tradition, with living presence—gives rise to an experience of language as corpse-like. (There's a similar moment in *All That Fall*, a play which maybe not coincidentally marks Beckett's own return to English, to his own mother-tongue, after so many years: Mr. Rooney remarks that he often feels, when he hears himself speak, as if he's speaking a dead language; the Gaelic issue is explicit here). . . .

EGOYAN: But the issue of silence is also important here. I'm thinking about when Krapp is talking about silence—profound silence—in describing that moment in the boat. To drop all sound, to cut off all ambient sound from the room: the moment that he begins caressing the machine you enter into a very different space. That was one of the real pleasures of this film: being able to locate the sound in a place that was not tied to the physical reality of the machine.

COMAY: Which is more or less true of all film, no? There's of course the convention that one thinks one is hearing a sound coming from a specific place—the eye needs to locate sound in a tangible source—but one is never truly hearing it from the place of the image. There's a crucial gap between sound and image, no matter how sophisticated the speaker technology, no matter how many points of sound emitted from behind the screen, there's still a gap. . . .

EGOYAN: And that's an issue in our time right now, and something I have huge problems with, generally. I had no problems with mono-sound: I think in a way that's how the ear actually works—sound coming from the front of the screen is entirely natural. I find it really problematic these days to go into the theatre and hear the sound coming from all around. That's not how the ear works at all. You have to be acoustically tied into what you're seeing: that's what you project into. Think of this incredible ability we have at a party to locate ourselves in a conversation and to focus on that. You can't hear everything—you'd go mad! You wouldn't be able to discern anything. So the idea of having this technology which tries to envelope you with sound is a bit silly. This is why I wanted to use the surround-sound technology in a very unconventional way. Technically, you're never supposed to put sound information in the surround speakers. You're allowed to put ambient crowd sounds in the surround—for example if you're showing a party on screen—but any dramatic dialogue is supposed to be located at the front. So, with Krapp, I thought to challenge this maxim by putting his voice all around you.

COMAY: This leads back to the question of the relationship between the tape recorder and the camera. What is specific about the camera is that it is located, it occupies a definite point of view: one is never not aware of its movement or of its position vis-à-vis the object. The camera occupies a point of view in a way that the tape-recorder does not, and this lack of location has been exploited by audio-technology from the outset. History books—and Friedrich Kittler most recently—tell us that magnetic tape-recorder technology was essentially developed and brought to a new standard by the Nazis, who used it to foil Allied intelligence efforts by emitting supposedly live radio broadcasts using pre-recorded tapes that had been manufactured at a completely different time and from completely different places than the time and place of the broadcast. (The Americans discovered this technology with the liberation of Radio Luxembourg, and turned it over to the movie and music industry, as well as to home-entertainment.) So the modern tape recorder comes into being in order to generate mobile acoustic images which are pretending to be rooted in space and time. Unlike the photographic image, which indexically distances itself from the referent, the acoustic image bears no inherent mark which would distinguish it from the "live" original. This radically distinguishes it from the camera as an archival instrument. And so I'm wondering about the effect of superimposing the camera on the tape-recorder. It's unclear at times whether the camera has a redemptive quality by functioning as a kind of embodied (situated) witness which will survive and document the "last tape." But there seems to be also something persecutory, at times, about the cinematography. This made me think of Beckett's own film, *Film*—in which Buster Keaton's flight from the camera turned into a kind of gag.

EGOYAN: When I was filming *Krapp*, I had two Beckett texts constantly in mind. First, there was the television film, *Eh Joe*, which shows a man being haunted by the voice of a past relationship. Whenever the woman's voice is heard, the camera makes a movement towards the man. And whenever she stops, and the haunting ceases, he physically relaxes, and the camera backs off. Then the voice begins again, and the camera moves closer, until at the end it's very close to his face. What's fascinating about *Eh Joe* is that it was intended for television: Beckett knew that he had to do a long take. It was a single move, captured on videotape—duration was not an issue. That's absolutely fascinating, given the issues crystallized in *Krapp's Last Tape*. Beckett himself perfectly understood the physical reality of videotape—the possibility of non-segmented time.

Beckett's incredibly sophisticated when it comes to the camera. The other text of course is, as you suggest, his notes for *Film*, which cites Bishop Berkeley's theorem *esse est percipi*—to be is to be perceived—and which explores the idea that even when all forms of perception are cut off, self-perception necessarily remains. When I watch it now it seems a bit theatrical, a bit clumsy—the Buster Keaton character physically fleeing perception and having to confront himself at the end. It's not ultimately successful as a film, I think, but the ideas in it are fascinating. The opportunity to reach into these two other works of Beckett's and to bring them to bear on *Krapp's Last Tape* was irresistible. In my film I tried to explore the idea of the camera representing self-perception, if you will, and the idea of this self-perception being activated by moments of reflection on the tape. My favourite shot in the film is actually not the final playback of the tape, but rather the scene that starts off with Krapp cursing the machine and being physically violent with it. The camera begins tracking as Krapp starts rewinding and madly skips over the story that he doesn't want to hear any more: when he starts hearing this moment of love, it's like a suspended epiphany, and the camera comes back to him in this gentle caress. And then he stops, and rewinds, and goes back very gently to the starting position, and he continues right through until he physically caresses the machine, just as the camera caresses this moment. That's all one shot—and all inspired by Beckett's notes on *Film*. I never really had any desire to remake *Film* itself, although someone did once suggest that I do so. I was more interested in taking some of the intentions of that work and applying them here. I think that this is much more coherent and interesting, and somehow much truer to the intentions of that film, than to have simply re-filmed *Film*.

Krapp is such a commanding text. I find it exceptional within Beckett's own corpus—it's almost autobiographical. He never reveals so much— he never writes this way. And perhaps one of the reasons he wanted the recording almost to be dismissed, or to be read through very quickly, is that he couldn't bear the implications of considering the text this way. My reading of it might have actually made him profoundly uncomfortable. But you know it is for this reason a somewhat sacred text for me.

COMAY: *Film* is all about trying to and failing to escape from the camera. There are shades of this even in the stage play *Play* as well, with its persecutory beams of light targeting the three characters in the urns— soliciting, regulating, interrupting speech, like an instrument of torture: the light almost functions like a surveillance camera on the stage. In *Film* we see Buster Keaton being hounded by the gaze, which turns out to be everywhere. Even when he thinks he's made his escape, shutting himself in the room, he finds himself surrounded by eyes. The whole universe becomes an eye—the eyes of the cat, the dog, the parrot, the goldfish, the eyes in the mirror, the eyes of God in the print on the wall, the two little circular tabs on the file folder, the carved round holes in the headrest of the rocking chair, the eyes in the photographs—everything around him becomes eye-like and threatening. He ejects the animals, covers the mirror, repositions the file-folder so the holes are aligned vertically rather than horizontally, becoming less ocular—but he actually has to destroy the print and the photographs, with an emphatic, difficult act of tearing—a gesture you find repeated elsewhere in Beckett (for example in *A Piece of Monologue*, or in *Malone Dies*, when Macmann rips up the photograph of his lover Moll and scatters the pieces to the wind). Which takes us back to the issue of deletion or erasure—and perhaps also back to the issue of the graven image, and all the anxiety this arouses: what do we make of this iconoclastic gesture? The photos seem to bear at least an implicit relationship to the movie camera; the gaze they embody is perhaps more virulent, if only because it is a reproduced, mobile gaze, a gaze that can come from anywhere: hence perhaps the singular, awkward violence of the act of destruction. Is there any need or desire to escape from the camera's gaze in *Krapp*? I'm also thinking of this in relation to the memory of his lover's eyes in the boat—his desire for her to open her eyes, to "let him in": here the gaze seems without persecutory affect. Is the camera similarly disarmed and disarming at this point?

EGOYAN: That's a really good point. I don't think Krapp is *self-conscious* of the camera in the film. It's interesting to think about a kind of self-perception—in the sense explored in *Film*—which doesn't involve self-consciousness. This became a major discussion with John Hurt as well. Is the camera a recording device or is it a participant? I always thought the camera was a participant. But I was also working with a performance which is tremendously self-contained. Hurt has lived with this play for so long: I don't know if there was time in our relationship ultimately to threaten his understanding of the text by means of the instrument I was bringing in. This again perhaps relates to the struggle between film and theatre.

COMAY: In many of the previous stage productions of *Krapp*—and this is something which is emphasized in Beckett's own production notebooks—there's a strange moment where Krapp becomes anxiously aware of some kind of invisible spectator who seems to have entered the space of the stage: he keeps glancing over his shoulder slightly backstage each time he sits down to listen to the tape recorder—as if someone else is suddenly in the room, listening in on what he's listening to. In his production notes, Beckett suggests that this is a figure of death, but it's also oddly suggestive of a virtual presence of a recording instrument having entered the scene (which may amount to the same thing). I didn't see that particular gesture in your production.

EGOYAN: No, we didn't use it.

COMAY: Was this because the camera was always already there, effectively performing the role of the invisible spectator? I'm thinking here of the difference between the stage and the television productions of *Not I*. The theatrical version calls for an amorphous, shrouded, anonymous, sexless auditor standing on a podium on stage, listening to the monologue, dead still except for the occasional arm movement: the Mouth seems to need a physical, embodied auditor to receive her words. Similarly, the Reader in *Ohio Impromptu* needs a Listener on stage. Whereas in the television version of *Not I* the auditor is already encoded in the medium of recording itself, and so perhaps doesn't need to be—and indeed shouldn't be—physically materialized or represented on screen. In stage productions of *Krapp*, the sense of the onstage gaze is very powerful, even though it is never embodied in an actual stage presence: we infer it from Krapp's head movements. But in your film, the gaze seems to be dramatized very differently—in part, of course, by the movements of the camera, but in part perhaps by these ambient gleams of light emanating from the surroundings, which seem to take on a kind of gaze-like density, and exert a kind of pressure on the speaker, as if from an unknown source. It's almost as if the light itself—the very medium of vision—is congealing into a reflective substance. This is one way in which the rather expressionist, high-contrast lighting seems to be working here. . . .

EGOYAN: Yes, and of course one of the most important ideas in both the play and the film is this notion of light and dark. As Krapp remarks, when he gets the new lamp over the table, ". . . with all this darkness around me, I feel less alone." There are repeated references in the text to light and darkness. I think that what we can do in film, which you can't do on stage, is to make those distinctions really physical. I think on stage the eye compensates, and you're never able to lose the character into black quite as easily as on film.

COMAY: And yet on film you can't get the same sort of black—there's always light coming through the projector—so in a way the darkness is more compromised. . . .

EGOYAN: It's true, you can't get the same sort of black. But what you can really get on film is the sense that when Krapp is moving away from the pool of lamplight he's losing light completely—you can literally see the light disappear. There's a scene where he's about to start recording—it's the moment where he talks about *Effi Briest*—when he falls back into the darkness and is lost in the frame, literally. So I think that the way that blackness works in this production is ominous, and creates a real pressure. For example, again, the moment Krapp turns on the light, when he's in the backroom. . . .

COMAY: This returns us to the issue of the disembodied voice. When Krapp goes backstage to get his drink, you hear his voice without seeing where it is coming from. The voice is not only disembodied, like the voice on the machine, but, unlike the latter, it is also completely non-articulated—coughing, grunting, gasping—pure phonic gesture. You hear this hidden off-screen voice very differently than you hear the invisible voice on the tape recorder, which has a very different tonality in its articulateness. And you're waiting for this voice to be embodied again, and to return to articulation, to meaning. As Krapp comes out from the backroom, you see his shadow projected before you see his actual person—like a ghost preceding the living body. This transition from disembodied voice to shadow to incarnated voice to articulated voice is interesting.

EGOYAN: Yes, and there's also this fortuitous moment where you hear this muffled cough coming from the backroom, and you're not quite sure why it is muffled, until he finally comes out holding the handkerchief in his hand—the sound gets rectified or explained at that point. We're really talking about a sense of anticipation. Again, this is one of the features of these technologies—the sense of time they give you: you look at those reels, you look at the boxes, or you look at the machine itself, and there's an anticipation of what they might contain. . . .

COMAY: An anticipation based on the crucial gap between seeing and hearing: the image is divorced from the sound, there's this fundamental non-synchronicity. You look at the machine and you anticipate the sound, or you hear the sound, and you can't help anticipating a view of the body—but the moment of synchronization is always in the future, always deferred; or it's always past, it's too late. Cinema, which has always worried about the nature of the relationship between sound and image, has always played with this non-synchronicity—waiting for the voice to get embodied or localized: a whole genre of film explores this—think of all these disembodied telephone voices, these radio voices, these tape-recorded voices, all coming from nowhere, attached to an invisible body, or to the prosthetic body of the machine. We have a foreboding that eventually a body is going to come along to fill the voice, and there is an inherent terror in this—the stuff of thrillers. Michel Chion has a wonderful discussion of this phenomenon of the detached voice, which he calls the *acousmétre*—the purely acoustic being which floats like a ghost. . . .

EGOYAN: The Cocteau play really shows this—it would be great to reinvestigate that as well, except it's not really written right—this idea of the one-way conversation and this anticipation of the other's face. You're right, it creates this spooky suspense. I'm now thinking also of *The Conversation* [Francis Ford Coppola, 1974].

COMAY: Or all the devices and tape-recorders in *Blow Out* (Brian de Palma, 1981]. Chion talks about Fritz Lang's *Testament of Dr. Mabuse*, [1933]—in which you keep waiting for this mysterious voice emanating from behind the curtain to acquire a body—until at the end the curtain is raised and you find out there's nothing but a gramophone behind the curtain: the ghostly terrifying sound turns out to be nothing but a mechanical device. All that suspense leads to this traumatically empty revelation in the end: the voice never finds a living, human body, and we're left with this radical disenchantment—an ending which deflates every expectation of closure. In a very different register, I'm also thinking of Fellini's *City of Women* [1980]—the museum of erotic audiotapes that the character saves and curates and replays, a low-tech audio-archive of sex scenes materialized in a physical space, but evoking a full-bodied experience that is either lost or projected to a future of pure fantasy. Returning to your film: is there a final synchronization of sound and image? One way of posing the question is to think about Krapp's relation to the camera at the end: does Krapp look at the camera at the end of the film? Is there a final encounter or moment of recognition between Krapp and the camera?

EGOYAN: We left that deliberately ambiguous. He might or he might not be looking at the camera—there's no way of telling. John Hurt was in fact not looking directly at the camera at the end of the film: he didn't want to push the ending in this direction. And in fact, to heighten the uncertainty, we lit the final shot so that you can't really see his eyeballs: you can't tell if he's actually looking at the camera or not. I think that ambiguity is absolutely right, in the end, and absolutely crucial in terms of our interpretation.

COMAY: I wonder what's at stake in this ambiguity. An encounter with the camera might have provided a kind of closure—as if the recorded voice might come to attach itself to the person listening to it, becoming a fully internal monologue which the audience in turn could internalize through a final encounter with Krapp's gaze. It's interesting that you chose to end the film with the camera trained on Hurt's face rather than on the red light or "eye" of the tape-recorder. Beckett's own stage directions of course call for a total black-out, with only the light of the machine visible at the end: all that's left to see in theatre productions is this mechanical indicator of an "on" switch glowing in the dark. Did you avoid this for technical reasons, to do with lighting, or was there some sense that you wanted to end with a human image, a face—even if that face is not directly returning our gaze?

EGOYAN: What I found really powerful in the movie—and again, it's something only the camera can do, something which you could never do on stage—was the moment when the camera frames Krapp and the machine, and then glides past the machine onto his face: at that point we hear—and it's an amazing effect—this voice coming from the machine. But it's not only tied to the machine: the moment the camera glides off the machine and moves onto Krapp's face, and is just held there, the voice so clearly becomes connected to an internal process in the man listening to it: and you yourself begin to hear the sound completely differently. At that point it really does become a matter of the ownership of experience: does this image, does this memory actually persist inside him? Or is it tied to this external device? I didn't want that question to be finally resolved. The ambiguity is of course further heightened by what we did with the sound. At that point, as you're watching Hurt's face and you're hearing the voice in this pristine digital surround system, there's nothing at all physically or visually tying it to the machine any longer—or even necessarily to Krapp himself, which is the twist. I love this passage culminating in the final image where the camera is moving onto his face, and we hear the voice coming from nowhere, until there is finally no voice—we're just letting the machine go completely, until we come aware simply of the sound of the room, and the empty movement of the reels, and then even that's cut in the end. There's such persistence here—that's what the red light is all about, on stage—sheer, mechanical persistence. The film is of course about mechanical persistence too, but it's adapted to the special properties of the camera. The camera is able to create a sense of persistence even after the performance is over. I think the very same issues are raised, but with a higher degree of reflection: it's a question here of an adaptation which is taking advantage of what the camera can specifically do. . . .

COMAY: The end of the performance yields a new kind of performance: the camera is essentially constituted in terms of after-image, after-effect. There's always some leftover in the archive to which the camera alone gives us access—again, we're getting into *Endgame* territory. . . .

EGOYAN: Yes, and there's also the ability of the camera to move through fields and to redefine one's relationship to a character's internal processes by virtue of what the camera is able to apply itself to. Of course in theory you could always lose the light on stage, and end up with a pin light trained on the actor's face, but the effect would not be as visceral as in the film; indeed, it would be too heavy-handed, too obvious. There are some readings of my film that will say how amazing it is that there are no cuts: that to me is a great compliment, because there are in fact nine cuts in the film, but there is an escalating intensity of experience which can give the impression of continuity.

COMAY: I thought we could come back to the specific relationship between film and theatre in this work. There is medium specificity here, but of a curious kind—the film marks off a very specific relationship to theatre. I was struck by a particular scene that you decided to cut from the final version of the film. In the deleted scene, the scene which you have threaded up on your editing table at the moment, the camera is positioned to the side and slightly behind Krapp's right shoulder. Whereas throughout the final version, with one notable exception, the camera always resolutely occupies a frontal position. It's as if there is a theatrical fourth wall which the camera is obliged to respect.

EGOYAN: Yes! It was shocking how persistent that obligation became: when we tried to shoot from this other angle, which for every technical reason should have worked—there's no crossing of axes, there's no logical shift, and so on—it was absolutely shocking how violent that shot turned out to be. There's no reason why it should have been as violent as it is—it's a nice composition and everything—but it turned out to be completely inappropriate. I've actually never encountered that before: that when you design a shot, and there's every reason why it should work, it simply doesn't work. Perhaps the play actually demands a fourth wall. And maybe it's Beckett's whole notion of perception that is operative here—that there's this fourth wall written into the text, which implies a certain distanced relationship with the viewer. So that even when you transcribe or adapt the play so as to incorporate a relationship with the camera, that fourth wall persists—the need for the fourth wall persists.

COMAY: It's interesting that while the play lends itself to cinema, with its multiple layers of archival registration—it almost demands cinematic treatment, it almost anticipates a movie camera in its formal structure—it rigidly maintains its theatrical character: indeed, perhaps it even ultimately forces this character on cinema itself. Even when you have a moment of pure cinema—for example, the close-up of Krapp looking up the word in the dictionary—the fourth wall remains in place: the camera angle never violates the fourth wall. And after the close-up of the dictionary, when there's a cut, the dictionary moves out of view but does not actually pass the camera—the camera never invades the space of the stage. . . .

EGOYAN: . . . Yes, and the camera moves back to that fourth wall position and you never, ever break through that fourth wall. . . .

COMAY: So I had a very strong sense of theatre—that your film is negotiating the tension between theatre and film. This also had to do with the lighting, which again struck me as very theatrical.

EGOYAN: Oh yes—that's another thing. At the end of the film we tried doing a theatrical fade—an optical fade to black, by means of the lighting, rather than, as one normally does it, through the camera itself. We had thought at first that a great way to end the piece would be to do a theatrical fadeout, to get that kind of slow, gradual black-out. But it was jarring how violently that affected the experience of the whole film: in this case, when you made a concession to a theatrical device, there was something in the chemistry which rejected that completely. In this case the problem was very different from the problem with the shot over Krapp's shoulder, which we had to delete because it was interrupting the fourth wall. With the theatrical fade-out at the end, we were indeed respecting the fourth wall, and therefore the theatricality of the piece—so let's have a theatrical end, we thought—but it was wrong, it simply didn't work. And so that's why it simply cuts to black at the very end of the film.

COMAY: Perhaps the theatrical fade tipped the delicate balance you were striving for. Another related moment: during the final recording sequence, when Krapp is sitting there speaking into the microphone, the foreground space suddenly opens up and the desk recedes into this stage-like distance: there's this immense emptiness in the foreground which is very theatrical, very atypical of cinematic space.

EGOYAN: Yes, and I'm not entirely happy with the composition of that shot—the other problem is that it's a static shot—and, yes, it's the most theatrical moment in the film. It's shot from just a bit too far back. The other shot I don't like is a short cutaway to the machine which I also find a bit jarring . . . I'm not sure about that one either. . . .

COMAY: The extreme close-up of the machine? Krapp is looking at the machine and suddenly we occupy his point of view: we see the machine from the same angle and the same distance as he is sitting—it effectively brings the spectator right up onto the stage. . . .

EGOYAN: . . . You know what—I just realized why I don't like that close-up: it would have been broaching the fourth wall—that's why it jars so much.

COMAY: I wonder if your efforts to maintain this uneasy boundary between theatre and cinema is connected to maintaining the tension between live performance and recorded performance—and if it ultimately relates to the kind of life-and-death issues that Beckett so persistently brings into focus. . . .

EGOYAN: Yes, I wonder. I'm thinking now about the Straub-Huillet renderings of theatre which are so static, and amazing in this way. That's the other extreme. There are really two ways to go. Either you acknowledge that you're working on theatre in film and you preserve and highlight that moment of theatre. . . .

COMAY: . . . Through film, you make theatre visible as theatre, with all the strangeness that this creates, cinematically. . . .

EGOYAN: Yes. Or else you somehow try to challenge that theatricality. Sometimes this strategy works, and at times it's mysteriously ineffective. I think it's because the camera has an uncanny ability to display not only what's going on in front of our eyes but also the intentions of the person behind the camera. If that person is in a frenzy of trying to make it "cinematic," this can become a distraction: you're constantly watching the camera work—it's as if the film is so insecure as to whether it even has a right to exist as a film—it has to keep on insisting, and this gets tiresome. Looking at a play like *Eh Joe* or at some of the camera gestures in the other Beckett pieces, you can see right away that you're dealing with someone who's completely aware of the camera, and what this means. And so all these issues become very sensitive when you're dealing with a text which is as tight and as perfectly considered as *Krapp*. Every gesture becomes magnified—there's nothing you can get away with. There are decisions that I made which still upset me because they're just not right—the text commands this immaculate interpretation. I'm still unhappy with these two shots: the closeup of the machine, and the retreat of the camera at the end, where we're too wide on the room. . . .

COMAY: It's as if the one is too filmic, the other too theatrical for you: the one broaches the fourth wall, the other reifies the fourth wall, turns the set into a stage. . . .

EGOYAN: Yes! But I also think that that's more than compensated for by some brilliant decisions that Peter Mettler [the cinematographer] made, for example during the long twenty-minute take—that almost violent switch-pan he makes at that point, down to the microphone: the camera then lingers over the machine until it finds John's face again. I'm so very grateful for that moment—a stroke of genius. When you're bequeathed a testament like this—if you had to pick one dramatic monologue from the last century, it would be *Krapp's Last Tape*, no question—you don't go into it lightly. There were moments when something was done as a bridge—both those shots were bridges, you see, and that's the problem with them: they *feel* like devices. . . .

COMAY: There were a couple of other interesting deviations that you made from Beckett's stage-directions. One was your decision to have Krapp walk away from the desk to pull down the window blinds before he sits down to listen to his tapes. The movement obviously anticipates the moment in the tape when Krapp describes the blinds going down in his mother's death chamber—a gesture which marks the moment of her death as well as Krapp's own self-exclusion from the scene as he waits outside her window. In this film the gesture creates a more interior space—it blocks out the rhythm of the rain, making for a claustrophobic intimacy. But it also evokes a strange sense of exclusion—puts Krapp into a kind of burial chamber to which we strictly should have no access. . . .

EGOYAN: The storm outside is also a contrivance. The gesture of pulling down the blind also serves to accentuate the play of light and dark which is so dominant in the text. Pulling down the blinds creates a darkness, but it also changes the room, making it more of a shrine. And of course we had the sound unnaturalistically dampened when Krapp pulls down the blinds.

COMAY: Suddenly you're in this dead, silent space—the room also suddenly turns into a kind of recording studio with the elimination of all outside noise. The effect of the rain is interesting: on the one hand, the reminder of a natural, cosmic, elemental environment. On the other hand, it introduces this driving, compulsive temporality—an almost machinelike repetition of light and sound effects: it forces a sense of time's mechanical passage at the very outset of the film, as if to anticipate the rhythm of the recorder. (Something similar is going on with the rain-effect in the radio play *All That Fall*.) It's interesting that this pulse-like rhythm is cut as soon as the actual ritual with the machine begins. . . .

EGOYAN: It's funny you should bring that up. The other thing I wanted to do, but John was adamantly opposed, was to have Krapp raise the blind just before he begins recording. I was intrigued by the idea that he could wander away from the machine and get far enough away from the microphone that it would have been quite possible that what he was going to say would not in fact get transcribed—that he might just get too far away, that his voice would lose itself in this way. He also would have ended up very close to the camera at that point, in the same position he was at the beginning of the film, when he went up to the window. But that idea didn't work out—John felt he needed to be behind the desk to do his recording. He might well have been right about that—I don't have any regrets.

COMAY: So you had the idea of having Krapp cut loose from his machine, with his voice untethered from the instrument which was supposed to capture it, but with his face closer to the camera and to the light of the window—pushed away from the tape-recorder and towards the camera. Hurt's decision to stay at the desk accentuates the visual continuity between the listening and the recording rituals and puts the camera in a parallel relationship to both. Another striking feature of your film was your emphasis on the intense materiality of the archive—your decision to do away with the traditional barren, empty, 1950s-style Beckett stage. That was quite shocking. Suddenly excess becomes the measure of the loss which is being registered, and the mark of the "lessness" which Beckett continually strives for. I've never seen such a clutter of stuff in any production of Beckett—the documents, the files, the boxes, the books, the papers, the drawers. . . . Instead of the typical minimalist stage set we're confronted with this mass of debris. On the one hand, this obsessional filing system; on the other hand, complete chaos and disintegration. This culminates in the tapes which Krapp violently sweeps to the ground: at this point the space becomes completely unnavigable. The heap of dead detritus becomes a physical obstacle for him—which also cuts off any further possibility of a circular movement around the desk: even if he wanted to, Krapp can't pass by the right side of the desk any more, can't wind himself up. There's almost an anticipation of jammed spools here, a mechanical breakdown. . . . A breakdown, too, of the powers both of mechanical deletion and of mechanical retention—the scattered tapes are neither accessible nor disposed of: they can be neither retrieved nor quite forgotten.

EGOYAN: Yes, and it seems absolutely clear here that he has just entered at a stage in his life when those tapes that have been pushed off will simply never—never—be collected or organized or accessed. I loved that moment of no return. I also like the fact that this is a person who had once had order—that there had once been a system, but which is now starting to fall apart. It would have been simply impossible to convey all this in an empty, black space. You've actually just touched on the three issues that I had to present to the Beckett estate to get permission to deviate from the stage directions: the sound effects of the storm, the business with the blinds, and the set itself. . . . I defended each of these changes by arguing for the need to respect the theatricality of the piece while simultaneously challenging it. If we had tried to combine the blank space with the digital surround sound, it would have been far too abstract. The entire tension of the piece would have been lost. I *liked* seeing the biscuit tin physically moving onto the dictionary. . . .

COMAY: The naturalism of the set only heightens the strangeness of the digital sound effects. Speaking of the dictionary, I was struck by your decision—which also deviated from the stage directions—to have Krapp simply turn around to look up the word. In the theatre, the dictionary is always secreted away in the dark, backstage—he has to clomp away to fetch it. It's interesting, visually, that in this film he retrieves his own half-forgotten language in this intermediate recessed space: neither fully present nor fully absent. Language has essentially become philology, at this point. One gets the sense here that one has to go physically back in space to go back in time—but not too terribly far back, just a little way back—the dictionary is just behind one's back. . . .

EGOYAN: Yes, there's certainly a physical movement towards the dictionary, but it's a question of maintaining the right distance. It's essentially about access: if the dictionary is right behind him, it suggests that he's deliberately placed it there, that he knows he will need easy access to it. It becomes a much more emotionally loaded prop than if it were simply put away in the back to be retrieved on the rare occasion that he might need it. It shows that he's someone who is in need of continual access to lost and forgotten meanings—it's a habitual gesture, turning around and looking up the meaning of a word. As opposed to the alcohol, which he's purposefully kept away in the back. . . .

COMAY: To time his drinks just as he times his recording sessions. But he can and must dip into a dead mother-tongue without any clock or schedule. . . .

EGOYAN: I didn't want to equate the dictionary with the alcohol. . . .

Ripple Effects

Monique Tschofen/2007

From *Image and Territory: Essays on Atom Egoyan*. Eds. Monique Tschofen and Jennifer Burwell. Waterloo, ON: Wilfred Laurier University Press, 2007. Reprinted by permission of the author.

MONIQUE TSCHOFEN: Your parents were artists before they moved to Canada. Your sister is a concert pianist. And you have been fully immersed in the arts since you were in your teens. You were writing plays that were actually performed at theatre festivals when you were as young as thirteen. You've performed classical guitar. Then when you were an undergraduate student, you started making short films for the University of Toronto's Hart House, which led to the features and the work in television. You have since expanded your repertoire into the worlds of opera and installation art. In addition, you've always been very much involved with writing. Your credits as a screenwriter are astonishing, and you have now adapted three novels to the screen. We have seen you flex your journalistic muscles interviewing writers like Michael Ondaatje and Russell Banks, and your academic muscles with essays and introductions to a number of books on film and art. Do you consider any of these modes of expression to be your "mother tongue"?

ATOM EGOYAN: I would say theatre is my mother tongue, because that's what I started out doing in school. I felt really drawn to the absurdists even before I knew who they were. An old teacher of mine just visited from Victoria. He reminded me of this early play that he had written I have a copy of, in which I was cast as a young boy playing myself. His name was Colin Skinner, and the play was called *Robot*. He couldn't imagine what an influence this would have. In the play, my actual best friend played my imaginary best friend. To have a teacher who was involved in writing drama, directing it, but who enjoined me and my friends and to make this a collaborative work left a huge impression

159

on me.[1] I began writing plays around this time just because I had this model; it was a very tangible thing for me to be able to do. I was also really drawn to the idea of how drama could deal with notions of dysfunctionality. If there were certain situations that I found untenable in my life, I was able to use drama as a way of dealing with some of the frustrations that arose. I loved the process—and maybe it's neurotically inspired—of making other people do things that they wouldn't do otherwise, and being able to organize people in a certain way that seemed to have some semblance of order.

The reason I made my first film is that I came to Toronto after having a wealth of plays produced at various schools in Victoria. I submitted a play to the Trinity College Dramatic Society, which was rejected. I was so outraged at this that I went to the Hart House Film Board and decided to make it as a short film, out of spite! Inadvertently, in making that film, I understood that the camera was a very powerful tool and could actually be another character, an active participant in the drama. That excited me.

At that time I also came to understand that all the drama I was writing was very derivative pastiches of Ionesco or Adamov, or Beckett, and later on Pinter. All these people had a huge influence on the plays I wrote, and I never really escaped from their shadow. Absurdist drama was something that informed the early films. I was fascinated by the harnessing of lunacy and despair, by the rituals that characters devised to deal with their pain or trauma. You see that absurdist influence in a film like *The Adjuster*—the use of repetition, role-playing, compulsive behaviour that touches on the violent and the grotesque. The absurdists believed that the assumptions of our civilization had been tested and were inadequate, and tried to find a way of expressing the senselessness of the human condition. Language and other modes of communication weren't reliable as mediums for real discovery and communication.

One of the things that I find so satisfying about returning to the theatre with *Salome* is that it offered me a chance to recover a brilliant piece of dramatic text by Oscar Wilde which probably doesn't work as well as a play as it does as a libretto. The psychodrama of that was—is—really compelling, and I'm really privileged to be able to go back to the theatre through opera because it was something that I originally aspired to do professionally.

MT: I've been reading through those early plays in the archive. Filed alongside many of them are what seem to be the comments of your earliest critics. Some of their criticisms are harsh, but very interesting. They accuse you of being too repetitious, or too abstract, or of cultivating too flat an affect. It seems to me that they are already noticing in your writing the core elements of what would later become your signature style. Along with thinking this is amazing, that a thirteen-year-old can have a signature style, I was wondering how you managed to survive the experience at that delicate age, and continued to write and put your work out there in your own voice.

AE: That was the Victoria Drama Festival, and those were plays I wrote, directed, and acted in. The plays were adjudicated, and you weren't let off easily just because you were young and wrote a play. Those early critics and their harshness, and the fact that I wasn't going to be able to get away with putting on any old play, were all really important. I was taken seriously. I think it's important to be rejected early on because you have to define why you want to continue doing something. And you also have to be able to place yourself into a context, to figure out what the work is that's being accepted and understand how your own ideas relate to that. The most damaging thing might be to be immediately accepted and not to have anything to work against. You develop muscles with criticism. The early films also received some really negative critiques. I always understood that I wasn't making films that were supposed to appeal to everybody, and that was just part of the package.

MT: In addition to returning to the theatre with *Salome* and your productions of the operas *Elsewhereless* and *Dr. Ox's Experiment*, you've recently had the opportunity to direct Wagner's *Walküre*, from the Ring Cycle, for the Canadian Opera Company in Toronto. The themes of this opera, such as incest and power (which echo so many of the themes your work turns to), make it a wonderful fit. But I'm wondering whether Wagner's views about the possibilities of the operatic medium have any special resonances for you?

AE: There are two ways of approaching the operatic projects. The first is purely sensual. I've always been excited by the fusion of music, drama, and spectacle, and Wagner certainly understood opera's extraordinary possibilities in this regard, with his idea of *Gesamtkunstwerk*. But the second factor, and the one that draws me at a deeper level, is the underlying psychology of these works. *Salome* is a powerful study of abuse and its aftermaths, and *Walküre* is one of the most complex studies of a father-daughter relationship in the history of dramatic art. I was recently reading an essay by Germaine Greer which states that the third act of the opera contains the only love scene in non-pornographic literature between a father and a daughter that explores the erotic power of parental love. She explains that Wagner boldly re-enacts the conventional scene of childhood—Daddy putting his daughter to bed—but imbues it with grandeur, majesty, and sexual power. He presents these two archetypal figures as their rich musical themes lift them to what she calls a "monumental intimacy." This is what excites me about opera.

MT: Let me ask about your work in television. One senses throughout your work that there is a real tension between the way you represent the medium of television in your feature films—as vacuous, facile, and yet prescient and powerfully manipulative—and the fact that your own credits included several short and feature projects for the Canadian Broadcasting Corporation (CBC) and Britain's Channel 4, as well as directorial credits for some popular American series such as *Friday the 13th* and *Alfred Hitchcock Presents*. What has the medium of television offered you?

AE: Television is about a communal event shared by millions of people yet watched alone, or in the intimacy of a familial setting. Maybe it's also about "monumental intimacy"! There's this tremendous fusion of the very public and the extremely private, and that's certainly at the dramatic core of a film like *Where the Truth Lies*—with the telethon—and even the cooking show *Felicia's Journey*. What fascinated me about the telethon is the almost mythological way it presents celebrity—testing the very physical limits of popular entertainers—and then juxtaposing this with an extremely intimate moment exchanged between a celebrity at the height of his fame, Lanny Morris, and this little girl who believes that he saved her. This moment of their exchange is witnessed by millions, yet its true meaning is completely concealed until the end of the film.

There is something almost banal about the ease of television broadcasting and reception that belies the psychological complexity of transmission and projection. I've explored this in a number of earlier films as well, like *Speaking Parts* and *Gross Misconduct*. On the other hand, there's the intimate video diaries explored in films like *Family Viewing*, *Calendar*, and, most recently, *Citadel*. These contain images that are made for private consumption, but which are then discovered and reformatted in other ways, depending on the needs of the particular receiver.

MT: Does the art of the theatre inform your other projects?

AE: There's definitely a theatrical element to the installations. For example in Montreal, the Musée d'Art Contemporain is a very theatrical space. It was able to do for *Hors d'usage* what I want any work to do, which is to create a sense of being able to enter into a space. This space could be a screen, or it could be physical if there's a degree of participation; either way, it plays with the curiosity of the viewer, and however much the viewer wants to invest in a piece, it can continue to unfold.

MT: That's interesting, because entrances are never straightforward in your work. Part of the theatricality you refer to in *Hors d'usage* has to do with the multitude of interstitial spaces one must pass through before reaching the main room of the installation. In installations such as *Close*, where the viewer's body is nearly pressed up against the screen, or *Hors d'usage*, where you tease the viewer with highly tactile images of people who are touching something your viewers are not allowed to touch, you seem to be physically prompting the viewer to assume certain intellectual and emotional positions vis-à-vis your work—in my experience, not only a position of curiosity, but also a position of doubt or uncertainty, and one that is never entrenched or static. So when you say you want your audience to "enter into" the space of your works and become participatory and invested as they would when entering the theatre, what do you mean? Is it safe to assume here you're talking about a more engaged kind of theatre, like the theatre of the absurd?

AE: I don't believe that the theatre of the absurd is any more "engaged" than other theatrical traditions, but I do find that the process of theatrical engagement is highly charged and inspiring. I love the idea of entering a theatre and being immediately aware of the artifice. There's something improbable about the idea that a viewer can overcome the clumsy idea of watching something blatantly artificial and embracing it. And yet that's the power of the medium. If the alchemy works—if the performances and the direction find the right pitch and tone—the viewer overcomes this initial distance and an extraordinary communion occurs. It's a rare and almost sacred moment.

MT: Yet as you say, being able to enter into a space is important. My own physical hesitations when I move through your installations—which I suppose aren't so dissimilar to the responses of viewers who have troubles with the narrative complexity or abstractions of your films—remind me of the scene in *Calendar* in which the photographer doesn't want to enter into the buildings he is photographing. Watching his awkward body, we have an acute sense of all the things he will lose because he hesitates to enter. And is this not a theme that recurs in your work, something bound up with a tension between seeing (the problem of images and screens, which in some ways remove us from embodied experience) and just being (in a body, time, and space)? Can you tell me about the relationship between the visual and the tactile in your work?

AE: I think that issue has been raised in a lot of the films. *Exotica* makes it most explicit with the idea that you can look but can't touch. Certainly it is also in *Calendar*, in Arsinée's questioning "Don't you ever feel like touching?" I think that it's even in *The Adjuster*—these very tentative ways in which Maury Chaykin touches the adjuster at one point, trying to make contact, as opposed to Don McKellar's character physically violating Arsinée with his hand. This idea of contact is so loaded, and I've certainly tried to broach the issue.

I've always felt that entrance into a screen is a physical act. In *Speaking Parts*, there are these moments where I almost would like to think of the screen as an installation site that you are able to interact with, that in a way questions what you know about touch. Likewise, in the recent installations I've tried to create ways in which people can physically manoeuvre themselves into the private and communal memories that are being investigated. There is a physical sense that the person is activating or initiating a process with their very presence.

I think this is something that happens very often in terms of the family construct—in certain social constructs, someone's mere presence initiates a process of revolution or change. I was very influenced by this notion, in, say, a film like Pasolini's *Theorema*; Terence Stamp's physical presence into that family just begins to initiate a whole series of shocks and shifts which lead to a whole redefinition of not only that particular family but also the entire social class that it functions within. With *Ararat*, the fact that there is this button missing in the photograph of Arshile Gorky's mother, which initiates this physical gesture to cover it, which initiates a certain pose in that photograph, which then, of course, may lead to this painting. A simple gesture either symbolically or literally can have a profound ripple effect.

MT: Yes. I see what you mean that it's not only a presence but often a particular gesture that sets up the real action of your films, unravelling the whole edifice of artifice. I can think of so many places in your films where somebody reaches out to touch somebody else, and that's often where the real action takes place, not in all the talking. Your work consistently turns to the motif of hands—reaching, touching, pulling back. Can you tell me more about this?

AE: Of all the different parts of my anatomy, I've always been very aware of the hand. I think my interest in hands probably comes from being a classical guitarist, of actually being aware of hands having two completely separate functions, and being very aware of positioning. And that's funny, because my son is now working on violin; there's a real consideration of how a hand is positioned to produce sound, and the different types of tonal effects that are produced by the shifts in hands and fingers. Fingers also fascinate me. Extremities. There's that line in *Family Viewing* as Stan is staring at his fingers and says, "It's strange to think we still have fingernails." As a musician, you're very aware of how you get a tremolo, or of the different positionings—on the guitar or violin you can play a G there or here, the same sound but down different strings. The notion of placement becomes a crucial consideration in terms of the tonal consequence.

MT: Moving out from there, you seem also to be fascinated by attendant notions like manipulation.

AE: Again, classical guitar is very intricate that way. What the right hand is doing is so different from what the left hand is doing. And it's also interesting too with the violin, where what the bow hand is doing is quite subtle. I'm thinking of instruments where the functions of the two hands and the muscles of the two hands are quite different. There's a moment where when you're studying a new piece. Initially, you're aware of what's happening: you're aware of going thumb, index, middle, index, middle, index, ring, index, ring. . . . You have to memorize these positions, and then you play them very rapidly until at a certain point you can't think about it. That is the point where it goes from a conscious manipulation to something that is completely intuitive.

MT: I wonder whether a process much like this, which proceeds from repetition to intuition, explains some of your characters' manipulative behaviours, like Hilditch in *Felicia's Journey* or the lawyer in *The Sweet Hereafter*?

AE: The passage of events and circumstances that lead to a ritualized activity, or a particular type of job or occupation, are fascinating. Certain professional pursuits—a litigation lawyer, a film censor, an insurance adjuster, a customs officer—allow an individual to indulge a neurosis that would otherwise not be socially acceptable, especially regarding how one can gain access to other people's lives.

MT: One of the images I've retained from your installation *Out of Order/ Hors d'usage* is the illusion that all of the tape being played on the reel-to-reels is linked. This vision of the interconnectedness of human experience—which seems to be an antidote to the equally powerful visions you produce about isolation, atomization, alienation—has a correlative on the level of the narratives you construct. You often pull together a number of storylines that seem disconnected, only to reveal that they are intimately connected. Many of your reviewers have a hard time with this complexity!

AE: A film like *Ararat* certainly seems to convolute issues that some people want to see as black and white. I've gotten into huge arguments over this with critics who found the film irresponsible; they argued that we're living in black and white times, and these issues have to be represented unambiguously so that people understand what the nature of genocide is. This completely flies in the face of (a) the fact that the enduring legacy of this particular genocide is denial and (b) the fact that we do have a whole body of holocaust literature and films that don't need to be supplemented by another reworking of an obvious statement—which is that human beings are capable of great evil, that they're able to abstract one another, that they're able to dehumanize each other. What happens in this scenario is that you inevitably find yourself in the middle of a lot of narrative stereotypes. As an artist, one is constantly trying to refine and purify one's own ideas and to distill what it is that one's trying to do. In my case, part of that distillation is an effort to generate a structural complexity, but to make that complexity as pristine as possible.

I had the experience right before *Ararat* of making *Krapp's Last Tape*, which was a very important text for me, and which I think in some ways the purest expression of what I do as a director working with one performance—working with a piece of text in one location. What astounded me were the shifts of time Beckett was able to deploy. We're working with three different periods of time: between Krapp as he is at the age of sixty-nine, reflecting on himself as he was twenty years before, which is also a reflection on who he was twenty years before that. So the idea of making the straight linear is something I came closest to with that project, and I allowed myself to do so because of the movements already there within that text.

MT: Around the same time as you put together *Steenbeckett*, an installation that is all about analogue media that are disappearing, you produced all these DVDs. What are your thoughts on the relationship between analogue and digital culture?

AE: The reason why I digitized all my films was a matter of convenience and accessibility: I want to make the work available to people. I think digital culture is enormously exciting. The tragedy is that most of the time it means watching something on a television screen, and no matter how progressive the landscape of digital culture is, it's sad to me that the conduit by which we watch it is very conventional. I think as that practice is challenged, we enter into something a lot more exciting.

The great virtue of digital culture is its democratization. It has made filmmaking available to anyone. To shoot *Next of Kin* in 1984 on a shooting budget of $25,000 seemed miraculous until a few years ago, when that's actually quite a healthy budget to shoot something digitally, which can be edited on your computer and still presented at a really professional level. The issue for me is that digital culture makes filmmaking, or image-making, quite ubiquitous. The risk is that there is nothing particularly considered about the act of shooting digitally because it's so easy and inexpensive to do, and that notion of consideration is hugely important to me.

This idea of the considered image—as opposed to the casual or "easy" image—is something I certainly bring up in a film like *Citadel*, the digital diary shot in Lebanon with Arsinée, which was an "effortless" film to make. On the other hand, when I was shooting *Krapp's Last Tape*, we had to bring in this special magazine that could accommodate 2,000 feet of 35mm film, so that the final twenty-minute shot was all done in a single take. That was a hugely physical act, something that is becoming so rare now because you can shoot so easily. With the tiny digital camera I used for *Citadel*, I could shoot an uninterrupted ninety-minute shot from the palm of my hand!

When you see the tape running through the whole space of *Out of Order/Hors d'usage*, which is also the idea behind *Steenbeckett* as well, I want you to have this idea of the physicality of the medium, so that there's a commensurate sort of relationship between the physical bulk and the amount of information that you're absorbing. We don't often get to experience that anymore. (That's even clear in *Hors d'usage*, because the sounds that you're actually hearing are not from the tape running through the players, but rather are stored digitally and are activated by a sensor.) What I find moving about the old technology is that it's at times supremely impractical, but that gives it a personality. But to state the obvious, the ancient idea that cinema or other recording technologies should only be defined by sheer physical bulk is a little ridiculous.

MT: Are you saying the analogue requires a particular kind of commitment?

AE: It requires commitment in a way that goes back to your issue about touching: you're aware that the physical properties of something define the relationship to its environment, or how that physical thing manoeuvres its way through the environment, either in purely practical ways or socially fraught ones.

MT: It seems as though you've always been very much aware of the social and physical relationships of things to their environment, drawing our attention not only to the specificity of media, but also to the specificity of social and public spaces. For example, you've linked several pieces to Montreal—a city in a province that honours remembrance on licence plates. Are you hyperconscious of its particular socio-political legacy?

AE: Yes, and I think that's why I've been so gratified by the success of *Ararat* in Montreal, because there was that whole other subtext in the film. In the film, the character of Celia is reluctant to use her native tongue—French—against Ani because she feels that ultimately this woman has the capability of intimidating her in her own native tongue. We get a glimpse of that tension in one conversation. I think that the Québécois ideas about how a collective memory is conveyed—it's fascinating that it's actually on the licence plate—connect to my own interests in these questions. Beyond this, my work has always found an audience there. The early films such as *Family Viewing* were really embraced in that city. And Montreal is also a hugely important city because most of my family lives there. Besides my parents, who went to BC when we moved to Canada, everyone else in my extended family settled in Montreal, so all my aunts and uncles and my cousins are there. *En Passant* in a way deals with this idea that Montreal is a place that's full of ghosts. It was great to be able to incorporate my two uncles into *Out of Order/Hors d'usage*.

MT: Ghosts are another theme that starts so early in your work. I came upon a grant proposal you did for your short film *Open House*, in which you talk about it as a ghost story—a haunted house.

AE: I'm interested in the idea of the physical spaces we build to insulate ourselves from certain issues. Instead of distancing us, these spaces may actually achieve the opposite by concentrating, even exaggerating and pummelling us with their presence. The same thing can happen with rituals we set up to deal with grief or mourning—again, they may only serve to exaggerate these feelings. The psychological term for this is "faulty mourning." The places we dream would make us happy and our actual relationship to what it means to be in those places intrigue me as well.

For all the uncertainty in my early life, I always knew that when my parents were making things, when they were involved in the production of art, there was refuge. So I have always had the sense that if people are involved in the process of making something together, there's something hopeful. So even in that film, *Open House*, the family is working together on this plan, and as the plan is being made, there is some joy in its creative aspect, even though it only defines their loneliness and their separation from the outside world. And that moment when the bell goes off and Frank goes to collect them, you know the glee, that sense of exhilaration that they're making something. And I think that process of making is infused throughout the work.

That's what *Ararat* questions: all these characters are trying to convey their past through these artifacts that they make, either Ani's book or Raffi's digital video or Rouben's screenplay or Edward's film—all with varying degrees of success. The film within the film may not be very good, and probably isn't—it's probably just going to disappear after that premiere. I think that's the difficult thing for people to understand. I'm not trying to be judgmental about it, but the fact is that there are things which disappear and there are things that endure. Gorky's painting has endured, but it's important to wonder about why it has endured and the degree to which people are prepared to investigate it. For years, it existed on the wall of the Whitney and the National Gallery of Art in Washington without people even knowing he was Armenian.

MT: Is there some other determinism here? That Gorky's work survives because it's a painting as opposed to something more transient like a photograph, high art rather than low art?

AE: That's interesting; I hadn't thought of it that way. I'm not so sure. I do think that I'm more drawn to the works that are more open to interpretation. I feel that you can invest more in them. There's much more interaction between that painting and the viewer than there is with Edward's film, which is very literal and doesn't really allow for a degree of interactivity. It bludgeons you, and I am suspicious of any sort of work that bludgeons you with an orthodoxy saying, "This is how this must be." What's interesting to me is how the customs agent is looking at a kid's diary and is trying to interpret the story behind what he's seeing literally. And Ani's book is an attempt to interpret an artist's life. In contrast, there's an arrogance to the Saroyan character, something almost self-satisfying and smug, in that he's finally getting a chance to tell this story. But I think that we can see in Rouben's character the sense that it's not telling the whole story. And certainly in Raffi's quest, he is trying to define authenticity: where, through the making of images, can you actually determine and find something that's authentic? I mean, that's such a fanciful idea, going to Turkey to get a 35mm image of Ararat. It's just ludicrous, but it's based on this emotional need to find authenticity. And for him it's not necessarily just in finding the artifact, in having the artifact there; it's being able to have it presented again in a physical way that allows for a degree of interactivity and which invites the viewer to participate.

MT: There is another kind of interactivity and physicality your films treat that I'd like to ask you about: incestuous motifs and the pornographic images have been part of your work from the beginning. They both attract and disturb your audiences, and you have invited your audience to participate in them at the same time as you have frustrated this participation. Your short *Peep Show* first dramatizes this kind of interaction. *Exotica*—which I understand was marketed as a sex thriller in some areas—takes it up even more explicitly. Have audiences in different parts of the world responded differently? I would guess that the French, for example, because of the legacy of de Sade, might be more inclined to make connections between this sexual dynamic and social, political, or revolutionary dimensions of your films.

AE: I would definitely say that the French have always been fascinated by the notion of perversity in my films. I found this most clearly in the early nineties, when I was in Paris for a retrospective of my work at the Jeu de Paume. It was very funny to be caught in the middle of an incredible discourse between Virilio and Baudrillard, the former saying the image is reality, the latter claiming that the image is a simulacrum of reality. But in France there is also the Sadeian notion—and I'm not just meaning to jump from one thing to the other!—but you are right in mentioning that there is also a tradition inherited from de Sade of the *staged* image, the Sadeian notion of the ritualized "scene," the positioning of indulgence in sensual extreme. What I find compelling in de Sade is how an unacceptable ritual gains in sanctity—through the sheer power of description and staging—from representing what, under ordinary circumstances, would undoubtably be considered a transgression.

MT: So are you working with the Sadean notion that a transgression in the form of sensual torment can express something that is socially or politically motivated?

AE: Yes. But in my work a lot of the time many of those characters are not aware of what they're doing. I think that in the Sadeian universe, the torment is done with such a degree of complicity and understanding. There is a breathtaking degree of predetermination in terms of how things are laid out in his world.

MT: Would you say these sets of themes about ritualistic sensual indulgence are put to the side in *Ararat*?

AE: Yes, except we're dealing with perversity on such a huge scale. I mean, the whole thing is actually dealing with a fundamental perversity. So yes, there is the sense that the film lacks some of the tonal registers of my other films—the sort of the humour that comes from seeing people deal with or negotiate their lust, or determine between their lust and their other needs. And I'm not quite sure why, but there is something decidedly neutralized about the erotic encounters in the film. I think it's just given the nature of the bigger issue here. The exploration of things sexual was secondary because I think that everything is set within the context of this monstrous cataclysmic event and somehow that is the central perversity in the film.

There's also something else here in the film, and I think a lot of people are reacting to, which is that in the other films the characters are not very adept at communicating their feelings. With *Ararat*, we're dealing here for the first time with characters who, because of their responsibilities, are very articulate: an actor, an art historian, a screenwriter, a director. They are people who are able to talk, and I'm using language here in a different way. There's a didacticism because people feel that they have an opportunity to speak, and a tension because it may be snatched away from them at any given time. So there's this young man, who during a customs inspection, just begins to go into the most arcane details about the film that he has been working on, because he's given licence—he's given the opportunity. And he doesn't know when he'll be silenced. That does make the work tonally different than the other films. This gives it a sort of earnestness. People are used to something else from my work; they associate the work with kind of a degree of emotional reserve, which is present here in a different way.

MT: Do you think the sex scenes in *Where the Truth Lies* that have generated so much controversy differ from this economy of ritualistic indulgences and perversity you have represented in earlier films?

AE: I really do think we have to think of those sex scenes as just that:

they are highly calculated *scenes*, set up by Lanny's voice-over narration. We spoke before of the Sadean notion of transgression and staging and predetermination, and how the sexual dynamics are constructed from the relation of power and politics. Lanny wants us to believe that he could have all the women he wanted, that the sex was vulgar, sleazy, compulsive, and impersonal. The more he can convince the viewer of this, the less implicated he is in Maureen's death. She was just another body, as opposed to someone who had some emotional consequence in his life. It's a masquerade. On the other hand, Vince's "sex scenes" feel exploitative because that's how he's choreographing the moment (the scene between "Alice" and Karen, for example). I was surprised that some people couldn't "read" these scenes for what they were. Perhaps it's because Lanny and Vince are such strong characters and that their personalities clashed too violently with my sensibilities as a director!

MT: What about humour in your films?

AE: The humour is often drawn at the expense of the viewer's comfort. It's about defining a sense of self-consciousness, and finding a droll humour in the sheer awkwardness of the execution. I'm not just speaking about the uncomfortable way the characters might have of going about things, but also my own discomfort in presenting events that are supposed to be monolithic in their meaning.

There are moments in *Ararat* that I think are funny, but they're often not understood that way—and some of them had to be cut. What is most darkly humorous about the piece is its use of kitsch, but I think that is something that people are uncomfortable negotiating. I certainly never wanted to make fun of the film within the film, but there are things which you can either look at from a distance or be implicated and very emotionally involved in. I just think it's difficult to be humorous about this particular event because it's a very sobering notion that something like this has not been addressed.

MT: Your films always seem to tread on a delicate line. For me, the bananas in *Howard in Particular* are very funny, as was the trick ending of *Citadel*.

AE: That's a good example of drawing the humour at the expense of the viewer's comfort. The event that concludes *Citadel* is partially staged. Defining the precise point at which the confabulation begins is extremely disturbing to the viewer who wants to believe that it must all be true. It creates a violent reaction. People don't know what to feel. I find this tension humorous, but other people won't find it funny at all. It's a bit like David Cronenberg's *Crash*—a film I adore, and which other people just detest—which I find very, very funny at moments. Other people just will not respond to that.

MT: You need to give yourself permission.

AE: Exactly, and then that's the issue for me as a director: How do you give permission to people? It's not just laughter. In *Ararat*, I'm exploring, how do you allow people to question, and feel? It's all about trust. I think that what happened with this film is that, given the historic, political perceived need of the movie, people were not prepared to trust that I could question certain things which are considered orthodox. And that surprises me, because it's so much a part of everything I've done, but in this particular case there's something sacrosanct about the presentation of the issue which I agree with. The issue of genocide has deeply affected me and has certainly tormented members of my family. But I also think that the idea that a film is going to change everything is something I just can't take seriously. Though, that being said, this film has changed some things, because there is now a degree of public discussion. If you read the *Washington Post*, which has never used the word *genocide* before, you suddenly see five articles come out in November 2002 which use that term very freely. Most journalists accept it as a fact, which wouldn't have been the case the year before.

MT: Since *Ararat*, you've produced two seemingly very different films. Your epistolary film *Citadel*, which as I understand was a private project—a kind of digital home movie you screened locally—seems to explicitly take up the question of politics and history again, investigating the devastating effects of the war in Lebanon, Arsinée's homeland, as well as the contemporary repression of Lebanese citizens. *Where the Truth Lies* appears to be much less political, through its forays into the entertainment business. Still, the two films are very much of a set through their obsession with the seductiveness of lying. What is your investment in this question of truth and lies that you keep returning to in your work?

AE: I'm fascinated by storytelling, by the moral consequences of telling a story. In our culture, the bombardment of information has completely transformed the way in which we respond to a story and how we define the truth of a narrative. I think it was Walter Benjamin who spoke of a story needing to achieve an amplitude that sheer information lacks. So then the question becomes how much trust we give a storyteller, what a storyteller needs to do to achieve this trust. That path—the storyteller needing to prove himself worthy of trust—forms an entirely different narrative, and it's a risky one. I think that *Citadel* and *Where the Truth Life* push those issues of trust. Who are the most reliable narrators of a story? Why should we believe them? At the end of *Where the Truth Lies*, as Karen assembles the "truth"—which in this case is the absolute cliché of the butler having done it—there is no absolute proof of what she concludes, much as Christopher Plummer finds there is no reason to believe Raffi's story at the end of *Ararat*. Plummer finds himself in a dark room at Canada Customs. Karen finds herself on the empty backlot of Universal Studios. Thousands of stories—fantasies and industrial fabrications—have emanated from the latter. The one that emerges from the dark room is absolutely unique. Is one story more valuable than the other? Why?

MT: So what are your next plans?

AE: I'll continue doing this for as long as I can, absolutely. One of the comforts of digital culture is that there is a way to continue to make this work in a more modest way. Like a lot of artists, I think that I work in a sort of garrison mentality: you just assume at all times that you are beleaguered and maybe that's the way it should be. This goes back to my earlier point about the critical comments about my work in theatre. You just assume that you're going to be met with resistance, and that defines your drive.

Note

1. Colin Skinner passed away shortly after this encounter.

Sight Unseen
Atom Egoyan

Tania Ketenjian/2009

From Resonance FM 104.4, 11 May 2009. www.radiotania.org/newspieces.html. Reprinted by permission of the author.

The San Francisco Film Festival has opened its doors presenting some of the best new films from around the world. When I noticed that Atom Egoyan was on the bill, I was especially excited. Atom Egoyan is an Armenian filmmaker born in Egypt, raised in Canada, and I'm of Armenian descent. Like most Armenians, I feel a sense of kinship, almost inexplicable excitement, when I meet another Armenian, especially a filmmaker I admire. I first interviewed Atom Egoyan seven years ago when his film *Ararat* was released. Like many of his films, *Ararat* represented the main character's attempt to understand a somewhat obscure past. It showed us a process of sifting through stories, memories, and history, to come to a present understanding of a present condition. Sounds a bit complicated? Well, it is, as are most of Egoyan's films, to his admittance. There are layers and layers of meaning, that we as viewers are invited to explore. His current film, *Adoration*, which is at the San Francisco International Film Festival, looks at similar themes. Who are we? What have we been told? What is truth? And how do we arrive at our own truth? In this case, however, the virtual world is involved.

This is the story: A young teenager, Simon, is doing a translation exercise in French class. In the exercise, the teacher is relaying a news story in English as the students translate it into French. The news story is about a couple who have fallen pregnant. The woman is on a flight to meet her partner's family in Jerusalem, and unbeknownst to her, her husband has planted a bomb in her bag. The bomb never goes off and the child is saved. In the French class, Simon takes on this story as his own, and shares it with his friends, as if it was his past. It goes viral, and suddenly Simon goes from being a student in a small high school, to a world-known figure based on fabricated facts. What's his real identity, is it separate from the one created online? And what are the dangers of this discrepancy?

My name is Tania Ketenjian, this is *Sight Unseen*, a weekly program that speaks with artists of all different mediums, uncovering the unseen sides of art and expression. I spoke with Atom Egoyan when he was here in San Francisco, please stay tuned.

TK: Well, I think it will be really interesting to screen your film here now because you're in the center of technology and the use of technology as a means to communicate and join together. I mean, San Francisco is an epicenter of that. Not to say that that is what your film is about, but that's a strong component of it.

ATOM EGOYAN: Oh yeah, it's a huge component. I mean, I think it's also . . . it's interesting to see someone move through that and then out of it. Because I think the technology is an amazing way of initiating a journey and the access to different opinions and ideas and different types of information systems, it's just overwhelming. But, for a young person who's trying to discover who they are, it's not going to be cathartic, the technology's not really designed to be cathartic. It can't really resolve because it's just so open, and that's the beauty of it as well. So, at a certain point, he decides that he has to go beyond that and take these objects and reformat them and actually create these physical rituals which are really important, I think, and will always be an important part of our human condition. But, I think what the technology opens up is really exciting for him and essential, because, you know, he's a young man who's been orphaned who doesn't really know who his parents were. The only access point he has is his grandfather, who idealizes his mother, who was this man's daughter. But the father is completely demonized, and that's all he's been raised with, is that the father might have been responsible for this accident, might have created it intentionally, and he doesn't really know how to focus that, and because it has been suppressed, he latches on to this other story that is presented inadvertently as a translation exercise. This actual story of this terrorist who, did this very extreme act, and this character, Simon, begins to imagine that he is this person's son. And it's a way of accessing this father image that he never had, and it's a very wrong-headed way perhaps, but it's also the only means he seems to have. So, and then he puts it on the Internet, and gets all sorts of different responses. It's a challenging film because I think in its essence it's a coming of age story, but it's dealing with a lot of other peripheral issues which the viewer has to assess and it's also full of scenes which are not in any way conventional, you know, and the audience has to also assess what the intention of these scenes are. Anyway, it's the type of film I make.

TK: Exactly. That's very true, and that's what so beautiful about it, is that it doesn't charge at you with what it's about; it allows you to unfold; it allows you to allow it to unfold upon you. There's definitely that common thread of Egoyan films of understanding your roots, understanding who you are. I mean, Simon is definitely digging for that. He doesn't really know what he is and we tend to see ourselves amongst our peers. So there's, as you see each person, him trying to understand himself within that. There is a very interesting scene where you compared a chat room of adults and a chat room of young people, and how different they were, how much more reserved the adults were. Could you talk to me about that?

AE: I think that that's particularly clear when you have families communicating with each other through Skype. You'll see the older members of the family are just much more awkward, and it's just a function of not quite understanding what the property is, but also not having been raised in an image-saturated culture and any kid is very aware of the performative aspect of who they are. As a matter of fact, you can even say that they have two different personas. We notice that with our son even. That the person that's texting and the relationship he has with his friends online is very different from the physical relationship he has and it's quite natural to have these, you know, this alternate persona and I think that's one of the reasons why Simon is able to sort of create this avatar, you know. It comes from not only gaming concepts, but also just the reality of how these kids relate on the 'Net. We did a lot of research with this and we went to these high schools and we set up cameras. I just wanted to see how kids would react to the story. What if a friend of yours purported to be the son of this terrorist, and then before I finished explaining it they were off and running and, you know, they got that. And they were able to, and a lot of the things you were seeing in the film with these high school students are not actors. It's just actually from those original research sessions, like choosing kids who were completely adept at going into these different concepts, and they all sound very considered, but they're not. And I think that's one of the issues about the Internet, a lot of people don't consider what they put out there, because it's so spontaneous. I think that comes to a peak in the film, at one point they're . . . The terrorist act involved a plane that might have exploded but never did, because the terrorist was caught before it could. But, suddenly, when Simon presents this story, there's a community of people who were on that plane, whose lives might have been taken away, but weren't. But they suddenly see themselves as victims, and again, that's only possible through the 'Net, where people can suddenly slip into this other zone and not consider the absurdity of what they're saying. These are not people who would get into a car and drive to a clubhouse and commiserate, but because they have such instant access, and because the possibility is there, they can create this subculture, and that's a culture that won't persist. It'll evaporate as quickly as it's created. But, for that moment it feels real.

TK: And, you know, you put something out there and it becomes a whole life of its own, in tandem with the spontaneity of it. It's just the way that people grab it and kind of re-created it and re-create it again and again. I think Simon had no clue that it would have this sort of development.

AE: But also, I don't think that Simon has any clue as to why he's being inspired to do this. I mean, there's this teacher who presents him with a story, who's also a drama teacher and who also inspires him to develop this persona, and she has a very specific agenda which he also doesn't understand and we can't understand until it's revealed gradually in the film. The film's full of those things where people are behaving in ways they can't really absorb and some of it is their own action like Simon, as you said . . . he wants to publicize it for his friends. It's not supposed to go into the wide world, but it does and he has to react to that and I think he figures out early on that, well, he stopped because I think he goes into this very extreme place and whether or not he will become as extreme as the character he's developing, I think not. You know, I think it's just something again that he's exploring because he's given that opportunity; he's given that room.

TK: You know, exactly, it's sort of before, we used to wear different outfits, go through a punk phase and go through, perhaps possibly, go through a drug phase or whatever it might be, and now maybe those are virtual phases that we go through.

AE: That's a very interesting way of looking at it. I do think we go through virtual phases and I think that they're compelling, because they are very exciting, but it's not sustainable. Though I think it settles down probably at one point and it actually becomes a way you might learn to communicate. I mean, clearly, in terms of the way in which we're connected. But this idea of it actually . . . I'm not so sure. There are places. There was this story in Florida, around the time we were shooting, of this young woman who had been raped and there was a trial. Do you remember this? The assailant was found to be not guilty, and she was so outraged, [that] she took it onto YouTube and she just, you know, told her story and it was so emotionally convincing and it got all this response and people believed her. And it was an incredible way for her to actually extract some sort of justice from this. Though I'm not sure how she emerged from that or if she felt that this actually was able to get her any sort of vindication, I don't know. It's an incredible instrument, but I still think that it doesn't resolve issues, and probably she might have ended up more confused than she was when she started it. I'm not sure. It is overwhelming to know that there is this incredible possibility of response, but at some point that still has to be made into something material, I think. It's just the way we're designed, until such time as we evolve into some place where we can exist only on that virtual plain.

TK: What I liked about Simon, now that I reflect back on it more, is his reaction when his story became really big and when everyone was really taking it very personally. He was somewhat aloof, in the sense that he kinda thought, "Well, OK look, that's your responsibility if you're gonna take it that seriously. I've just put out a story; I'm just trying something else."

AE: I think it's aloof because he's so aware of what it is he's really trying to find out, and no one's really addressing that, and they can't. They're spinning in their own circles, but he really needs to find out who his parents are and he has to deal with his incredible pain. And, as diverting as these things might be, I mean, they're not really responding to what he's looking for, even though he may not know that's what he's looking for, and I think that that wasn't important to convey. That he's not the type of character who gets excited merely by the fact that other people are reacting to him. I mean, if he was that sort of a kid, then that would be . . . needed a different type of response, but that's not; he's quite a soulful young guy who needs a specific response that he's not gonna find on the Internet. The reason why he's projected himself into this story is so specific that absolutely no one else can really understand it.

He probably doesn't particularly understand it himself. Sabine might, but she's not in a position to address that because of her own issues and the way she has to camouflage who she is. So, yeah, it's a complex movie.

TK: Well, in thinking about the first scene of Simon filming his grandfather, and the sort of static nature of that small image on his digital camera and the dynamic nature of actual real life, and all the inferences there are in, you know, the scent of the room, or all these things we miss out when we really believe the virtual or the recorded and not so much when we're living in that sort of belief. It was really, it was fantastic to see that dynamic, and I'm sure as a filmmaker it must be interesting for you to move between what you're looking at in real time and real world and then how it gets drawn into this contained space and it must confuse you as to what's real.

AE: Well, it's a very interesting perspective about that sort of scene, and I think that he wants something, which is that he can archive where he has that final story and he goes to that room expecting that he's gonna get it, and he doesn't. And, you know, I think that he actually gets this very extreme statement, which he then uses as evidence for this purported story, and ultimately it's this statement he has to eventually to erase from his own memory of what the father might have been. But that's an interesting perspective. You're talking about it more from just the visual plan and the way it's actually designed. And of course that's the big issue in terms of any filmmaking practice. There's an infinite number of places you could place your lens and an infinite numbers of ways you could frame a scene and you choose one frame and when the character within that frame chooses another, that's always fascinating. And I think that in a lot of the films I've made there are characters who are making directorial choices in terms of how to photograph either their lives or their family lives, sometimes how to photograph epic scenes in a film that they're making, or that there are a number of people who are making decisions which are not dissimilar to the ones I'm doing. When I started making films in the mid-eighties that was a little contrived, because there weren't really that many opportunities. I remember when I made *Family Viewing* I had to explain that the reason the father had home videos was because he worked for the company that pioneered them, or something like that. But obviously that technology has caught up and everyone can make images and everyone makes those decisions all the time, and not only that but everyone becomes distributors. Everyone becomes capable of finding audiences for their work and it's not rarified anymore. And the world is not as divided as it was in the eighties between people who had the privilege of making images and controlling those images and people who were condemned to just watch them. Like now, in our culture, there's no exclusivity and I think that's a good thing. You know, you can become nostalgic and it's wonderful and I think it's had very questionable effects on cinema culture, but in a larger sense in terms of democratization and the ability to exchange ideas, it's been extraordinary.

TK: And that's happened of course through the Internet as well, this whole democratization of just being able to share ideas, being able to create networks, have friends, be very popular. It's the access of being able to be on a similar plain, and it's not class-based.

AE: Yeah, it's not. But then there are artists that are dealing with the fact there's still class issues. There's an Indian artist whose name escapes me, but who sets up these security systems of communities that are actually just a few blocks from each other, and who are reacting in a closed-circuit way and you realize that we take it for granted that it's not class-based, but of course in other cultures it still is, very much so. Access to technology has been, especially in cultures that are very involved with the systems in developing, or maybe manufacturing systems that we use in the west, but don't actually have access to themselves. That's all very loaded, so there's still these global inequities, but, you know, yes it's true that within our own culture . . . there is that sense that it's not really class-based at all.

TK: That's true; I do always forget you actually need a computer.

AE: But they are trying to develop very inexpensive computers in some of these countries so that people will have access to basic programs. But, yes, it's one of these things we take for granted. It's like the equivalent of Marie Antoinette saying, "Well. Let them at the cake." Well, let them use their Internet. Well, they don't have an Internet, so yeah, yeah.

TK: When your son saw the film, . . . I'm assuming that he did see it.

AE: Yeah, it's one of the first films I made where he got to see it as I was making it, because he's old enough, and yeah, he had a really emotional response. It was great, actually, his response to it. It's not necessarily that he identifies with the characters, because he's a little bit, I guess now he's about their age, but he was younger, like, last year when he saw the film. But I think it was just the whole understanding what his parents do, and just the whole process of it. And I think . . . the type of storytelling. You know, he wants to write himself, and it's seeing how much you invested of yourself in any story you tell.

TK: What did you learn about him in his reaction? When you saw his reaction, what did you discover about him?

AE: It's something I already understood, he's just very attuned to . . . you know, he's very sensitive to complex stories and he has a great attention span, which is just different from a number of his friends. He's seen a lot of difficult movies, and that's one of the things that we did, to show him films that were challenging, so he has no problem with pacing and not necessarily following certain formulas. I don't necessarily know that it's the type of film that he would go see on his own, but he certainly is able to read it. What I'm realizing is that there's something with this film, which is my twelfth feature, that I'm coming to an end with, and I'm not quite sure where I evolve next. But, I started writing plays when I was fifteen at school, and I just got very consumed with this idea of being able to create these narratives and that this film is very much based on a reflection of seeing our Arshile become fifteen, and think about if I was fifteen now. I wouldn't be satisfied with writing plays for friends and parents. But I would want to put it on the 'Net. And now that we've got to this place where I'm now creating a character who is like I was at that point, I sort of feel like some sort of cycle has come to some sort of an end. I'm not quite sure where one goes after, but it's been interesting. And also, there's been a movement in the way these technologies were dealt with in the earlier films and I think now there's much more optimism about what they suggest . . . and that people can actually make the decision. That was there in *Family Viewing* though, as well, where you had a character in '86, who used the technology which was actually set up to oppress him and kind of like destroy his history, but he was able to actually claim that what he needed to find out was who he was, and I think that's something similar in that character of Van and this character Simon.

TK: When you speak about things coming full circle, I think it's always interesting to be able to present your work to your child. Someone asked me who I would want most to be recognized by. I don't have children yet, and I said, "My children." So, there's something about A) seeing yourself in your child in a very tangible way, where you would be at their age, not like eight and playing around, but really understanding yourself. And B) being able to present something to them and actually see their reaction.

AE: Yeah, but you don't want to project too much and you don't want to become too much of a burden for them, either. This is a whole conversation we have. Maybe you do; maybe that's good to have that. You want to have expectations of a child, but you don't want those expectations to also traumatize them, obviously. So it's tricky bounds.

TK: Very much, it's parenthood.

AE: Yeah.

TK: So, when I was doing research about you online, all these different things came up. Someone called you an Egyptian filmmaker, someone said you're an Armenian filmmaker, there were quotes that had been isolated, and I know that, again, it's actually just the fact that it's from print to the computer; it's not so much about the online world, the virtual world. But there is this sort of "Who are you?" kind of situation when you're a persona online. Do you have dual, triple, or quadruple personas that you play with, whether it be here or virtually? Are they created by you? Are they created by others?

AE: Well, I do think that part of the experience of being an immigrant and coming to a country and figuring out how to assimilate . . . teaches you that character or personality is a construct at some level. And especially my parents' decision to move to Victoria, British Columbia, which is a small city on the west coast of Canada, and there was no Armenian community there. So, they were very assimilationist. So even though Armenian was my mother tongue, and I had this very strong relationship with my grandmother, I wanted to be like everyone else, and so you learn how to become that way. As to whether that ever becomes completely natural is an issue, and it's very specific to the way I was raised, and it's very different from the way most Armenians are raised, and certainly my cousins who came at the same time to Canada were raised in Montreal, where they were raised in a community. So it depends. They have their own issues, I suppose, because they're being raised with three cultures in Montreal, say . . . between French through the Québécois sort of culture, and English and Armenian. So, I think we are all, you know, a series of composites in a sense that, do any of those individual templates emerge until they become separated and they probably do at some point, depending on what we're going through. If that happens all the time it's dangerous because it becomes quite schizophrenic, of course. But there are probably moments we can, and need to, be different personalities. I don't know whether or not that's a natural process or it's just a survival mechanism and maybe it's both.

TK: And do you still find that you discover new personas? New personas when you do new stuff? Or do you feel that you kind of . . . I'm Armenian, as you know, my family's from Lebanon and they're French educated and they speak Turkish as well, so they're all these and they live in America now and they're all these things going on. And they completely resonate and understand. And I often wonder, "Is my mom still discovering another Christine within her? Or is my father discovering another Otto within him?" Do you find that there are these other Atoms you discover now that we can actually create, or that can actually be created about us?

AE: You certainly discover ones that other people are creating about you when, to me the most shocking one was when *Ararat* came out, and I don't know if you read any of that literature, but there is a Turkish site which analyzes and presents a version of who I am, which is kind of shocking and interesting, though. There's a site called Turkish Review and it's pages of this sort of analysis of the transformations of my life, from what happened to me when I met my wife and how . . . it's really weird because it's very, it's studied. It has a very political reason that they're presenting it, and it's troubling because their theory is that I'm somehow a decoy, that my entire setup as an artist is actually to extend a political agenda and that it's somehow designed. And they're trying to kind of call the bluff. But it's really weird because it's actually serious and I think it's one of the more extreme examples, and it could only happen, you know, in the political context of Armenian-Turkish relations, probably. But it's still interesting, and it's a mild form, perhaps, of what a celebrity goes through, where people are analyzing why they act the way they do. Fortunately, I'm not in that zone. But I was from a certain Turkish perspective around the time of *Ararat* certainly, considered very threatening. So I don't know if . . . and as a result of that you certainly want to dismiss it, but it's also an interesting thing to actually look at an alternate version of who you are. And certainly we go through that every time we form a new relationship. I mean, we are seeing ourselves through the other person, or are guarding ourselves or opening ourselves up. That's the nature of human relations, and it's certainly something that comes up a lot in the films—the essential mystery of those meetings between individuals, between two people, and what has to be negotiated.

TK: That's exactly what I think; it's completely what comes up for assignment, this really seeing himself through these other eyes. Ultimately, like you say, having to let all that go and have something more tangible.

AE: Yeah.

TK: Those were the words of filmmaker Atom Egoyan speaking about his film, *Adoration*. To learn more about the film and all of Egoyan's other work, please visit egofilmarts.com. My name is Tania Ketenjian and this is *Sight Unseen*, shedding light on the creative world through candid conversations with the artists of our time.

Atom Egoyan Interview

Eleanor Wachtel/2009

CBC Radio's *Ideas* (produced by Sasha Hastings), 12 May 2009. Printed by permission of the interviewer.

INTRODUCTION: I'm Paul Kennedy and this is *Ideas*. On this edition, our regular monthly feature "Wachtel on the Arts," with the host of *Writers and Company*, Eleanor Wachtel. Tonight, family, identity, and memory: why voyeurism can be good and why denial never works. Armenian-Canadian filmmaker Atom Egoyan talks about his life, his career, and his new movie, *Adoration*.

ELEANOR WACHTEL: I'm Eleanor Wachtel. Welcome to "Wachtel on the Arts." You're listening to the opening music of Atom Egoyan's new film *Adoration*. It's about a Toronto teenager who re-imagines himself as the son of a terrorist, and then he has to deal with the reaction when his story hits chatrooms on the Internet. In the process, though, he does come to terms with his own family history and he's able to redefine his understanding of who he really is. Personal identity, how it's formed, how it can fall apart, and how it's reconstructed, has always fascinated Atom Egoyan, and that may be partly because of his own personal history. Egoyan was born in Cairo in 1960 to Armenian parents. His family moved to Victoria, British Columbia, when he was still a toddler. Like most kids, young Atom just wanted to fit in, so he more or less rejected his Armenian background. He even refused to speak the language. But when he moved to Toronto to attend university, Egoyan reconnected with Armenian culture and history. Armenia, especially the legacy of the Armenian genocide of the early twentieth century, has been an important part of his life and movies ever since. Egoyan is especially interested in how history and memory shape identity. Most of his films examine what happens when we try to suppress or deny the past, both personal and collective. And he has a rare gift for combining intellectual rigor

186

with emotional complexity. I had the chance to talk to Atom Egoyan in Toronto recently and we began with his earliest experiences in Egypt.

EW: You lived your first couple of years in Cairo, the first few years of your life were in Cairo. What do you remember of that time?

AE: I always find it difficult to understand what I remember and what I remember having seen because my father took home movies from a very early point. And after we came to Canada and settled in Victoria, I clearly remember watching these images of my early childhood in Cairo. So, images of me being placed on top of a chimpanzee in the Cairo zoo or images in our apartment there, and images of my parents' store in Cairo—I don't really understand the delineation between what I remember having experienced and what I remember having watched. My parents had this, my father especially, have a very nostalgic view of that period of his life. They were both born there as well and they had to leave in a hurry, so there was this sense of having left something behind, and I was made aware of that. So, those images were something that were very important to me in my early childhood. I don't know. I can say something about what I think I remember, but I'm not sure if I actually remember it or whether or not I'm remembering something else.

EW: You realize this is key to your entire *oeuvre*. (laughter)

AE: It is. You know, I always think that formation of those first few years, obviously from a Freudian perspective, is crucial, so that idea of being displaced and coming to a place where you don't have language and you are trying to locate yourself and then having that strange recording of your early childhood, which was quite meticulous. I think my father was really enamored with this Brownie camera that he had that he shot everything with. And also that sense that when you're leaving something, I suppose, you want some record of what your life was there.

EW: You said your parents had to leave in a hurry. Why?

AE: Well, there was a rise of Arab nationalism at that time and they were like many members of the Armenian community fearing for their business and there was a large exodus of Armenians from Egypt in the early sixties to Canada. Most of them settled in Montreal, where most of my family moved. It was, I think, probably a very difficult period for them because they had a certain sense of what their community was in Egypt. In retrospect, they perhaps were hasty, because the Armenians that stayed behind were able to thrive and have actually done quite well. There were a lot of people, especially middle-class shopkeepers and people who were in manufacturing who felt that their businesses could be nationalized at any point, there was certainly a very real fear.

EW: During Nasser's period? [Nassar was president of Egypt 1956–70.]

AE: Yeah, this was a very volatile period. They befriended someone at the Canadian embassy who helped them come to Canada.

EW: Why Victoria?

AE: Well, that's a really interesting point. My parents are both painters. My father was one of the first people from the Middle East to get this full scholarship to study at the Art Institute of Chicago, and so when he came back to Egypt from Chicago, he had this sense that the community was very parochial and conservative. And he made a decision when they moved to Canada to move away from the community. So, while everyone else settled in Montreal, they moved to Vancouver and my father was going to teach in Vancouver and then a business opportunity came up. They had an art gallery/furniture store in Cairo called Ego Arts, which they wanted to use as a gallery space for their work, but they also designed furniture and found that people were more interested in buying the furniture than the art, necessarily. They tried to set up a similar type of establishment in Vancouver and then Victoria, which was an art gallery. They had one of the first private galleries in Victoria, where they moved because someone who had a Scandinavian furniture store was closing down that operation and offered my father to take over and he saw the opportunity and moved to Victoria, which was very, very strange. We were probably the only . . . we were the only Armenian family there and my sister and I were raised in this very . . . Victoria at that time was a very different place than it is now.

EW: It was very Englishy and Ye Oldey. . . .

AE: Well, faux English and everything was Ye Olde. There was like Beef-eaters and I was also working at the Empress Hotel from a young age as a busboy, so all of those traditions, which are quite artificial but were very much a part of what Victoria was at that point.

EW: High tea. . . .

AE: People speaking with English accents who had never been to England. This idea of it being the last bastion of the British Empire, which was something that was able to present in a very theatrical way and court, and so seeing all of that, seeing the construction of this false identity as well, a cultural identity which wasn't really rooted in anything. . . . There were a number of people who had moved to Victoria from

England because it resembled the weather there, but then there was this whole other subculture of people who aspired to that Englishness and I think that that was very formative as well. And certainly when I came to Toronto in '78, the idea of a multicultural city was something which was very fresh and exciting. It wasn't really part of my experience in Victoria. That being said, of course, I came here to study at Trinity College, which was . . .

EW: . . . a sort of Anglo bastion.

AE: Yes. But it was also fascinating. I came not really knowing what Trinity meant. I came because it was the smallest college and it seemed at that time I had visions of becoming a diplomat and it was a place to go for international relations. So, the black academic gowns and all the strange rituals at Trinity were something that I was not prepared for, but experienced with wide-open eyes because it was all very interesting from an ethnographic perspective.

EW: And people thought you were Jewish, I think you said?

AE: Of course, there was this . . . I had a really close friend there, Doug Cooper. Douglas Cooper, who has since become a novelist and we . . . at one point there was this person that we both really regarded with contempt who was applying for a Rhodes scholarship, which seemed so ridiculously appropriate given how prejudiced and racist he was, and the very slurs he directed towards us. So we actually actively campaigned for him to win, because we felt the Rhodes scholarship would be perfect given Rhodes's . . .

EW: . . . history as a racist.

AE: He never got it actually. He actually was one of these people who just didn't quite understand when something was being done in a satirical vein. But, you know, it was a strange place. I must say I loved it there. I have always thrived in a place where I have felt slightly outside and I like that process of trying to integrate into something that you're not really a part of and trying to understand how the laws and rules work and how far you can go in stretching them and playing with them, so Trinity was great for that. And they had a dramatic society where I got to begin to put on plays, but also at Hart House there was a film board and that was a revelation for me. I wasn't really steeped in film culture; I started writing plays when I was quite young at school. But when the Trinity College Dramatic Society turned down one of my plays, I was so arrogant and kind of ridiculous at the time, but I remember running across the field outside of Hart House and collapsing on my knees and thinking, "Okay, what do I do now that my play's been rejected?" And then a light bulb went off, because I remembered there was Hart House film board and I thought, "Okay, I'll make it as a film," out of spite more than anything else really. Then, I had a spring-wound Bolex Camera, and the moment I started filming this play I realized that there was something very unusual about how a camera could assume the role of a character that was watching something. That seemed really novel and original at that moment. Now, I think very often that you are seized with the idea that you're breaking new ground and you may not be, but you need to believe that, especially when you're young, to sustain this creative energy. So, perhaps because of my naiveté and lack of familiarity with pre-existing films canons, I thought I was doing something new. And a lot of those early films were about family paradigms where someone is missing and the spirit of that missing person, represented by the camera, may be watching them.

EW: I want to pick up on a lot of what you just said very soon.

AE: Sure.

EW: But just to get back to Victoria and your parents, as these new immigrants, and your father as a kind of artist-manque, and your mother was also a painter.

AE: She just recently had shows at the Winchester Gallery in Victoria at the age of seventy. She had her first one-woman show, so she's gone back to it, and it was their love and I very aware of the fact they were both happiest when they were painting, even though that was not something that they could devote themselves to. They had to raise a family, of course. So, this idea of creativity as being something which could bring joy and release and which was sacred, really, was something I gathered through osmosis, if nothing else. Even to this day, I think especially in the Armenian community, there's that sense that the culture is very important but there's this trepidation in encouraging kids too much sometimes because it's so unpredictable and there is this pressure on the children to become doctors or engineers and lawyers and to have a respectable profession. It's tough. I think it was tough for my parents because they sensed that very early on that the two of us, my sister and I, were both really geared towards artistic livelihoods.

EW: Growing up in Victoria, how did you feel about your Armenian heritage?

AE: Well, my link with my Armenian culture was most clear to me in terms of my relationship with my grandmother. She didn't speak

English, and when she was in Victoria, she was very important to me, she was. I do remember the two of us wandering around Victoria while my parents were busy trying to construct their business; I just spent a lot of time with her. I remember this feeling of drifting, really, and her trying to orient herself in this culture she could never really become a part of. Because there was no community, I didn't understand this idea of having a heritage which was important at that moment. I understood that there were certain aspects that would become important, but I wasn't raised to be proud of it, necessarily, and I certainly wasn't an assimilationist. I wanted to become English, I wanted to lose and submerge my mother tongue. I wanted to speak the language better than my friends, and I wanted to really shed everything that had to do with anything that made me different, which is what a lot of kids are like. You don't really get a sense of your identity as being something valuable until much later on in your life, unless you are raised in a social setting or a familial setting where that is thrust upon you, and where you were told that narrative from a very young point. I wasn't.

EW: So you didn't want to speak the language?

AE: No. Absolutely not. No, no. I lost it really until I came to Toronto and I began to pick it up.

EW: What moved you to do that?

AE: In Toronto in those years, there was at the university an Armenian Students Association, and I was feeling a little lost at Trinity and I came into contact with that group. It was a very volatile period because there was the presence of a more radical element, in terms of seeking historical recognition for Armenian genocide. There was this more extremist position and within that student group there were a lot of heated discussions about that. That was something I was suddenly thrust into, it was very . . . I was torn by it, and yet it was something that . . .

EW: Was it news to you?

AE: I was aware of the history, but I wasn't really aware the details of it. And to suddenly be surrounded by people who were so vehement was something that overwhelmed me and I tried to absorb as much as I could as quickly as I could, and to catch up on things. Most of my studies at university were geared towards the issue of the Armenian genocide, and I wrote my undergraduate thesis on how that question came up at the Paris Peace Conference. I became aware of this as being this extraordinary legacy and that it's still was very much an open wound. Then, of course, in the early eighties it began to explode into violence.

There were Armenian—either terrorist groups or freedom fighters, you know—people who were really doing whatever they could to push this case forward. That began to have a very strong effect on me as well. I understood my parents' decision to not bring me up with that, and certainly wasn't something I was seeking at that point, but then when I came here at the age of eighteen it became essential to understand the history and also to understand how that related to my identity as a Canadian. Then, of course, on top of that with this idea of becoming a diplomat, there were all sorts of issues and all sorts of politics that hadn't informed the denial which were fascinating to me and continue to be fascinating to me to this day. It's a very unusual case.

EW: The denial by the Turkish Republic?

AE: By the Turkish Republic, but also this sense that the West has given the Turkish Republic the permission to deny it. I think that that is the part of the equation that's not really talked about very often. If the West was able to maintain its position in regards to this history as everyone understood it at the time, then Turkey would not have been allowed to deny. I think that there was this whole regime that came in with Ataturk, where in exchange for access to the extraordinary oil riches of the former Ottoman Empire, there was a pact that was signed where this issue would go away and it was alarmingly effective. Anyway, that's a whole other story we can get into, but it seems to me the mechanics of that and the way the issue has not gone away to this moment . . . It's quite remarkable to see, for instance, President Obama now being able to have one position as a private citizen and then go to Turkey and not be able to use that word. And it's a loaded word, and the semantics of that are also fascinating to me, the way people dodge that and the way alternate narratives are constructed around it. Also, the very tortured relationship that a whole class of Turkish intellectuals has towards the issue as well and it continues to be fascinating and very emotionally loaded and very much on the agenda.

EW: Atom Egoyan, in 1983 you made your first feature called *Next of Kin*. It's about an upper-middle class boy, young man, who pretends to be the long-lost son of an immigrant Armenian couple and who seems to actually fool them into believing him. Was this a scenario you could in some way relate to yourself?

AE: Yeah, it's some sort of . . . I guess, a Freudian term is sort of a family romance, right? Where you construct an alternate family, and I think that that happens in a number of those early films where someone decides that a structure that they're living in isn't really viable for them anymore, so they create something as an alternative. They reconstruct, or they reformat their own lives and that's an exciting concept for me.

EW: Why do you think that is? You've said you're fascinated by role-playing in family situations. Why?

AE: Because I think that every family has a certain mythology that it wants to say defines itself. And the way that's extended, the way that's embellished, the way that's challenged is so important to the way we form ourselves, and the family is at the core of how we build up our society. The examination of any family is very much an examination of the society that family lives in. It's a dynamic that we all understand and I think we're all raised with these archetypes, and for someone who's fascinated by the mystery of any meeting between human beings, I think that that primal meeting we have with our parents and with our children and our siblings, the meeting that we can't really control in some way, is going to define us. And the fantasy of being able to reconfigure, that is something which I think both becomes possible at a certain point in one's life, and also incredibly oppressive if you don't act on it. I think what it comes down to, this notion of control, right? Many families are torpedoed by some character who thinks that they can control that family narrative. It could be a patriarchal or matriarchal figure that imposes something on characters who suffer from it at some level. That can be done with the best of intentions, but it can still have a very marked effect on certain people's development. The tragedy of many families is that people don't understand until it's far too late that they may not be in the right setting and they have to continue to function in a certain way that might not conform to what's best for them. That is incredibly painful. It's almost like people who are born into the wrong sex . . . who are looking for that transplant, that way of being able to conform to what they feel they need and what they own. And I think the reason why many of the leading characters in the films are younger is because they are at a point where they are still quite idealistic about what is possible.

EW: Atom Egoyan, in 1992 you and your wife, the actress Arsinée Khanjian, traveled to Armenia to shoot the film *Calendar*. And you're both children of the Armenian diaspora. What was that like for you?

AE: That was an extraordinary experience because we came to it with such different histories. I, again, not having been raised in an Armenian community, had no sense that this was really a sacred trip. In any way, for Arsinée, who was raised in a very nationalist environment in Beirut where there was a very strong Armenian community, she was raised to believe that Armenia was heaven, that it was paradise, that it was the promised land. And the characters that we ended up playing in this film were actually quite different from what we experienced on a personal level. I was very excited to be there, very charged, and there was nothing I was remotely disappointed with, because I had no real expectations. She had to deal with this—at that point, you can't say post-Soviet, because it was still very much . . . really it had just become independent, so it was a culture that was very different from the one she was led to believe would be there. The character she plays in the film is very romantically attached, and I don't think that's what she was feeling, while I was much more open. We played against ourselves and . . .

EW: It was made very cheaply. You play the photographer who's going to Armenia to shoot these images for a calendar. He's accompanied by his girlfriend, played by Arsinée, and she also translates between the photographer and their guide, who speaks no English. You, the photographer, speak no Armenian and then gradually the girlfriend begins a romantic relationship with the guide.

AE: And he watches his relationship slip away. In front of his lens, this relationship begins to fall apart. He watches his wife fall in love with someone else.

EW: Through the lens.

AE: Through the lens.

EW: And you draw a parallel between not understanding language and the distance that that creates and the distance and loss of the relationship.

AE: Well, I think any relationship is probably challenged by the idea that there is a language in which that other person might speak, either literally or figuratively, that we won't understand at some level. And that is both the source of an attraction, but it can also be the moment of alienation in a relationship as well, that there is something about that person which you can never quite get. And when it's within a culture, it becomes even more threatening in a way. I think that my character plays up his alienation from what he sees as a way of creating a defense mechanism against what he sees his wife falling into.

EW: I'd like to play a short scene from *Calendar*, and this is part of a three-way conversation. And *conversation* must be in quotations because there's a lot of misunderstanding between the photographer, his girlfriend, and the guide, who can't understand why the photographer remains behind the camera the whole time.

Film dialog:

Guide: (speaks Armenian)

Translator: [translating] He says you seem to be interested in what you're seeing. You're asking a lot of questions.

Photographer: I guess that's part of why we're here.

Guide: (speaks Armenian)

Translator: [translating] Don't you feel the need to come closer? Feel, like actually touch and feel?

Photographer: Touch and feel the churches?

Translator: [translating] Realize how it's made, constructed.

Photographer: To touch and feel the churches?

Translator: Yeah.

Photographer: Um, hasn't occurred to me.

Translator: Hasn't occurred to you?

Photographer: No.

Translator: You didn't feel the need?

Photographer: What, he'd like to caress them or something, or . . .

Translator: No, you know what he means.

Photographer: Well, I I . . . no, I don't really.

Translator: [speaks in Armenian to guide]

Guide: [speaks Armenian]

Translator: [translating] He says if you had seen someone else's photographs of these places you wouldn't have wondered like what it must be inside? What it would look like inside?

Photographer: No, I'd just think that they were very, very beautiful places, and I'd think that they were very, very well composed, beautifully lit, and very seductive. Is that what he wants to hear?

Translator: [speaks Armenian to guide]

EW: That was Arsinée Khanjian, Ashot Adamian, and Atom Egoyan, in Egoyan's 1993 film *Calendar*. There is something very voyeuristic about *Calendar*. We watch all the Armenian sequences through the eyes of the photographer as he looks through his camera or through video replay. What interests you about voyeurism?

AE: Voyeurism is the act of looking at something which doesn't know that you're, in most cases, that you're looking at it. There's a detachment, there's an objectification, but I also believe that it challenges an idea of what it means to be activated. Because there is a decision one has made to engage with something in a clinical way. But that raises a number of emotional issues because you might find that it is more inspiring to you to have that level of detachment than to actually be in that place, and it might allow you to engage in that place with an intimacy that you may not have were you not watching it in a certain way. So, it's not all it's made out to be. We usually think of voyeurism as something which is abhorrent, which divorces us from any real feeling. But I think in many of these films, it's that act of voyeurism which enlivens the character in a certain way because they understand a responsibility and in some cases a responsibility that they've forfeited by becoming a voyeur and that then motivates change. But, to get to that point, you have to really be in that place. You have to understand what is at the core of their scopophilia, which is the clinical term for it. It's like this idea of watching as a practice, which is very engaged at some level and protects them. It's a protective mechanism as well. It's not really just to take advantage of someone else, though it can be as well. In many of the films, that's part of it.

EW: But it detaches you from life. It puts you at one remove.

AE: Only to then find a way to move past that. It's a passage which I'm really fascinated by, and I think that it's that passage between the intellectual detachment that you sometimes need to understand a situation and the emotional engagement you need to resolve the issue that exists within it. So, you can't really have one without the other.

EW: You're listening to "Wachtel on the Arts" on *Ideas* on CBC Radio 1 on Sirius Satellite Radio 137 and around the world on cbc.ca. I'm Eleanor Wachtel and I'm speaking to Canadian filmmaker Atom Egoyan. Atom Egoyan, in 2002, you made *Ararat*, about the Armenian genocide of 1915. And after years of making films that broached the subject indirectly, there are various oblique clues here and there if someone tracks your work, but what made you want to deal with it head-on.

AE: What made me want to deal with it was an opportunity that was offered to me and it was irresistible. There was an event at the Armenian Community Center where I was being honored, and they asked me to suggest someone who could introduce me and I chose Robert Lantos, who was very involved in my career as a distributor and producer of my work. He got up in front of this crowd, and as Robert often does, he took a moment to gauge the feeling in the room, and he said, as a Jewish producer who has been raised on depictions of Holocaust that were indelible to him, he could not understand why a film hadn't been made about the Armenian genocide, and if I was ready to make this film, he would support it. And the room erupted in applause and I thought, "Oh my God, Robert, why have you done this to me, why at this point?" Because I could see the energy and Robert sat down and I got up to the podium and, of course, anything I said at that point was going to be a letdown after what he was able to infuse these people with. Yet, I thought this was an incredible moment where I was being challenged to deal with this. I went back to a script I'd written in my early twenties in this period when I was being re-engaged with this historic issue. It was a very melodramatic retelling of this particular episode with an American missionary, Clarence Usher, based on his memoirs of what he witnessed. I looked at it and I thought, "What is it about this story that doesn't engage me?" I realized it wasn't really dealing with what I had been raised with, which is not a direct experience of the genocide, but the denial of it, and how the denial of it had become the most important issue in my experience and negotiating that. So, I began to think of this film that could be the story of these four generations. You would have the story of a survivor, represented in the era by the figure of Ashile Gorky.

EW: The painter.

AE: The painter, the abstract expressionist painter. And then you would have the figure of a survivor's child, who is represented by Charles Aznavour, who's a film director engaged in making this large historic epic on the Armenian genocide based on the script I had written in my early twenties. You have the grandchild of the survivor played by Arsinée's character, who's an academic who specializes in the work of Arshile Gorky. And then you have her son whose name is Raffi and he, through his mother, gets a job working as a driver on a film that's being shot in Toronto, this historic epic. His job is to drive home the actor who plays this Turkish monster. That becomes really one of the central ideas in the film of how these traumas are somehow transferred from one generation to the other and also through these parts that people are expected to play, either literally within the film or in these, again, these family structures. There's a tremendous weight that's put on Armenian kids, as I'm sure with Jewish kids, or kids who have experienced any collective trauma to remember, and if it's not remembered it will disappear. In the case of the Armenian genocide that's actually very true. If the issue had not been kept alive by successive generations, it would have disappeared, effectively. Yet, that doesn't really come to terms with what it means to impose this history on a young Turkish person who may have never heard of it, and how you actually accommodate that in the fabric that we have in this country. Where we're all trying to negotiate certain histories and what I wanted to do with *Ararat*, which has been very controversial both within my own community and certainly from a Turkish perspective, is to put that issue into the structure of the film.

EW: Now, I understand why it would be controversial from a Turkish perspective, and in fact, you have that Turkish-Canadian actor respond to this young Armenian who says, "You portray such a brutal Turkish official in the movie" within the movie. He says, "That isn't what I was taught in school . . . and it wasn't a genocide. It was during the first World War. The Armenians were in that part of the country. It was during the Ottoman Empire. [The Armenians] were allied with the Russian Empire, who were our enemy, and in any case this is a new country. Let's just drop history and get on with it."

AE: Well, that is a reality that person has been raised to believe. Now, it is also reprehensible because it's not as easy as that. Also, that relativist argument, that both sides suffered, is something that as Armenians we've had to endure. And it's malicious because it doesn't really account for the fact that there was a state-organized genocide against the Armenian population that was living in Turkey at that time. Whether or not there were Turks who might have suffered is not really the point. However, that can quickly become the point in a relativist society where different narratives are being juggled.

EW: Why was the Armenian community objecting to your film?

AE: I think many Armenians felt that they wanted something that was simpler, and which would serve the film that Aznavour's character is making within my movie . . .

EW: They wanted the movie within the movie . . .

AE: They wanted something that would finally once and for all ascertain what happened, as though any work of art can actually live with that responsibility. And certainly it does not account for the fact that the predominant condition that I was dealing with was denial and confronting this notion of how denial is perpetrated, but also how it filters through and how maybe some of the Armenian characters may have not learned from their own history in terms the corrosive effects of what denial might be. It's also using a very powerful word in Armenian mythology. Ararat is the holy mountain, so the fact that that mountain is only viewed from one angle—from Armenia . . . You know, part of the project of this film was to see it from this other side, quite literally when the boy goes to try and create a digital diary of what Ararat might have looked like, because he senses as he watches this historical pageant being made that it's not going to serve the function, that there's something about it that seems antiquated and it doesn't really relate to what he feels. He's very concerned about this and he wants to make it as authentic as possible and goes with this crazy, again, young idea that he can go with his digital camera, create imagery which might enjoin itself somehow into this very old-fashioned historic epic.

EW: We have that scene actually, where Raffi's . . .

AE: Oh, what a great set up.

EW: Exactly . . . Raffi's pulled over by a Canadian customs official at the Toronto airport as he's returning from Turkey, and although he insists he was shooting footage for his movie, the official suspects he's smuggling drugs, especially when he learns that Raffi's father was killed trying to assassinate a Turkish diplomat years earlier. The customs official, played by Christopher Plummer, he's also moved by Raffi's story of the Armenian genocide and particularly when Raffi shows him this video diary that he made for his mother at Ani, a medieval Armenian city of which almost nothing remains.

Film dialog:

Raffi: (on video) I'm here mom. Ani. In a dream world, the three of us would be here together. Dad, you, and me. I remember all the stories I used to hear about this place. Glorious capital of our kingdom, ancient history. I think the story that dad was a freedom fighter fighting for the return of this, I guess. Many died and now something in me died, too. What am I supposed to feel when I look at these ruins? And do I believe that they're ravaged by time, or do I believe that they've been willfully destroyed? Is this proof of what happened? Am I supposed to feel anger? Can I ever feel the anger that dad must have felt when . . . (video turned off.)

Customs official: When he tried to kill a Turkish diplomat?

Raffi: How did you know?

Customs official: Well, you gave me your passport. Files are kept. You happen to be the son of a terrorist. Will you turn that back on please?

Raffi: (on video) . . . you tried to kill that man. Why was he prepared to give us up for that? Mom, what's the legacy he is supposed to have given me? Why can't I take any comfort in his death? When I see these places, I realize how much we've *lost. Not just the land and the lives, the loss of any way to remember it. There is nothing here to prove that anything ever happened.*

EW: David Alpay as Raffi and Christopher Plummer as the Canadian customs official in Atom Egoyan's 2002 film *Ararat*. Raffi raises a serious question, which is, "How do you remember when there's nothing left to prove that anything happened?"

AE: Well, I think that also leads back to what I was also saying before about voyeurism, which is that Raffi's also engaged in looking at and recording this evidence of destruction and trying to understand it. Also understanding that there's very little that he can actually evoke through this and that's why he has to go further, he has to find some other way. Because what he's looking for is not tangible in this manner and we have to be able to re-imagine; we have to find some way to allow ourselves to re-imagine something as it might have been, as it could have been, to create a condition for ourselves which allows history to thrive and to become clarified and often that means creating an alternate structure. I think Christopher Plummer's character does this in a remarkable way in the movie, in terms of his own family history. What Raffi cannot understand, and again through the exuberance of his youth doesn't really even question, is why this customs officer would take such an interest in him. Why he's asking him to tell this story. Well, we know as viewers that Plummer is experiencing a complete breakdown in his family in terms of his relationship with his son and projects something into Raffi. It's the last night he's working as a customs officer, which Raffi also doesn't know. So there's this . . . it's a very loaded meeting. Often in the films there are these meetings between people who are not really aware of what the true agenda might be, and feel that there is an energy and either don't want to ask those questions or are too absorbed with their own pain to go there. But history is often changed in these meetings between individuals. It's not in these grand gestures or in the epic films that are made or in these large public demonstrations. It's really in the way two individuals negotiate and redefine a very particular history, which can then have reverberations and can find unexpected results in places that you wouldn't think of. So, what happens to Raffi on this night is absolutely redefining. First of all, he gets to tell his story to someone who's engaged and who's invested in it for reasons he doesn't understand, and that is empowering to him. And I think that is how history is redefined. It's in this ability . . . it's a creative gesture, of course, it is the fantasy of art that you can, through the retelling of something, through the beautiful retelling of something. I don't mean objectively that it's beautiful, but rather that it's perceived with care and is something that's sacred and special, that that dignifies a history with a character. I think that those are very precious moments, moments that have to be really guarded, that people might be afraid to reveal because they may not be taken seriously or it may be discarded. And those are also moments that I find very touching in drama, where someone is very cautiously extending some aspect of themselves, and their ability to define who they are is dependent on that other person's ability to receive that gesture.

EW: Atom Egoyan, your newest movie is called *Adoration*, and it's about a Toronto teenager who writes an account of how his father tried to blow up a plane with his pregnant wife on board. The teenager, Simon, projects himself into the role of the unborn child and inhabits this news article as if it were his own autobiography, and things soon spin out of control when the story, Simon's fiction, his invention, hits these Internet chat rooms and everyone seems to know about it and take him seriously. What inspired this movie?

AE: Well, it's inspired by an actual event which left an impression on me. In 1986 a Jordanian man talked his Irish girlfriend, who was pregnant with his child, onto an El Al flight, and promised that he would meet her in Tel Aviv and take her to meet his family. And unbeknownst to her, he had planted a bomb in her handbag. At the very last moment, El Al security was able to discover this and she was in complete shock. She had no idea that this bomb had been planted. It was impressive because it was one of the first times when you realized that someone could go that far. I mean, what could be more horrifying than being able to plan something that methodically. Was it planned from the moment he made her pregnant? Was this whole thing really a way of constructing this perfect detonating device, a pregnant woman? It was very troubling. And I'd forgotten about it until it came up again. Robert Fisk devotes a number of pages to it in his book *The Great War for Civilization*, and what's remarkable is that the man, Nezar Hindawi, is currently serving the longest prison sentence ever given to anyone in Great Britain and is completely unrepentant. In an interview with Fisk, he says no one will ever understand why he did what he did. I thought that there was just something so provocative about a character who is raised in a situation where his father has been completely demonized by his grandfather for reasons that he cannot really understand and he doesn't have access to that history at all. The grandfather's made it absolutely unavailable to him.

EW: These are your characters . . .

AE: These are the characters in *Adoration* . . . and that the boy would encounter this story in a French class as a translation exercise, but suddenly realizes that through this imaginary role he can begin to explore this figure of his father as the embodiment of evil in a way that he would not be able to have access to otherwise. He can actually redefine this entire relationship. He's been made an orphan because his parents died in this car crash, which his grandfather is sure the father created. There's no one who can witness that event, the only possible person who can give him any sense of what happened that night is a grandfather who will never change that story, even on his deathbed, quite literally.

EW: And part of his antipathy to his son-in-law is the fact that he's an Arab.

AE: That he's an Arab, and that his daughter is a golden child who had this ideal career and that was somehow sullied by this encounter with this man. And Simon is at a point in his life when he needs to explore this and he explores it in this very unconventional way. And I think that one of the more remarkable things about the Internet is that it does allow these very alternate narratives to make themselves available. And not only that, but it also creates these amazingly intense encounters with others who might share that belief for a particular period of time. One of the groups that he encounters are the people who were on this plane whose lives would have been taken away if this tragedy had unfolded, but it didn't.

EW: We have that scene.

AE: Oh, you have that scene, too? I've been setting these up so incredibly well. I mean, people think I was able to kind of anticipate this, but anyway, OK, we'll listen to the scene now.

EW: This is where Simon's story gets out to the mother of one of his friends who tells her friends and there's this sequence in a video chat room where these people who don't know Simon personally, but they try to own the trauma of a plane-bombing that didn't actually happen.

Film dialog:

Woman 1: Why is that so shocking, so surprising to you that you feel you have a sense of entitlement in this story?

Woman 2: I was on that plane. I was on that plane. I don't call it a sense of entitlement. It happens to be that if it is evil, whatever it was, whatever Simon's father intentions were, I could feel on my own skin once I learned about it. I'm not sure that it was a trauma at the time, I think we just . . . living it in our minds the way Simon is trying to live it in his mind.

Man: Yes, I think that the trauma happens later on, that it grows on you as time goes by, almost like a cancer. Whether it's real or fictional, as soon as we imagine it, then it becomes something that we have to deal with.

Woman 3: I don't understand what's so seductive about being a victim. We embrace the sense of being a victim almost to the extent that it blinds us to the pain of others. It's like a suit of clothes that's so comfortable today.

Man 2: His father ruined . . . basically ruined my life. I mean, I've been pretty much since, you know, since it happened I've been pretty much . . . complete . . . my eating has is completely out of control, has been, I've gained about a hundred pounds and I just can't seem to get, you know, get it together to just basically do anything.

EW: A scene from Atom Egoyan's new movie *Adoration.* One of the characters in that scene says that, "Whether the trauma is real or fictional, as soon as we imagine it, it becomes something that we have to deal with." I can see the part about the real trauma, but why do we have to deal with fictional trauma?

AE: Because it unleashes a number of possibilities that can provoke a response, and that response is very real. I think that that's the power of fiction; it is that it is very volatile, it provokes very strong responses, and it allows the imagination to be directed in a certain way. And that there's regimes that are built around the suppression of that particular trajectory. You know, people imagining things and especially with the Internet and with technologies which make access to forming groups around people who might have a similar predisposition, that becomes a real force. And also the way it creates, in this case, a culture of victims as well, people who want to assign blame and feel that they have the right to something. And there's no hindrance to imagine that, because there are other people who support and give credence to that path. This community could not be formed in the real world. In the real world, people would not get into their cars and go to a clubhouse because they are victims of a tragedy that never happened. They would have time to think about it and on that drive to the clubhouse they'd realize it's absurd. But because the technology's so immediate, it provokes these very

very strong reactions which are not really considered but can be very real and sometimes quite violent. I think Simon in *Adoration* is at the forefront of that. He's somebody who understands that the new media is a way of creating a tremendous amount of excitement, but it doesn't really solve certain issues. That still needs to be done in the physical world. I don't think the Internet is a place where you find catharsis. It's certainly a very engaging and diverting and entertaining place, but as Simon finds, you still have to actually construct and reconstruct these things in a physical way for them to have bearing and meaning. And I think that that's just a fundamental aspect of how we're formed. We need to actually, as the character, the guy, says in *Calendar*, you need to actually touch and feel things for them to have resonance and meaning. Though, the new media is wildly exciting as a way of engaging and gaining entry into other worlds, it doesn't complete the journey, it can't. It's just not designed to do that, I don't think.

EW: It's great to have a chance to talk to you again, thank you.

AE: Thank you.

EW: That was my conversation with Toronto filmmaker, Atom Egoyan. *Adoration* is in cinemas now. Egoyan's earlier movies including *Next of Kin*, *Calendar*, and *Ararat*, are all available on DVD. And that's this edition of "Wachtel on the Arts." I'm Eleanor Wachtel and I'll be back again next month.

Index

LaVergne, TN USA
30 April 2010
181063LV00001B/1/P